CALVINUS EVANGELII PROPUGNATOR

Calvin, Champion of the Gospel

Papers Presented at the International Congress on Calvin Research
Seoul, 1998

Edited by
David F. Wright
Anthony N. S. Lane
Jon Balserak

Published for the Calvin Studies Society by
CRC Product Services
Grand Rapids, Michigan
2006

Cover: Calvin's letter to Edward VI, facsimile in *Letters of Calvin*, trans. Jules Bonnet (Philadelphia: Presbyterian Board of Publication, 1858), vol. 1, title page.

The image of Calvin is from Emile Doumergue, *Iconographie Calvinienne* (Lausanne: Georges Bridel & Cie Editeurs, 1909), plate V, 34.

Library of Congress Control Number: 2006900845
ISBN 0-9700028-4-X

Contents

Welcome from the Praesidium

W. H. Neuser

First of all, I would like to welcome, on behalf of the Presidium, the participants of the Seventh International Congress on Calvin Research. Personally, I am pleased to see many familiar faces again. Apart from the participants from Korea, Japan and Taiwan (Republic of China), you have all had a long journey in order to be able to take part in this Congress, and also hopefully to curb your curiosity and get to know this wonderful country.

As Secretary, I am the only one who knows the contents of most of the lectures and seminars, and I can tell you this: the long journey has been worth it; interesting days of listening and discussion lie ahead.

Now I would like to mention two names in particular, the first of which is that of the Honorary President of the Asian United Theological University, Dr Han Chul-Ha. When I asked him about six years ago whether the Calvin Congress could perhaps take place in Korea sometime, he immediately agreed and tried to talk me into arranging the Congress here rather than in Edinburgh. We have to thank you first of all, Dr Han, that we are here today. On behalf of everyone, I thank you.

The second name is that of Professor Dr Lee Sou-Young, who undertook responsibility for the organizational burdens on the spot. Through the correspondence with him, you all will have been aware for a long time that he is a great organizer. One of the difficulties is that we find ourselves here in a country whose culture and language are unfamiliar to us. Professor Lee has spared no trouble in making us feel happy and has even taught us some Korean words. We say to him a big "Gam-sa-hamnida."

Christian faith proves to be a unifying bond over all cultural and linguistic hurdles. The opening service ensured that we felt at home here at once. We thank President Dr Rhee Jong-Sung for his message. We are his guests here in the splendid Presbyterian College and Theological Seminary. Very many thanks! The President of the Torch Trinity Graduate School of Theology will welcome us tomorrow.

Finally, I must confess that I was a little worried some months ago whether the Congress would be able to take place for financial reasons, in view of the economic crisis in this country. If I have understood correctly, the Preparation Committee and especially the Korea Calvin Society were responsible for the financing. We thank your President, Rev. Lim Ok, for this tremendous effort and hard work.

A Search for the Roots of Korean Calvinism in the Religion of John Calvin (1 John 5:18)

Han, Chul-Ha

Dear Professor Wilhelm Neuser, members of the Presidium, and all participants of the Seventh Congress on Calvin Research! I would like to extend to each of you a warm welcome to Korea, on behalf of the Rev. Lim Ok, the Chairman of the Preparation Committee, and all the Members of the Committee who represent the Korean Church and the members of the Korea Calvin Society. It is a memorable event for this great Congress to be held for the first time in a so-called mission field. This indicates that a younger church has grown out of the missionary effort of a sending church and has now reached a stature which is able to bear the burden of holding this Congress. It is also meaningful for the Congress on Calvin Research to be held in a land of Calvinism.

I. Two Missionaries

In 1885 two missionaries: one Presbyterian, Horace G. Underwood, and one Methodist, Henry G. Appenzeller, landed together in Jemulpo. A century later we today find ten million Presbyterians, while Methodists number only about one and half million. Presbyterians are 70% of the entire Protestant population of about twelve million. There are about three million Catholics, and consequently the entire Christian population is about fifteen million out of a population of forty-three million (35%).

II. Enthusiasm

What was the reason for such outstanding growth of the Calvinistic Church in this land? Many reasons have been indicated for that remarkable church growth. I would like to indicate, however, one indispensable factor for any rapid church growth: enthusiasm. Often shamanism has been indicated as the source of the enthusiastic character of Korean Christianity. That may be a partial reason for it. But one ought to search into a deeper source of the enthusiasm in Korean Christianity. Over against the Presbyterian Church, the Methodist Church in Korea has taken up the more rationalistic and moralistic side of Christian religion throughout her history. Consequently religious enthusiasm could never develop in that church.

The very root of enthusiasm in Korean Calvinism seems to be the evangelistic type of Christian religion of the early Presbyterian missionaries themselves. Though this is not the result of accurate research, I can give some evidence for it.

1) The fifth article of the Nevius Plan called for the "intensive biblical and doctrinal instruction" of pastors, whose education was not necessarily equal to that of missionaries. This article seems to reflect the presence of early missionaries from the New School of American Presbyterianism, who were more evangelistic.
2) The Great Revival Movement of 1905 started among missionaries and was promoted by them.
3) There is an article written about 1918 in *Shin Hak Ji Nam,* the theological periodical published by the Presbyterian Seminary in Pyung Yang, which was entitled "All Pastors Must Be Revivalists."
4) From the early period, Bible conferences were widely held in the mountains and were similar to the eighteenth-century field revival meetings held by George Whitefield, John Wesley and Jonathan Edwards.
5) The hymns in the Korean Church's *United Hymn Book* are mostly the revival hymns of the eighteenth and nineteenth centuries. Of 558 hymns, 391 are from the eighteenth century, and 105 from the nineteenth. Only 62 are from earlier or later.
6) The Rev. Dr. Park Hyung-Nong can properly be called the defender and promoter of Calvinism in Korea. Many thousand pastors were educated by him with his Reformed dogmatics. Despite his calm and grave external manner of treating doctrinal topics, his religious enthusiasm did not escape anyone's notice—from his trembling voice, from his earnest high tone while speaking, sometimes from his tears. He was indeed a man of passion.

It is my intention to say that religious enthusiasm is the very cause of the amazing Korean Church explosion and that the source of this religious enthusiasm ought to be traced back to the American evangelical tradition, which can be further traced back to John Calvin himself through John Wesley's Great Awakening of the power of living faith in Christ.

No one can deny that Calvin's religion was a religion of enthusiasm. For Calvin Christian doctrine was not a matter of the tongue but of the inmost heart:

> For [the gospel] is a doctrine not of the tongue but of life. It is not apprehended by the understanding and memory alone, as other disciplines are, but it is received only when it possesses the whole soul, and finds a seat and resting place in the inmost affection of the heart.[1]

To Calvin the doctrine of the gospel is the very principle of a Wesleyan inner change of our heart as well as of our entire life:

[1] *Inst.* 3:6:4.

> We have given the first place to the doctrine in which our religion is contained, since our salvation begins with it. But it must enter our heart, and pass into our daily living, and so transform us into itself that it may not be unfruitful for us. *[Verum ea in pectus transfundatur atque in mores transeat oportet, adeoque nos in se transformet ut sit nobis non infructuosa.]*[2]

The very source of this burning heart is the Holy Spirit himself, who seals our heart with love and assurance:

> The Spirit accordingly serves as a seal, to seal up in our hearts those very promises the certainty of which it has previously impressed upon our minds; and takes the place of a guarantee to confirm and establish them. After "you believed" (the apostle declares), "you were sealed with the Holy Spirit of promise, who is the guarantee of our inheritance."[3]

For Calvin faith is a matter not of apprehension but of certainty sealed by the Holy Spirit. "From this we conclude that the knowledge of faith consists in assurance rather than in comprehension *[unde statuimus, fidei notitiam certitudine magis quam apprehensione contineri]* ".[4]

To Calvin faith was the innermost conviction of God's benevolence toward us. God assures us of this love in Christ who establishes the testament with his blood. This love of God is sealed in our heart by the Holy Spirit in the form of a burning heart. Calvin defines faith as follows:

> Nunc iusta fidei definitio nobis constabit si dicamus esse divinae erga nos benevolentiae firmam certamque cognitionem, quae gratuitae in Christo promissionis veritate fundata, per Spiritum sanctum et revelatur mentibus nostris et cordibus obsignatur.[5]

We can find enough parallels to Wesley's extraordinary enthusiasm in Calvin. Not only in small society meetings but also often in John Wesley's large assemblies, many were cut to the hearts, screaming and crying out with agonies of death, often falling into fits.

"Coram summo judicio" is the very basic religious principle for both Calvin and Wesley. Calvin's description of "man in the presence of God" convicts us of our sin of insensibility in our nominal faith and makes us understand how such strange works could occur in the Wesleyan religious movement. A true picture of man is the starting point of everything. It is, however, visible only *coram Deo.* Thus, Calvin starts his *Institutio* with "the knowledge of God and the knowledge of self." Calvin indeed depicts a true picture of man before God, not only in the beginning but also at every point of his life!

---

[2] Ibid.

[3] *Inst.* 3:2:36.

[4] *Inst.* 3:2:14.

[5] *Inst.* 3:2:7.

> Hence that dread and wonder with which Scripture commonly represents the saints as stricken and overcome whenever they felt the presence of God. Thus it comes about that we see men who in his absence normally remained firm and constant, but who, when he manifests his glory, are so shaken and struck dumb as to be laid low by the dread of death—are in fact overwhelmed by it and almost annihilated.[6]

Calvin's accumulations of expression: "dread and wonder," "stricken and overcome," "shaken and struck dumb," "laid low by the dread of death," and "overwhelmed ... and almost annihilated" in the presence of divine majesty are no different from Wesleyan enthusiasm.

To Calvin such a sense of misery and agony is not a matter of particular moment, but he declares that as believers we ought to feel tormented with "a deep-seated conviction of our own misery" at each table of the Lord's Supper. In order not to pollute the Holy Supper we ought to be diligent in examining ourselves:

> He who knows the turpitude of his sin and the wretchedness of his state and condition while alienated from God, is so ashamed that he is constrained to be dissatisfied with himself, to condemn himself, to sigh and groan in great sadness.[7]

Here again Calvin does not spare the strongest expression: "eternal death," "a kind of perpetual hell," "already in the abyss of death," "vex and torment us," "more than miserable," "great sadness and anguish," "groaning and sighing," and "tormented and unquiet." The strange features of the Wesleyan movement, such as "strong cries and tears," "falling into a violent agony," and "falling into fits" at the moment of inner change, are more than natural if all these events described by Calvin occurred in a soul in a moment.

In fact biblical religion itself, we find, is an enthusiastic religion. The God of Israel introduces himself as a jealous God who does not tolerate any idolatry. The zeal of Phinehas turned aside God's wrath from the adulterous children of Israel (Numbers 25:7). Isaiah prophesied that the zeal of the Lord of hosts would fulfill the Messianic prophecy (Isaiah 9:7). The risen Lord prefers that we be either cold or hot rather than lukewarm (Revelation 3:16).

Korean Church growth was called from the beginning "a wild fire" as the church grew to 300,000 by the time of Liberation in 1945, out of a population of 28 million (about 1%), 60 years after 1885, the year Protestant mission started. If so, Korean Church growth after the Liberation may be called "a much more fierce wild fire," because within 50 years it reached fifteen out of forty-three million, some 35%. Concerning this continued growth after the Liberation, we cannot deny the pronounced influence of Dr. Park Hyung-

---

[6] *Inst.* 1:1:3.

[7] *Short Treatise on The Lord's Supper* 22.

Nong, through his founding of the Nam-San General Assembly Theological Seminary at the Japanese Shinto Shrine site at the time of Liberation. The outstanding church growth came from this source, not the Han Gook Theological Seminary, nor the Koryu Theological Seminary, not to mention any other non-Presbyterian Theological Seminaries.

III. Defense of Faith

I indicated that religious enthusiasm, which is the basic cause of Korean Church growth, is clearly visible also in Park Hyung-Nong. We must, however, also indicate some other factors in his theology which we see as the source of Korean Church growth: conservatism, that is, zeal for the defense of faith and a non-analytical, but truly scientific, approach to the center of reality, which is the true source of power and enthusiasm.

A church stands and falls with faith. If faith weakens the church declines. If faith revives the church revives and grows. The whole corpus of revelation is for the sake of faith. The word of God is not for itself, but to give birth to faith and to make it to grow. The word of God supports faith and strengthens it. By faith alone a sinner is justified. To believers, where sin abounds, grace abounds even more.

Jesus came to us to establish our faith: faith in his Father as our Father; faith in his God as our God. He taught us that God is "our Father which is in Heaven." He lamented the smallness of our faith (Matthew 6:30, 8:26, 14:31, 16:8; Mark 4:40; Luke 12:28). He confirmed faith through immediate fulfillment, with commendations (Matthew 8:10, 9:22, 9:29, 15:28; Mark 5:34, 10:52; Luke 8:48, 17:19). He gave numerous promises that prayer with faith is heard (Matthew 7:7). Jesus associated this faith with the forgiveness of sins and its fruits, peace and joy (Matthew 9:2). Paul worked out this central truth of our religion in the doctrine of justification by faith alone (Romans 3:28). This doctrine of the grace of the forgiveness of sins has been handed down to us through Augustine, Luther, Calvin and Wesley as the central truth of the Christian religion.

The very greatest tragedy in human history was the rise of liberal theology in the West and the total disintegration of Western Christianity in the last two centuries. Churches in Europe began to empty already long ago and even numerous church buildings in the U.S. are sold to Korean American congregations. This total decay of the old dead trunk is now daily accelerated. It was to my great surprise to hear that the proportion paying church taxes in Germany has declined from 98% to 60% and church attendance is deceasing by 120,000 every year. It was Immanuel Kant who started to undermine the Christian faith as *Gunstwerberei* (favor-seeking religion) in favour of a moral religion. Since that time all theologies have followed his example of compartmentalization: noumena and phenomena; *Sein und Dasein; Geschichte und Historie;* the kerygmatic Christ and the historical Jesus. Though there are numerous different forms of abstract theological Christianity, they are all united in rejecting the simple faith of the biblical unitary truth of reality as "wild metaphysics" and "confused myths." Thus true and sincere faith in the reality and power of God has been denied. It was a grave mistake of Western Christianity to have started the twentieth century with a great acclamation to Adolf Von Harnack's *Das Wesen des Christentums,* which is actually a total rejection of the Apostolic Creed as a Pauline Greek doctrinal construction upon the soil of the gospel of Jesus of Nazareth, which he saw as the teaching of the universal fatherhood of God and the universal brotherhood of mankind. How could the Western Church, having been taught this utter unbelief for a century, be maintained without being emptied? It is the time for Western theologians, facing the twenty-first century in only sixteen months time, to stop teaching Kantian unbelief and to start teaching the true religion of John Calvin and John Wesley.

Dr. Park Hyung-Nong was the sole defender of faith in his generation, together with a very small number of conservative theologians. The first half of the twentieth century was the darkest age of the Christian faith. The General Assembly of the United Presbyterian Church, U.S.A. of 1927, following the Auburn Affirmation of 1924, marked the total defeat of Fundamentalism in that church. Dr. Park went to America in 1923 for his theological studies at the young age of 26. He studied at Princeton from 1923 to 1926. It was the time when the Fundamentalists were making their last efforts to keep the church on the line of faith, totally without success. Dr. Park already showed his passion for the defense of the faith in the ship on his way to the U.S. He happened to read a Korean book, published by leftist Korean students in Japan, entitled *An Irreligionist's View of Religion* and, he said, "he could not suppress his indignation." This resulted in his writing his doctoral dissertation on "Anti-Christian Inferences from Natural Science." If he had been wise he would not have taken the side of the defeated group at Princeton. Later on he sent his own student, Park Yun-Sun, the leader of Koryu Church, to Westminster Theological Seminary instead of Princeton.

When I went to the U.S. for theological studies in 1955, conservative seminaries were still of negligible status. What does it mean that nowadays those then tiny seminaries (Westminster, Faith, Dallas, Fuller, Trinity, Gordon Conwell) have became giant institutions, while renowned centers such as Harvard, Yale, Union, etc. barely maintain their existence? Again the mainline churches are altogether declining, while giant individual congregations are arising through evangelical preachers.

The point that I am making about Korean Church growth, is that it is indebted entirely to Dr. Park Hyung-Nong's heroic victory in the defense of faith for the Korean Church. He was an outspoken Calvinist and following his example Korean Presbyterians accept Calvinism: a conviction as to biblical inerrancy, the sovereignty of God, allegiance to orthodox doctrines (particularly the "five points of Calvinism"), strict church discipline and strict observance of church ordinances.

Sola fide was the very core of the Reformation. Needless to say it was also the center of Calvin's teaching. The entire work of the *Institutes* was organized around this one word, faith. He summarized Book III as follows: "It is by the faith in the gospel that Christ becomes ours and we are made partakers of the salvation and eternal blessedness brought by him."[8] Here we see that "faith in the gospel" takes the key role in Calvin's religion. Then, he continues, "Since, however, in our ignorance and sloth (to which I add fickleness of disposition) we need outward helps to beget and increase faith within us, and advance it to its goal, God has also added these aids that he may provide for our weakness."[9] This means that the whole of Book IV is on the external means of grace, provided by God for the sake of "faith." Consequently we can arrange the entire *Institutes (religionis summa)* in all its parts *(omnibus partibus ... eo quoque ordine*[10]*)* as follows:

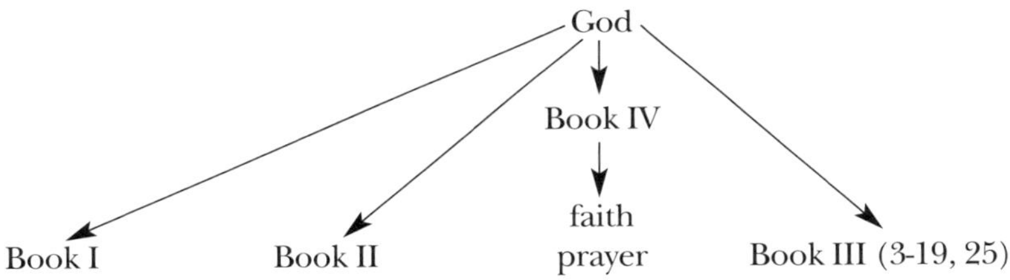

Needless to say, God is the only ultimate reference point of everything. However, God is concerned with our salvation. Repentance (3:3-10), forgiveness of sins (3:11-19) and resurrection (3:25) are given to us only through faith in the gospel of "Christ and all his benefits." Thus, faith and its chief exercise occupy the very core of the *summa.* If faith is removed, nothing will remain. Is it then an exaggeration to say that Korean Church growth is entirely due to Dr. Park Hyung-Nong's heroic defense of the faith?

IV. Evangelicalism

Now, I am going to take up the second factor in Dr. Park Hyung-Nong's theology which we consider to be the prime source of Korean Church growth. That is, his non-analytical, but truly scientific approach to the center of reality, which is the true source of power and enthusiasm. Mere defense of the faith would not make any church grow. Very often Western conservatives stopped with mere defense of doctrines. Dr. Park Hyung-Nong also defended all the important doctrines, because these are the very framework by which faith can be defended, indeed the organic components of faith. Dr. Park's theological

[8]*Inst.* 4:1:1.

[9]Ibid.

[10]*Inst.,* To the Reader.

method was, however, different from all Western theologians, whether liberal, conservative or modernist. *Dividamus ut uniamus.* This is the common approach of Western theologians. The West has reaped a great success in various fields of the visible world, through an analytical approach, that is, an inductive-deductive method of dealing with the objects it handles. Modern Western theologians made a grave mistake, however, by applying the same empirical scientific method to theological objects. Karl Barth and T. F. Torrance have well worked out the principle of the "Wissenschaftlichkeit der Theologie." But, according to my observation, they did not make much progress, though they spoke well on the question of the "Wissenschaftlichkeit" of theology. The scientific character of theology does not depend upon its rationality but upon its truthfulness to *res ipsa.* I am not going to discuss this very important matter here, in relation to the theology of Dr. Park Hyung-Nong and John Calvin. The point which I am making is to indicate that the only true theological methodology is that taken by both Dr. Park and John Calvin, which is, I feel, a most important element of our religion and the very source of Church growth.

Though Dr. Park was an outspoken Fundamentalist, his real concern was with "apostolic theology" or "Pauline thought," on the basis of 2 Timothy 2:2. He located the fundamental unity of the entire church throughout history at this very point. In this sense he was a real ecumenical theologian. Because of the ecumenical creeds and the apostolic tradition, the ancient apologists and the Greek and Latin fathers "all attempted to follow and faithfully preserve the apostolic theology, that is, Pauline thought."[11] He even accepts medieval scholastic theology as an attempt to clarify apostolic theology, i.e. Pauline thought, though with grave errors and deviations. He applies the same ecumenical approach to the Reformation churches and to all those later churches which maintain traditional Christianity:

> In general, historical traditional Christianity can be recognized practically as the same religion as the religion of Paul. Millions of both men and women who became Christians were actually not aware of the fact that the Christianity in which they believed was the thought of the same Paul whom they respected greatly as an Apostle.[12]

I feel that history itself supports this great theologian's view. Luther and Zwingli agreed on fourteen and a half out of fifteen articles of faith. Concerning this half article, that is about the mode of presence, Melanchthon worked out a *Variata* of the *Confessio Augustana* which all Reformers of that time, including John Calvin signed. The *Consensus Tigurinus* between Bullinger and Calvin was a real consensus, not a compromise as Paul Rorem suspects. Wouldn't these historical facts be enough for us to take Dr. Park's approach

---

[11] *Works,* 13:220.

[12] Ibid., 13:221.

toward the ecumenical unity of Christian Churches? He indicates two things as the basis of Church unity, the gospel and essential doctrines:

> Evangelical Christian faith is the "good news" or "glad tidings" that God has prepared a redemption for us mankind. This faith affirms that salvation from sins is not given by any merit of good works but totally by the grace of God alone.[13]

This is the Pauline thought or apostolic theology which, according to Dr. Park, is the very center of the Christian religion. At the same time he insists that basic doctrines must be maintained by the church:

> This faith persists in the following doctrines as the fundamental truths of the Christian religion: the Trinity, the divinity of Christ, the personhood of the Holy Spirit, the perfect inspiration of Holy Scripture, miracles, the substitutionary suffering and death of Christ which atone for the sins of his own people, his resurrection, ascension and glorious bodily second coming, the resurrection and final judgment of all men, heaven and hell![14]

Then, we can see that Dr. Park was above all an evangelical, even though he was a defender of the faith. We can call him an evangelist. Consequently, the Korean church is an evangelical church, which puts revival and evangelism foremost, before anything else.

I learned from Calvin how to read the Bible:

> I have so embraced the sum of religion in all its parts, and have arranged it in such an order, that if anyone rightly grasp it, it will not be difficult for him to determine what he ought especially to seek in Scripture, and to what end he ought to relate its contents.[15]

Whenever I open the Bible, there I can worship my God the Creator and Redeemer in Christ. I try to hear the glad tidings of salvation in the words of God and apply it to my own salvation and the salvation of all others through faith in Christ. Calvin was an evangelical theologian. Needless to say that God, "the only true God" (John 17:4), is concerned with the salvation of fallen mankind. Consequently, "faith in the gospel," as already indicated above, occupies the very center of all religion.

V. Prayer

The Korean Church is a praying church. Prayer is the chief exercise of faith. If prayer does not take place fervently, faith becomes dead. Faith receives its power and fruits only through prayer life. We may dare to say that the faith of

---

[13]Ibid. 13:304.

[14]Ibid.

[15]*Inst.,* To the Reader.

the Korean Church is *Gunstwerberei* (favor-seeking religion) over against Kantian unbelief. So far as I see, among theologians Calvin and Karl Barth pre-eminently define "prayer" as "petition." So far as I see, however, it is Calvin alone who believes seriously that we can obtain something from God through prayer. How many things believers need to ask to receive from God! Above all Korean believers seek material as well as spiritual blessings from God. That is the reason why they come to God in the name of Christ early each morning to cry to him. On every mountain where clean rivulets flow there is certainly a mountain prayer house, full of people praying all year around. There are more than 500 mountain prayer houses in Korea.

Calvin was a man of prayer. Calvin's manner of prayer seems to have been "fervent" *(heiss),* like Korean believers praying aloud in unison. As he said, "More than 20 times in these days I have eagerly prayed to God that he may let me die."[16]

Of the last moments of Idelette, Calvin wrote, "those present hardly noticed the transition from life to death," while Calvin could not do anything but "took flight into prayer."[17] In other word, while Calvin was praying fervently, they did not know when Idelette passed away. We are told that Calvin himself concluded his life with prayer. "So Calvin shows the image of man of prayer, which he recorded diligently in the biblical books, in his own person up to the last hours of his life."[18] To Calvin prayer was the chief exercise of faith. If prayer is the chief exercise of faith, we can see the predominant place that it holds in Calvin's religion. If our life is to be a life in faith, we ought to engage in prayer without ceasing. Thus, Calvin was a Christian man of prayer.

Tomorrow morning we will visit Myung-Sung Church. Myung-Sung started eighteen years ago and grew to a congregation of fifty thousand. It is particularly renowned for its early morning prayer meetings. Every morning throughout the year four to five thousand members gather three times: at four, five, and six o'clock. Twice a year in March and September, special prayer meetings are held with an average daily attendance of twenty thousand. Kum-Ran Methodist Church is the leading growing church of eighty-five thousand members. In 1997 Rev. Dr. Kim Hong-Do admitted 2,626 into catechism and baptized 1,874. Last April I attended a baptismal service for 537 with 985 admitted to the catechumenate. This takes place three times a year. These are simply the results of these pastors' ministry of manifestation of power in the presence of living God.

---

[16]Hans Scholl, *Der Dienst des Gebetes nach Johannes Calvin* (Zurich & Stuttgart: Zwingli Verlag, 1968), 206 ["Mehr als zwanzigmal habe ich in diesen Tagen in heissem Gebet zu Gott gefleht, er moge mich sterben lassen"].

[17]Ibid., 204 ["die Anwesenden den Ubergang von Leben zum Tod kaum merkten. ... nahm ich meine Zuflucht zum Gebet."].

[18]Ibid., 207 ["so zeigt Calvin das Bild des Beters, das er mit Fleiss in den biblischen Büchern registriert hat, in seiner Person bis in die letzten Lebensstunden"].

In other words God himself manifests his power of salvation through these pastors' ministry of the word of God. Thus, we can conclude that a Wesleyan type of evangelical pastoral ministry is the true cause of Korean Church growth.

It is clear to me what is the cause of Korean Church growth: enthusiasm, zeal for the defense of the faith, sole and total devotion to evangelism, a fervent prayer life. If any element of these is lacking, the church will decay! This is the time, I believe, for this Congress, being held for the first time in a mission field, to pay more attention to faith, not merely to historical research. It is my hope to see in the next Congress more of the gospel in the valuable presentations for world evangelization.

VI. Mission

Missionary outreach of a church is the result of empowerment by the Holy Spirit, that is a full conviction of salvation by Jesus Christ. As the Korean Church had been empowered in faith through her prayer life and devotion to evangelism, the next step was to reach out for the evangelization of the world. Indeed, the Korean Church is a missionary church. Zeal for foreign mission is alight throughout the Korean Churches. "National Evangelization" is one of the most familiar catch-phrases. Thus, the phrase "World Evangelization" is a synonym which became the life goal of every Korean Christian.

Up to 1980 about 100 missionaries had been sent out to foreign lands. Ten years later, we can see rapid increase of missionaries sent by the Korean Churches.

1990:- 1645   1992:- 2576   1994:- 3272   1996:- 4402

By this year, 1998, they count about 6,000 missionaries being sent out.

Calvin's theology has often been misunderstood as lacking mission interest. At the last Congress in Edinburgh Peter Wilcox well demonstrated from Calvin's exposition of the Prophets his concern for the progress of the Kingdom of Christ, "the rule of God over 'the nations,' and the extension of worship 'to the ends of the earth.'"[19] Now, in the apostolic era, Gentiles were brought into the Church from all sides, through the gospel.[20] In a sense Calvin's theology as a whole can be seen as a mission theology.

What is mission? As already indicated, "faith in the gospel" occupies the center of Calvin's *Institutes*. However, faith comes from hearing *(fides ex auditu)*. Thus, the evangelical passage: How beautiful are the feet of them that preach the gospel of peace, and bring glad tidings of good things! This occupies

[19]W. H. Neuser & B. G. Armstrong (eds.), *Calvinus Sincerioris Religionis Vindex. Calvin as Protector of the Purer Religion*, Sixteenth Century Essays and Studies 36 (Kirksville: Sixteenth Century Journal Publishers, 1997), 318.

[20]Ibid., 319.

indeed the center of Calvin's religion. If Calvin's theology was mainly concerned with the salvation of mankind through the ministry of the gospel, that is, the good news of forgiveness of sins and repentance, Calvin research also ought to be concerned with more pastoral and missionary ministry.

As the one who invited you to Korea, I am afraid, I am preaching too much in this opening address. My primary responsibility is rather to provide you with our best hospitality. I hope you enjoy your stay here and have a comfortable time and good fellowship!

Thank You.

Calvins Denken in Relationen*

Michael Beintker

I. Einige Vorüberlegungen zum Thema

Wo auch immer gedacht wird, werden Beziehungen und Verknüpfungen sichtbar gemacht und hergestellt. Das Denken setzt stets Relationsgeflechte voraus, innerhalb derer es sich bewegt und entfaltet. Es folgt den unterschiedlichsten Relationen zwischen Begriffen, Dingen oder Ereignissen. Ebenso kann das Denken solche Relationsgeflechte transformieren oder transzendieren, und es vermag neue Relationsgeflechte hervorzubringen. Der Umgang mit Relationen gehört zu den allgemeinen Merkmalen des Denkens: "Denken heißt überhaupt Beziehen," und zwar als Prozeß der "Vereinigung des zugleich Geschiedenen, Differenzierung des zugleich Geeinten" (Paul Natorp).[1]

Man drückt also anscheinend etwas ganz Selbstverständliches aus, wenn man von einem "Denken in Relationen" spricht. Das Interesse an Relationen ist so alt wie das philosophische Denken. Seit Aristoteles das *pros ti* ("das, was in bezug auf etwas ist") als eine der grundlegenden Kategorien bzw. Prädikationen der Aussage entdeckt hat, beschäftigt sich vornehmlich die Logik mit den Relationen.[2] Im Laufe ihrer Geschichte, in der sich zugleich auch die allgemeine Geschichte des menschlichen Denkens widerspiegelt, manifestierte sich eine deutliche Tendenz zur Aufwertung von Relationen und relationalen Phänomenen. An der Wende vom 19. zum 20. Jahrhundert entstand sogar eine eigene Relationenlogik. Man kann das darauf zurückführen, "daß die antike

---

*This paper has already been published in *Zeitschrift für Theologie und Kirche* 99 (2002), 109-129 and is reproduced here by kind permission.

[1]P. Natorp, *Die logischen Grundlagen der exakten Wissenschaften* (Leipzig & Berlin: B. G. Teubner, 21921), 67 sowie 26; vgl. Ch. von Wolzogen, "Relation IV. 20. Jahrhundert," in *Historisches Wörterbuch der Philosophie* (= HWP) 8 (Darmstadt: Wissenschaftliche Buchgesselschaft, 1992), (602-606) 603.

[2]Vgl. G. Patzig, "Relation," in *Handbuch philosophischer Grundbegriffe* 4 (München: Kösel-Verlag, 1973), 1220-31; M. Erler, B. Mojsisch, M. Baum, Ch. von Wolzogen, H.-G. Steiner, "Relation," in HWP 8:578-611. Ch. S. Peirce: "... relatives have, since Aristotle, been a recognized topic of logic" ("Notes on Symbolic Logic and Mathematics," in Ders., *Collected Papers III,* hgg. Ch. Hartshorne and P. Weiss (Cambridge, MA: Harvard University Press, 1960), 609-45, Zitat: 643).

Wissenschaft mehr auf die Einteilung der Gegenstände nach Art und Gattungen, die neuzeitliche Wissenschaft mehr auf die gesetzmäßigen Beziehungen zwischen Ereignissen gerichtet war."[3]

Wir werden uns im Folgenden allerdings nicht auf der abstrakten, mathematisierbaren Ebene der Relationenlogik bewegen. Denn das, was bei Calvin unser Interesse herausfordert, läßt sich nicht einfach mit Hilfe formaler logischer Operationen klären. Im Gegenteil: So selbstverständlich es auf den ersten Blick erscheinen mochte, das Denken prinzipiell als ein Denken in Relationen zu bestimmen, so wenig selbstverständlich ist es bei genauerer Betrachtung, daß das Denken auch tatsächlich in Relationen verläuft.

Wenn wir nämlich sagen: Uns interessieren primär die realen Prozesse, in denen wir uns bewegen und von denen wir bewegt werden, die Interaktionen und Kommunikationen zwischen den Polen einer Relation, und uns interessiert die Frage, wie die Beschaffenheit dieser Pole auf eine zwischen ihnen waltende Relation zurückwirkt und wie umgekehrt eine Relation die jeweiligen Pole beeinflußt, dann können uns die logischen Theorien kaum weiterbringen. Denn diese formalisieren und abstrahieren, sie katalogisieren und fixieren, um zu logisch kohärenten und konsistenten Aussagen zu gelangen. Aber ein Denken in Relationen, das die Dynamik von Prozessen und lebendigen Interaktionen erfassen will, muß sich an Bewegungen orientieren und sich selber den Bewegungen aussetzen. Es verträgt keine Statik. Es bahnt sich seinen Weg nicht über die Entitäten des Seins, sondern in den Dynamiken von Prozeßabläufen. Es analysiert die Relationen nicht aus der beobachtenden Distanz, sondern es weiß sich durch eben jene Relationen engagiert, die es zu beschreiben versucht.

Ein bemerkenswertes Modell solchen Denkens hat der theologische Personalismus geliefert, der im 20. Jahrhundert vor allem durch die Ich-Du-Dialogik Martin Bubers inspiriert worden ist.[4] Mit der Ich-Du-Relation stößt das Denken des Glaubens auf die Basisrelation aller Wirklichkeit: die Relation zwischen dem Du Gottes und dem Ich des vom Du Gottes angeredeten Menschen bzw.—umgekehrt—dem Ich Gottes und dem Du seines menschlichen Gegenübers. Zwischen Ich und Du und erst recht zwischen *diesem* Ich und Du herrschen überaus ereignishafte, dynamische Relationen. Gerhard Gloege hat Subjektbezogenheit, Relation und Aktualität als die besonderen Kennzeichen dieses Personalismus sichtbar gemacht.[5] Und er hat prägnant den Wesenszug der *dialogisch qualifizierten Relation* verdeutlicht: "Personale Beziehung 'ist' nicht ruhende Korrelation, sondern ereignet sich in bewegter

[3]Patzig, "Relation," 1228.

[4]Vgl. M. Buber, *Ich und Du* (Heidelberg: Schneider, [10]1979 [[1]1923]).

[5]Vgl. G. Gloege, "Der theologische Personalismus als dogmatisches Problem. Versuch einer Fragestellung," in Ders., *Heilsgeschehen und Welt, Theologische Traktate I* (Göttingen: Vandenhoeck & Ruprecht, 1965), 53-76, bes. 65.

Korrespondenz."[6] Gloege attestierte der Theologie Martin Luthers eine auffällige Affinität zum personalen Denken. Angesichts der konkreten Anrede des Wortes, der *viva vox Evangelii,* stellt sich die theologische Unbrauchbarkeit des metaphysischen Seinsdenkens heraus, das die von Aristoteles geprägte Denktradition beherrscht.

Vermutlich haben wir es hier mit einer Eigenart der genuinen reformatorischen Theologie zu tun. Die dialogisch qualifizierte Relation, die nicht als ruhendes Verhältnis, sondern als "bewegte Korrespondenz" in Erscheinung tritt, taucht bei Calvin gleich am Anfang seines dogmatischen Hauptwerks auf. Die bekannte Zuordnung von Erkenntnis Gottes und menschlicher Selbsterkenntnis, die als Leitmotiv wie als Gliederungsprinzip der ganzen *Institutio christianae religionis* verstanden werden muß,[7] fügt ja zwei Erkenntnisakte bzw. -prozesse ineinander, die zumeist auseinanderfallen und in ihrem Auseinanderfallen das Elend des Menschen auslösen und kennzeichnen. Die *cognitio Dei* und die *cognitio nostri* "hängen vielfältig zusammen [multis inter se vinculis connexae sint],"[8] und sie sind wechselseitig miteinander verknüpft ("mutuo inter se nexu sint colligatae"[9]). Wie auch immer wir die Gotteserkenntnis und die menschliche Selbsterkenntnis entfalten—als Erkenntnis Gottes des Schöpfers und als Erkenntnis des Geschöpfs in seiner ursprünglichen Integrität einerseits *und* als Erkenntnis Gottes des Erlösers und als Erkenntnis des an die Sünde geketteten, der Erlösung bedürftigen Geschöpfs andererseits:[10] wir haben es in jedem Fall mit einer höchst bewegten, zugleich dramatischen und heilvollen, Dynamik zu tun. Gott und Mensch existieren in multiplen, interaktiven, lebendigen Relationen. Das muß sich immer auch auf das diese Relationen deutende und auslegende Denken auswirken. Hingegen muß die Ignoranz gegenüber der Prozeßqualität dieser Relationen unweigerlich zu Verzerrungen und Verzeichnungen des Gott-Mensch-Verhältnisses führen. Nach Calvin können Gott und Mensch nicht betrachtet werden "as statically irreconcilable entities or as unrelatable types of being. Rather, God and man are seen together in a continual story of the one's effort persuasively to

---

[6]Ebd.

[7]Vgl. dazu bes. G. Ebeling, "Cognitio Dei et hominis," in: Ders., *Lutherstudien I* (Tübingen: J C B Mohr (Paul Siebeck), 1971), 221-72; E. A. Dowey, "The Structure of Calvin's Thought as Influenced by the Twofold Knowledge of God," in W. H. Neuser, hg., *Calvinus Ecclesiae Genevensis Custos. Die Referate des Internationalen Kongresses für Calvinforschung vom 6. bis 9. September 1982 in Genf* (Frankfurt/M. u.a.: Peter Lang, 1984), 135-48; K. Barth, *Die Theologie Calvins [1922]* (Zürich: Theologischer Verlag, 1993), 214ff.

[8]*Institutio* [1559] 1:1:1 (J. Calvin, *Opera selecta* (München: Chr. Kaiser, 1926ff.) [im folgenden als OS] 3:31, Z. 8-9).

[9]*Institutio* [1559] 1:1:3 (OS 3:34, Z. 1).

[10]Zur doppelten *cognitio duplex,* vgl. *Institutio* 1:1:1; 1:15:1; 2:1:1.

relate himself to the other and of the other's growing self-knowledge and maturity as the subject of his persuasive history."[11]

Calvins Denken wird also durch eine spezifische Dynamik geprägt. Relationen stellen die maßgeblichen Aktions- und Bindungselemente dieser Dynamik dar. Ein "Denken in Relationen" ist im Hinblick auf Calvin also als ein Denken zu erläutern, das von der Dynamik seines Gegenstandes erfaßt ist und der Bewegtheit seiner Themen in den Akten des Denkens zu entsprechen versucht.

II. Beobachtungen zum Gebrauch des Ausdrucks "Relation"

Calvin kann auf den Ausdruck *relatio* zurückgreifen, um die Mutualität und Reziprozität im Verhältnis zwischen Gott und Mensch zu verdeutlichen.

> In der Interpretation des Ersten Gebots bemerkt Calvin zu der Selbstprädikation Gottes "Ich bin der Herr dein Gott": Diese Aussage bezeichne "eine gegenseitige Beziehung [mutua relatio], wie sie in der Verheißung [in promissione] enthalten ist: 'Ich will ihr Gott sein und sie sollen mein Volk sein' [Jer. 31:33]."[12] In der Auslegung des Prologs des Johannesevangeliums erläutert er die Rolle des präexistenten und sich dann inkarnierenden Logos so: Das Wort, durch das Gott die Welt geschaffen habe, stehe in einer "duplex ... relatio: prior ad Deum, altera ad homines."[13] Damit wird die konstitutive Bedeutung Jesu Christi—des Mittlers—für die Beziehung zwischen Gott und Mensch hervorgehoben.

So interessant die Verwendung des Relationsbegriffs an solchen, theologisch zentralen, Stellen auch ist: es muß deutlich gesagt werden, daß er bei Calvin verhältnismäßig selten begegnet. Unsere Überlegungen können sich also nicht einfach auf Untersuchungen zum Begriffsgebrauch beschränken. Vielmehr müssen vor allem die relationalen Phänomene und Sachverhalte im Denken Calvins studiert werden, die eindeutig nicht an das formale Vorkommen des Ausdrucks *relatio* und seiner Derivate gebunden sind. Es ist aber durchaus instruktiv, zu beobachten, wie Calvin mit dem Ausdruck *relatio* umgeht, wie und wo er ihn einsetzt.

---

[11]E. D. Willis, "Rhetoric and Responsibility in Calvin's Theology," in A. J. McKelway and E. D. Willis, hgg., *The Context of Contemporary Theology. Essays in Honor of Paul Lehmann* (Atlanta: John Knox Press, 1974), 57-58.

[12]Institutio [1559] 2:8:14 (deutsche Übersetzung von O. Weber [J. Calvin, *Unterricht in der christlichen Religion* (Neukirchen-Vluyn: Neukirchener Verlag, 21963)]; vgl. OS 3:355, Z. 19-21).

[13]J. Calvin, *Opera quae supersunt omnia* (Braunschweig & Berlin, Schwetschke, 1863-1900) [im folgenden als CO] 47:2 (*Kommentar zu Joh.* 1:1).

Unter den 14 Belegen in der *Institutio* von 1559 sind für unser Interesse zehn Fälle relevant.[14] Ein gewichtiges Beispiel wurde bereits genannt. Die übrigen Anwendungen verteilen sich auffälligerweise auf zwei thematische Schwerpunkte: (1.) die Relationen zwischen Wort und Glaube mit drei Stellen, (2.) die Relationen zwischen Vater, Sohn und Heiligem Geist in der Trinität des *einen* Gottes (sechs Stellen).

(1.) Zwischen der Anrede des Wortes Gottes und dem Glauben des Menschen, der diese Anrede hört und erwidert, bestehen selbstverständlich lebendige, dynamische Beziehungen. Die Dynamik ist an die Voraussetzung geknüpft, daß sich der Mensch das Zeugnis der Schrift gesagt sein läßt und aus diesem Zeugnis lebt. Der Glaube existiert nur in ständiger Relation *(perpetua relatio)* mit dem Wort, "er kann von ihm ebensowenig getrennt werden, wie die Strahlen von der Sonne, aus der sie hervorgehen."[15] Ja, das Heil des Glaubenden folgt aus der "fidei ad verbum relatio."[16] Die Dynamik in Calvins Schrifthermeneutik ist durch solche Äußerungen unmittelbar vorgezeichnet. Es ist kaum erstaunlich, daß Calvin an späterer Stelle dann resümiert: " ... relationem constituimus inter fidem et Evangelium."[17] Da sich der *lebendige, gegenwärtige* Gott durch das biblische Zeugnis an uns mitteilt, hören und lesen wir die Schrift im Horizont seiner *Gegenwart,* im Medium der existentiell präsenten Ich-Du-Beziehung. Aus diesem Grund weist die hermeneutische Relation auf eine intensive, überaus bewegte, spannungsreiche Kommunikation mit dem Wort.

(2.) Statistisch betrachtet erreichen die Belege für den Ausdruck *relatio* in der Trinitätslehre Calvins die höchste Frequenz—fünf Stellen allein im einschlägigen Kapitel 13 des ersten Buches der *Institutio,*[18] während ein weiterer charakteristischer Beleg in der Christologie auftaucht, als Calvin in einer Auseinandersetzung mit Servet an die trinitarischen Prämissen christologischer Reflexion anknüpft.[19] Calvin muß die "unica Dei essentia"[20] im Sinne des

[14]Als für unser Thema nicht charakteristisch bewerte ich die Verwendung des Ausdrucks in OS 3:235, Z. 14 (es geht um die logische Beziehung zwischen Satzgliedern) und ebd., Z. 3-4, wo die Adam-Christus-Typologie nach Röm. 5:12ff. als eine "relatio" charakterisiert wird. Auch hier wird übrigens relational gedacht, aber das erschließt sich nicht über die Terminologie! Ferner können wir die Rede von der "relatio" zwischen den irdischen und den himmlischen Dingen (vgl. OS 3:256, Z. 25-26) vernachlässigen. Unspezifisch ist auch die Verwendung in OS 4:201, Z. 31.

[15]"Principio admonendi sumus, perpetuam esse fidei relationem cum verbo, nec magis ab eo posse divelli, quam radios a sole, unde oriuntur ... Tolle igitur verbum, et nulla iam restabit fides" (*Institutio* [1559] 3:2:6 (OS 4:14, Z. 7-9, 27-28); vgl. auch die Auslegung zu Röm. 10:17 im *Kommentar zum Römerbrief* (CO 49:206-207)).

[16]*Institutio* [1559] 3:2:31 (OS 4:14, Z. 28-29).

[17]*Institutio* [1559] 3:11:17 (OS 4:200, Z. 28-29): Calvin bezieht sich vor allem auf 2:9:2 und 3:2:16.

[18]OS 3:116, Z. 24; 132, Z. 19; 132, Z. 22; 134, Z. 7; 135, Z. 3.

[19]*Institutio* [1559] 2:14:7 (OS 3:469, Z. 3).

[20]OS 3:108, Z. 20 u.ö.

biblischen Zeugnisses differenzieren: einerseits darf die Einheit Gottes nicht verletzt werden und andererseits dürfen die besonderen Spezifika der drei göttlichen Seinsweisen nicht nivelliert werden.[21] Es ist bemerkenswert, daß er diese Differenzierung im Wesen des einen Gottes in die besonderen göttlichen *subsistentiae* als Vater, Sohn und Geist über den relationalen Zugang erreicht.

Vater, Sohn und Geist sind in der *unitas essentiae*[22] vereint und haben ohne die geringste Einschränkung an ihr Anteil. Der einfache Gottesname *(simplex Dei nomen)* läßt eine Relation nicht zu, deshalb kommt er dem Vater, dem Sohn und dem Heiligen Geist ununterscheidbar in gleicher Weise zu.[23] Sobald aber das Verhältnis zwischen Vater, Sohn und Geist beachtet wird, kann man über die jeweilige Relation zwischen ihnen ihre Unterscheidung in der Einheit erfassen. "Tritt neben den Vater der Sohn, dann kommt die Relation zum Vorschein: und so unterscheiden wir zwischen den Personen [der Trinität]."[24] Calvin steht damit in einer bewährten Tradition: Er kann sich für diese Rezeption des Ausdrucks *relatio* auf Augustinus berufen und erweist sich diesbezüglich als sein adäquater Schüler.

In der Kontroverse mit Peter Caroli, die eine wichtige Etappe auf dem Weg Calvins zu einer reifen immanenten Trinitätslehre darstellt, bezog sich Calvin auf Augustinus und auch auf den Relationsbegriff.[25] In der *Institutio* zitierte er unter anderem seit der Ausgabe von 1543 aus Augustinus' Auslegung des 68. Psalms:[26] "Christus wird an und für sich Gott genannt, in seinem Verhältnis zum Vater aber Sohn. Und andererseits: der Vater wird an und für sich Gott genannt, in seinem Verhältnis zum Sohn aber Vater. Wenn er also dem Sohn gegenüber Vater ist, so ist er eben nicht der Sohn, und wenn der Sohn gegenüber dem Vater Sohn heißt, so ist er eben nicht der Vater; der aber an und für sich Vater und der an und für sich Sohn genannt wird, der ist derselbe Gott!"[27] Sie unterscheiden sich gerade in ihrem jeweiligen Gegenüber von Ich und Du und sind doch immer Eines. Calvin schlußfolgert: Ohne Bezug auf den Vater können wir den Sohn sogar den einzigen Ursprung *(unicum principium)* nennen, "wenn wir aber seine Relation zum Vater *[relatio quae illi cum Patre est]* beachten, so sagen wir mit

---

[21]Vgl. dazu H. H. Eßer, "Hat Calvin eine 'leise modalisierende Trinitätslehre'?" in: W. H. Neuser, hg., *Calvinus Theologus. Die Referate des Europäischen Kongresses für Calvinforschung vom 16. bis 19. September 1974 in Amsterdam* (Neukirchen-Vluyn: Neukirchener Verlag, 1976), 113-29.

[22]Vgl. OS 3:116, Z. 33.

[23]Vgl. OS 3:134-35 passim.

[24]"... ubi autem adiungitur Filius Patri, tunc in medium venit relatio: atque ita distinguimus inter personas" (*Institutio* 1:13:20 (OS 3:134, Z. 6-7)).

[25]Vgl. *Adversus Petri Caroli calumnias* (1545) (CO 7:323-24 (293-339)).

[26]Vgl. CChr.SL 39:905-906 (Auslegung zu Ps. 68:5).

[27]*Institutio* 1:13:19 (deutsche Übersetzung von O. Weber; vgl. OS 3:133, Z. 11-16).

Recht, daß der Vater der Ursprung des Sohnes [Filii principium] sei."[28] Ausdrücklich beruft sich Calvin für diese—von ihm als unspekulativ bewertete[29]—Relationentheorie auf Augustinus' Ausführungen im V. Buch von De trinitate.[30]

Die trinitätstheologische Prägung des Ausdrucks *relatio* verdankt sich also der Schule des Augustinus. Calvin hat aus dessen Trinitätslehre reichlich geschöpft. Dennoch sollte man besser nicht sagen, daß "die Trinitätslehre Calvins jeglicher Originalität entbehrt."[31] Es läßt sich nämlich auch zeigen, daß gerade das trinitarische Denken die dynamischen Potentiale von Calvins Theologie befruchtet und gefördert hat.[32] Wenn sich Calvin gegenüber der trinitarischen Denkweise nur rezeptiv verhalten hätte, wäre das kaum vorstellbar. Schon sein innovativer Beitrag zur Pneumatologie impliziert eine bestimmte trinitätstheologische Originalität. Man kann außerdem sagen, daß Augustinus nicht nur das begriffliche Instrumentarium zur Verfügung stellte, sondern auch Calvins Sensitivität für relationale Phänomene förderte.[33]

III. Dynamik und Relation in der Wirklichkeit Gottes

Ähnlich wie die anderen Reformatoren hat Calvin eine deutlich spürbare Aversion gegen die spekulative Reflexion der Wirklichkeit Gottes entwickelt. Die Absage an "frigidae speculationes"[34] gehört zum methodologischen Repertoire seiner Theologie. Sie taucht bevorzugt dort auf, wo unser Intellekt durch den Schwierigkeitsgrad des jeweiligen Themas zur Überschreitung seiner

---

[28]Ebd., vgl. OS 3:133, Z. 16ff.

[29]Vgl. OS 3:133, Z. 23.

[30]OS 3:133, Z. 20-22; vgl. CChr.SL 50:210ff.

[31]So F. Wendel, *Calvin. Ursprung und Entwicklung seiner Theologie* (Neukirchen-Vluyn: Neukirchener Verlag, 1968), 145.

[32]So mit guten Gründen Ph. W. Butin, *Revelation, Redemption and Response. Calvin's Trinitarian Understanding of the Divine-Human Relationship* (New York & Oxford: Oxford University Press, 1995), bes. 51ff. ("The Trinitarian Basis, Pattern, and Dynamic of the Divine-Human Relationship") und 76ff. ("Human Response. The Trinity as the Dynamic of God's Relationship with Humanity").

[33]Die trinitätstheologische Aufwertung der Relation durch Augustinus begünstigte zweifellos eine Entwicklung, innerhalb derer die Relation aus dem Schatten der sie ständig abwertenden Aristotelischen Prädikamentenlehre herausgeführt wurde. Markant ist die Fokussierung der trinitätstheologisch rezipierten Relation durch Boethius: "Ita igitur substantia continet unitatem, relatio multiplicat trinitatem" (A. M. S. Boethius, *Quomodo trinitas unus deus ac non tres dii* 6, in Ders., *Die Theologischen Traktate*, hg. M. Elsässer (Hamburg: Meiner, 1988), 24, Z. 7-9; vgl. auch B. Mojsisch, "Relation II. Spätantike, Mittelalter und Renaissance," HWP 8:586-87 [586-595]). W. Pannenberg diagnostizierte hinter der trinitarischen Relation den Ursprung des Personbegriffs (in personalem Sinne): "Der Sache nach war schon die altkirchliche Christologie dahin gelangt, Person als *Relation* zu verstehen ..." (W. Pannenberg, "Person," in RGG3 5:231 [230-235]).

[34]*Institutio* [1559] 1:2:2 (OS 3:35, Z. 11).

Grenzen regelrecht provoziert wird. Sei es die Frage nach der Beschaffenheit des göttlichen Wesens,[35] sei es das trinitarische Problem,[36] sei es das Nachdenken über die Welt als Schöpfung,[37] oder sei es die Kommentierung der biblischen Schöpfungsberichte:[38] regelmäßig werden die Erörterungen mit einer deutlichen Warnung vor fruchtlosen, abstrakten Theorieanstrengungen eingeleitet. In erster Linie sind die Reflexionsgebäude der scholastischen Theologie von dieser Kritik betroffen. Gegen sie wird eine vor allem aus den biblischen Quellen geschöpfte und am Wirken Gottes orientierte Betrachtungsweise gerückt. Calvin will—im Wissen um die Grenzen unseres Intellekts—die jede irdische Komplexität übersteigende und umgreifende Komplexität des dreieinen Gottes[39] respektieren. Er stellt die "Unermeßlichkeit" *(immensitas)* des göttlichen Wesens, dessen "immensa et spiritualis essentia," heraus[40] und läßt sich stets von dem im Genfer Katechismus aufgestellten Grundsatz leiten: "Neque enim essentiae eius capax est mens nostra."[41]

Calvin formuliert hier deutlich in antimetaphysischer Stoßrichtung. Er kann zwar ontologisch profilierte Ausdrücke wie *essentia* oder *substantia* unbefangen benutzen—z. B. in der Trinitätslehre—, aber zugleich dekonstruiert er die kognitiven Anmaßungen, die sie begleiten. Die menschliche Gotteserkenntnis ist auf die Initiativen und Aktionen *Gottes* angewiesen. Sie fußt auf seiner uns zugewandten Selbsterschließung in seinem Wirken und ist ganz davon abhängig, daß Gott sich uns mitteilt und öffnet. Wo dieser Fall eingetreten ist, hat Calvin keine Scheu mehr, sehr direkt, sehr persönlich die Erkennbarkeit Gottes zu betonen und sogar davon zu reden, daß Gott sich in Christus *in sein Herz schauen läßt.* [42] Ist es nur ein Zufall daß er bei der ersten Auseinandersetzung mit der metaphysisch instruierten Theologie in der *Institutio* aus dem Stil der Darstellung unvermittelt in die Du-Anrede übergeht?

> "Was hilft es ..., einen Gott zu erkennen, mit dem wir nichts zu schaffen haben? Zweck und Ziel der Gotteserkenntnis soll doch vielmehr sein, daß wir

---

[35]Vgl. ebd., Z. 11ff.; vgl. auch *Institutio* [1559] 1:5:9 (OS 3:53, Z. 20).

[36]Vgl. *Institutio* [1559] 1:13:1 (OS 3:108, Z. 23ff.).

[37]Vgl. *Institutio* [1559] 1:14:1, 3 (OS 3:152-53, 154ff.).

[38]Vgl. *Kommentar zur Genesis,* Einleitung (CO 23:7ff.).

[39]So heißt es etwa in der Auslegung des Vaterunsers: Die Wendung "in den Himmeln" bezeichne einen göttlichen Vater, von dem gesagt werden müsse, daß er "universum orbem complecti et continere, suaque potentia moderari" (*Institutio* [1559] 3:20:40 (OS 4:350, Z. 4-5)).

[40]*Institutio* [1559] 1:13:1 (OS 3:108, Z. 32 sowie Z. 23).

[41]*Genfer Katechismus 1545,* Frage 25 (OS 2:77, Z. 25).

[42]Vgl. den *Genesiskommentar:* "Christus enim imago est, in qua non modo pectus suum nobis Deus conspicuum reddit, sed manus quoque et pedes" (Einleitung, CO 23:11-12). Oder: "sciamus in evangelio nos habere quasi apertum Dei pectus" (*Kommentar zu Joh.* 1:18 (CO 47:20)).

es lernen, Gott zu fürchten und zu ehren, ferner: daß wir unter ihrer Leitung alles von ihm erbitten und ihm alles in Dankbarkeit zuschreiben lernen. *Wie sollte denn der Gedanke an Gott anders in deinem Herzen Raum gewinnen, als daß du sogleich bedächtest: Du bist sein Gebild [figmentum illius sis] ..., dein Leben verdankst du ihm, all dein Tun und Planen soll sich nach ihm ausrichten? ...*"[43] Die ontologische Distanz wird durch den existentiellen Bezug auf das Du aufgebrochen, hier das Du des Lesers, der sich vor dem Du Gottes erfassen soll.

Wenn es um die Eigenschaften *(attributiones)* Gottes geht, bemerkt man die gleiche Tendenz.[44] Die sogenannten Majestätsattribute wie Aseität *(autousia)*, Ewigkeit, Macht *(potentia)*, Heiligkeit und Wahrheit werden nicht mittels einer Kombination von theologischen und philosophischen Denkbewegungen gewonnen, sondern direkt aus der Schrift abgeleitet. Zugleich werden die Attribute der Zuwendung zum Menschen (der Relation also!) wie Barmherzigkeit, Gnade, Geduld, Freundlichkeit, Gerechtigkeit deutlich in den dominanten Vordergrund gerückt. Gott wird über die Attribute der Relation *erkannt*—wir brauchen uns nicht damit zu beschäftigen, "wie er in sich selber ist, sondern wie er sich uns zuwendet [non quis sit apud se, sed qualis erga nos]."[45] Auffällig ist es auch, daß Calvin die einzelnen Eigenschaften Gottes nicht schematisch katalogisiert, sondern ineinander verschränkt und dialektisch aufeinander bezieht (z. B. mit Jeremia 9:23 Gottes Barmherzigkeit, Recht und Gerechtigkeit[46]).

Natürlich konnte sich Calvin nicht an allen Punkten vom Erbe der metaphysischen Gotteslehre lösen. In mancher Hinsicht blieb er ihm auch verhaftet. So fällt es etwa mehrfach auf, daß er gewisse Schwierigkeiten damit hat, das Wesen *(essentia)* Gottes und die Möglichkeit einer Veränderung in Gott miteinander zu vereinbaren. "Gott bleibt sich immer gleich;"[47] seine Natur kann nicht der Veränderlichkeit *(mutatio)* oder gar der Leidenschaft *(passio)* unterworfen sein.[48] Ihn kann nichts reuen.[49] Wenn in der Bibel berichtet wird, daß Gott gelegentlich seine Beschlüsse ändert—wie z. B: angesichts der Buße der Leute von Ninive—, so ist das als eine metaphorische Redewendung zu

---

[43]*Institutio* [1559] 1:2:2 (deutsche Übersetzung von O. Weber, kursiv vom Vf.). Formal wird der Wechsel zur Du-Anrede wohl durch den Rückgriff auf die *Institutio*-Ausgabe von 1539 ausgelöst. Aber wichtig ist: Calvin hatte keine Probleme, unvermittelt in den—überraschenden—Dialog mit dem Leser überzugehen.

[44]Zum Folgenden vgl. *Institutio* [1559] 1:10:2 (OS 3:86-87).

[45]*Institutio* [1559] 1:10:2 (OS 3:86, Z. 17-18).

[46]AaO., 86-87.

[47]*Institutio* [1559] 1:4:3 (OS 3:42, Z. 29-30): "Deum vero ipsum semper sui similem manere ...."

[48]Vgl. *Institutio* [1559] 1:15:5 (OS 3:181, Z. 13-14).

[49]Vgl. *Institutio* [1559] 1:17:12 passim (OS 3:216-17).

betrachten ("Mutatio figurate traditur"[50]), unabhängig davon ("absque figura") gelte Gottes "immutabilitas."[51]

Solche Schwierigkeiten mit der konsequenten Überwindung des metaphysischen Theismus sollte man nicht dramatisieren. Es handelt sich bekanntlich um ein zeitübergreifendes Grundproblem der christlichen Gotteslehre. Wenn man genauer hinsieht, kann man sogar entdecken, daß Calvin nach solchen metaphysischen Eierschalen greift, um Gottes Beständigkeit und Treue auszudrücken. Eine Einzelanalyse wird nachweisen können, daß das relationale Denken Calvins eine spürbare Erosion der metaphysischen Traditionselemente bewirken *mußte.* Untersuchungen zum Verständnis des Ausdrucks "Ewigkeit" können zu dem Resultat gelangen, daß Calvin die Ewigkeitsvorstellung biblisch konzipierte und demgemäß von dem ontologischen Status des Ewigen *(Neutrum),* wie er von Parmenides von Elea formuliert worden war, abzugrenzen vermochte.[52]

> Schon Joseph Bohatec hat gezeigt, daß Calvin die Ewigkeit nicht als ein starres Sein aufgefaßt habe und sich in dieser Hinsicht seines Gegensatzes zur griechischen Antike bewußt gewesen sei.[53] Aus Calvins Deutung gehe klar hervor, "daß nach ihm die Ewigkeit nicht bloß ein ontischer, sondern ein dynamischer Begriff ist."[54] Indem die Ewigkeit Gottes sich nicht allein auf sein transzendentes Wesen bezieht, sondern auf das providentielle Wirken Gottes, gehöre auch sie "in die Reihe der weltbezogenen Eigenschaften [Gottes]."[55]

Den eindrucksvollsten Beleg für die relationale Transformation des metaphysischen Erbes in der Gotteslehre bietet die Providenzlehre Calvins. Zwar polemisiert er prima vista gegen die Religionsphilosophie der Renaissance, wenn er sich von der Vorstellung des *Deus otiosus* abgrenzt, "der die Sorge für die Welt von sich wirft und sich nur an der Muße erbaut."[56] Faktisch ist aber von dieser Kritik auch die Aristotelische Denktradition getroffen, die Gott in der reinen Selbstbezogenheit des *actus purus* angesiedelt hatte und daher Schwierigkeiten bekam, konkrete Interaktionen zwischen dem Schöpfer und

---

[50]OS 3:217, Z. 21.

[51]AaO., Z. 24-25.

[52]Das kann man getrost geltend machen—trotz der zu vermutenden Reverenz für Platon in *Institutio* 1:5:6: "Iam ipsa potentia nos ad cogitandam eius [Dei] aeternitatem deducit: quia aeternum esse, et a seipso principium habere necesse est unde omnia trahunt originem" (OS 3:51, Z. 21-23).

[53]Vgl. J. Bohatec, *Budé und Calvin. Studien zur Gedankenwelt des französischen Frühhumanismus* (Graz: Hermann Böhlaus, 1950), 309.

[54]Ebd.

[55]AaO., 310.

[56]*Institutio* [1559] 1:2:2 (vgl. OS 3:35, Z. 14-15).

der Welt der Geschöpfe auszusagen. Gegen das apersonale Gottesbild der Philosophie, für dessen Fragwürdigkeit er einen scharfen Blick hatte, setzte Calvin den unermüdlich aktiven *gubernator* bzw. *moderator mundi.* [57]

Ihm geht es um die *Gegenwart* des Schöpfers. Wir blicken nicht auf einen vergangenen Anfang zurück, sondern schauen auf die kreative Dynamik seines Wirkens im Hier und Heute. Die *providentia* Dei realisiert das multirelationale Spektrum *aller* Beziehungen zwischen Gott und der Welt seiner Geschöpfe. Aus diesem Grunde traktiert Calvin die Lehre von der Erschaffung der Welt eher sparsam und beiläufig.[58] Aber er bietet seine ganze theologische Leidenschaft auf, um gleich in drei großen Kapiteln über die göttliche *gubernatio mundi* nachzudenken und den Leser der dynamisch agierenden Allgegenwart und Allwirksamkeit Gottes zu vergewissern: "Der Artikel von der Schöpfung steht dominierend im Zeichen der *Vorsehung.* "[59] Ähnlich wie im Genfer Katechismus[60] hebt Calvin die *Gegenwart* der Dynamik Gottes ("praesentia divinae virtutis"[61]) hervor: "Gott zu einem Schöpfer für den Augenblick zu machen [momentaneum creatorem], der sein Werk ein für allemal hinter sich gebracht hätte [absolverit], wäre eine kalte und unfruchtbare Sache; und wir sollen uns gerade *darin* von den Weltmenschen unterscheiden, daß uns die Gegenwart der Kraft Gottes im fortdauernden Bestehen der Welt ebenso hell entgegenleuchtet wie in ihrem Ursprung [ut non minus in perpetuo mundi statu quam prima eius origine praesentia divinae virtutis nobis illuceat]."[62] Die *providentia* ist als aktives Wirken zu interpretieren—ein Wirken "in actu,"[63] und zwar "in continuo actu,"[64] nicht in müßiger, träger Zurückhaltung, sondern äußerst "vigilis, efficax, operosa."[65] Der lebendige Gott sorgt für alles Geschaffene—er agiert gleichsam als die aller Wirklichkeit zugrundeliegende

---

[57]Darin besteht ein Charakteristikum des kompletten Kapitels 1:5 der *Institutio.*

[58]Genaugenommen nur in fünf Unterabschnitten von *Institutio* 1:14, nämlich in 1:14:1-2 und 20-22; dazwischen finden wir die Angelologie und die Dämonologie. Die Beschäftigung mit der Erschaffung des menschlichen Geschöpfs in 1:15 ist Ausgangspunkt vorrangig anthropologischer Klärungen.

[59]Ch. Link, *Schöpfung. Schöpfungstheologie in reformatorischer Tradition,* HST 7 (Gütersloh: Mohn, 1991) 1, 122, vgl. 157ff. Zur Providenzlehre Calvins siehe auch: E. Saxer, *Vorsehung und Verheißung, Vier theologische Modelle (Calvin, Schleiermacher, Barth, Sölle) und ein systematischer Versuch* (Zürich: Theologischer Verlag, 1980), 25ff.

[60]Vgl. OS 2:78 (Frage 27).

[61]*Institutio* [1559] 1:16:1 (OS 3:187, Z. 14).

62 *Institutio* [1559] 1:16:1 (deutsche Übersetzung von O.Weber; vgl. OS 3:187, Z. 10-14).

[63]"Unde sequitur, providentiam in actu locari ..." (OS 3:192, Z. 20-21).

[64]OS 3:190, Z. 16-17.

[65]AaO., Z. 16.

spirituelle Energie. Selbst die unscheinbarsten Kleinigkeiten—und sei es auch nur der Regentropfen[66]—werden von ihm bewegt und gelenkt.

Das Wirklichkeitsverständnis Calvins ist also weit von der Unbeweglichkeit ontologischer Strukturen entfernt. Hier dominiert vielmehr die Bewegung. Genauer: Es sind Bewegungen, Aktionen und Interaktionen, die—im Positiven wie im Negativen—aus ihren lebendigen Relationen zu Gott verstanden werden müssen—zum Creator und Gubernator, den Calvin gerne als Quelle aller Realität, als "fons omnium bonorum,"[67] bezeichnet hat.

IV. Der Horizont der Pneumatologie

Dynamik und Relation in der Wirklichkeit Gottes lassen sich bei Calvin noch in einer anderen Perspektive nachzeichnen: in der Perspektive der Pneumatologie. Ja, unsere bisherigen Ausführungen blieben unvollständig und darin fehlerhaft, wenn wir diesen Aspekt übergehen würden. Gottes Aktualität, seine Präsenz, sein Wirken in allen Dingen sind für Calvin trinitätstheologisch identifizierbar—sie tragen den Namen des Heiligen Geistes. Alles, was Gott wirkt, und alles, was mit diesem Wirken im Zusammenhang steht, ereignet sich in der Gegenwart des Heiligen Geistes. Wenn wir die Relationen im strengen Sinne *theologisch* verstehen wollen, müssen wir sie als pneumatologische Kategorien begreifen.

Geist bedeutet für Calvin immer: *Gott in Aktion,* in Wirkung, in dichtester, intensivster Nähe, aber ebenso auch in anonymer, verborgen bleibender Vitalität. Man muß sich vergegenwärtigen, wie Calvin in der Trinitätslehre die Spezifika der drei Seinsweisen Gottes bestimmt hat: Dem Vater wird der Anfang des Handelns ("principium agendi") zugeschrieben; er ist aller Dinge Quelle und Brunnen ("fons et scaturigo").[68] Dem ewigen Sohne eignen Weisheit, Rat und "dispensatio in rebus agendis."[69] Dem Geist aber werden Kraft und Wirksamkeit im Handeln zugeordnet: " ... at Spiritui virtus et efficacia assignatur actionis."[70] *Virtus und efficacia de*ssen, was der eine Gott als der Vater und als der Sohn tut, bezeichnen die Eigenart des Heiligen Geistes im Geheimnis der Trinität. Gottes Geist wird von Calvin also als diejenige Seinsweise des dreieinen Gottes charakterisiert, in welcher das göttliche Planen und Handeln zur aktuellen Wirkung gelangen. Der Geist tut gegenüber dem Tun des Vaters und dem Tun des Sohnes nichts Eigenes, er präsentiert kein

[66] *Institutio* [1559] 1:16:5: "... certum est non cadere pluviae guttam nisi certo Dei mandato" (OS 3:195, Z. 25-26).

[67] *Institutio* [1559] 1:2:1 (OS 3:34, Z. 29); vgl. *Institutio* [1559] 1:13:9 (OS 3:121, Z. 20-21); *Institutio* [1559] 1:13:18 (OS 3:132, Z. 9); *Kommentar zu Joh.* 1:16 (CO 47:16); *Kommentar zu Gen.* 2:9 (CO 23:39). Calvin hat Gott sehr gerne als "Quelle/fons" bezeichnet.

[68] *Institutio* [1559] 1:13:18 (OS 3:132, Z. 9).

[69] AaO., Z. 10-11.

[70] AaO., Z. 11.

neues *Thema,* das ergänzend zu den großen Themen von Schöpfung und Erlösung hinzuträte. Das Eigene des Geistes—so Werner Krusche—ist gerade das, "daß er nichts Eigenes tut, sondern das Tun des Vaters und des Sohnes verwirklicht."[71] Im Geist kommen das Handeln des Vaters und des Sohnes zur *Wirkung.*

In seiner großartigen Monographie zu Calvins Pneumatologie hat Krusche Calvins pneumatische Präzisierung des göttlichen Wirkens kongenial erfaßt und beschrieben:

> Gott ist für Calvin Heiliger Geist "als der wirksam Handelnde und der handelnd zur Wirkung Gelangende."[72] Darin bringt Gott als Heiliger Geist "das Wirken des *Vaters* und des *Sohnes* zum Ziel."[73] "Alles, was Gott wirkt—und er wirkt alles und wirkt immer! -, ist in seiner *Wirkung* Wirken des Heiligen Geistes. Es gibt schlechterdings kein Handeln des Vaters und des Sohnes, das wirksam würde ohne das Wirken des Geistes. Alles göttliche Wirken ist in seiner Spitze pneumatisch. Der Geist ist die Dei manus, qua suam potentiam exercet.[[74]] Und es gilt auch die Kehrseite: wo Gott seinen Geist entzieht oder vorenthält, beläßt er sein Wirken in der Negativität, benimmt er ihm seine Wirksamkeit. Im Kreaturbereich heißt das: Aufhören der Lebendigkeit—also: Tod; im Heilsbereich: das große 'frustra' über dem gesamten Heilsgeschehen—und also: Verwerfung."[75]

Calvins Pneumatologie entfaltete sich folgerichtig in zwei Dimensionen—die der Schöpfung und Erhaltung und die der Neuschöpfung und Erlösung. Da alles göttliche Wirken in seiner Spitze pneumatisch ist, sind *creatio* und *gubernatio* der Welt als *aktuelle* Relationszusammenhänge *immer* pneumatisch gewirkt. Die Pneumatologie bildet hier die trinitarische Brücke zur Providenzlehre, denn Gottes Geist ist selbstverständlich der *effector providentiae.*[76] Mit seiner allgemein wirkenden Kraft ("virtus generalis"), "wie sie an der Menschheit und auch an der ganzen übrigen Kreatur in Erscheinung tritt, belebt und erhält er uns."[77] Damit ist das Wirklichkeitsverständnis Calvins gleichsam pneumatisch grundiert.

---

[71]W. Krusche, *Das Wirken des Heiligen Geistes nach Calvin* (Göttingen: Vandenhoeck & Ruprecht, 1957), 11.

[72]Ebd.

[73]Ebd.

[74]Zitat aus *Institutio* [1559] 3:1:3 (OS 4:4, Z. 21-22).

[75]Krusche, *Das Wirken,* 11-12.

[76]Vgl. Krusche, *Das Wirken,* 17, 122.—Zur kosmischen und geschichtlichen Entgrenzung der Pneumatologie durch Calvin siehe auch Link, *Schöpfung,* 125-26, 131-32, sowie M. Beintker, "Creator Spiritus. Zu einem unerledigten Problem der Pneumatologie," *EvTh* 46 (1986), 12-26, zu Calvin 20ff.

[77] *Institutio* [1559] 3:1:2 (deutsche Übersetzung nach O. Weber; vgl. OS 4:2, Z. 12-14).

Von noch viel größerer Bedeutung ist natürlich das Wirken des Geistes als effector salutis und darin als *effector electionis* und als *effector sanctificationis.*[78] Denn die durch die Sünde des Menschen dem Tod und dem Verderben ausgelieferte Welt hat nur eine Hoffnung, wenn Gottes Geist Menschen aus ihrem Elend befreit und sie in den Stand der Kinder Gottes versetzt.[79] Als "Wurzel und Samen des himmlischen Lebens in uns" heißt er "Spiritus sanctificationis."[80] Von ihm erfaßt, wird der Mensch zum Glauben erweckt und dem neuen Leben geschenkt. In ihm kommen der Vater und der Sohn zu uns, um uns zu sich zu ziehen.

Auf diese Weise wirkt der Geist des Pfingstfestes die direkteste, intimste Nähe, die zwischen Gott und den Menschen denkbar und—lebbar ist. "Der Heilige Geist ist das Band, durch das uns Christus mit sich wirksam und ganz fest verbindet [Spiritum sanctum vinculum esse, quo nos sibi efficaciter devincit Christus]."[81] Gottes Geist bringt das Heilshandeln des Vaters und des Sohnes zur Wirkung. Er erzeugt Relationen, wo völlige Beziehungslosigkeit herrschte. Aber nicht nur das: Wenn der Geist als das "Band" bezeichnet werden kann, durch das sich Christus mit uns "zusammenbindet," dann stellt er nicht nur Relationen her—dann ist er vielmehr in seinem spezifischen Wirken die Relation, die er herstellt: *Gottes Geist ist Gott in Relation und als Relation.* Als Geist *sind* der Vater und der Sohn die Relationen, von denen die ganze Wirklichkeit gehalten und getragen wird und durch die ihr das Licht der Erlösung aufleuchtet. Nach Calvin muß jedenfalls eine theologisch begründete Relationenlehre pneumatologisch einsetzen, pneumatologisch akzentuieren und pneumatologisch—schließen.

V. Der soteriologische Horizont

Daß gerade die Soteriologie von den Relationen zwischen Gott und Mensch beherrscht ist und hier ihre spannendsten Seiten offenbart, setzen wir als bekannt voraus. Man muß allerdings ein wenig schwindelfrei sein, um hier nicht zu kapitulieren. Die Antithesen von Gnade und Sünde, von Fleisch und Geist, von Leben und Tod, von Heil und Verdammnis verlangen nach einem Denken, das auf Bewegungen und Kontraste eingestellt ist, und verweigern sich jeder linearen, undialektischen Denkweise. Auch den, anders gelagerten,

---

[78]Wir gehen hier nicht auf die christologische Reichweite der Pneumatologie ein. Natürlich hat Calvin dem Wirken des Geistes auch eine Funktion in der Christologie zuerkannt: Gottes Gegenwart im irdischen Jesus läßt sich ebenfalls pneumatologisch erfassen und darstellen (vgl. etwa *Institutio* [1559] 2:15:2; oder vgl. die Rede von der "virtus" des Heiligen Geistes in der "persona Mediatoris" in OS 4:2, Z. 38-39).

[79]Vgl. hierzu pars pro toto die eindrückliche und dichte Auslegung von Röm 8 im *Kommentar zum Römerbrief* (CO 49:136-68).

[80]*Institutio* [1559] 3:1:2 (OS 4:2, Z. 11, 14).

[81]*Institutio* [1559] 3:1:1 (OS 4:2, Z. 5-6).

Dualen von Rechtfertigung und Heiligung, von Glaube und Ethos, von Zeit und Ewigkeit oder von Zukunft und Gegenwart des Reiches Gottes werden wir nur gerecht werden, wenn wir uns in der anspruchsvollen Kunst üben, mehrdimensional zu denken, d.h. die diversen Dimensionen und Perspektiven solcher und ähnlicher Phänomene zu erkennen, sie in Bewegung zu halten und sie ständig aufeinander zu beziehen. Calvin hatte diese Aufgabe klar erkannt. Wir können sagen, daß seine Beiträge zu ihrer Lösung bis heute als vorbildlich gelten müssen.

Im Folgenden kann es nur darum gehen, einige besonders signifikante Beispiele herauszugreifen. Wir konzentrieren uns auf drei Punkte: (1.) die Christus-Relation des Christen, die als die tragende Achse aller soteriologischen Themen zu beachten ist, (2.) die unter dem Kreuz gelebte "vita hominis Christiani"[82] und (3.) die Frage, ob und in welchem Ausmaß in Calvins Soteriologie Entwicklungen, Prozeßdynamiken und Fortschritte anzutreffen sind.

(1.) Nachdem der in die Sünde geratene Mensch jede Möglichkeit verloren hat, von sich aus in eine Beziehung zu Gott zu treten, kann eine Beziehung zwischen Gott und ihm nur von Gott her gebildet werden. Die Rechtfertigung des Sünders eröffnet eine neue, Leben gebende Beziehung, die *solo Christo* exklusiv aus Gnade geschenkt und im Glauben ergriffen wird. Im Blick auf seinen Grund und auf sein personales Gegenüber hat Calvin den Glauben als lebendige Christusgemeinschaft beschrieben. Auch wenn—pneumatologisch betrachtet—Christus diese Gemeinschaft durch den Geist herstellt,[83] handelt es sich nichtsdestoweniger um die dichteste, tiefste, innigste Gemeinschaft *mit Christus.* An ihrer Authentizität darf nicht gezweifelt werden. Die *unio* bzw. *coniunctio cum Christo,* nach Emil Brunner "die Mitte des ganzen calvinischen Denkens,"[84] schmilzt uns mit ihm zusammen. Indem wir mit ihm zusammenwachsen ("cum ipso in unum coalescimus"[85]), teilt er uns durch die Kraft seines Geistes sein Leben und alle ihm vom Vater geschenkten Güter mit.[86] Solange wir mit Christus verbunden sind, droht uns keine Gefahr der Verdammnis,[87] aber ohne ihn würden wir hoffnungslos dem ewigen Tod verfallen.[88]

---

[82]So in der Kapitelüberschrift von *Institutio* 3:6 (vgl. OS 3:146, Z. 12).

[83]Vgl. *Institutio* [1559] 3:1:3: Christus "solo autem Spiritu unit se nobiscum. Eiusdem Spiritus gratia et virtute efficimur illius membra, ut nos sub se contineat, vicissimque illum possideamus" (OS 4:5, Z. 10-12).

[84]E. Brunner, *Vom Werk des Heiligen Geistes* (Tübingen: J C B Mohr, 1935), 38. Vgl. auch Krusche, *Das Wirken,* 266, der sich Brunner ohne Vorbehalte anschießt.

[85]*Institutio* [1559] 3:1:1 (OS 4:1, Z. 18-19).

[86]Vgl. *Kommentar zu* Joh. 17:21 (CO 47:387).

[87]Vgl. *Kommentar zu Röm.* 8:1 (CO 49:136).

[88]Vgl. *Institutio* [1559] 3:14:4 (OS 4:222, Z. 31ff.).

In der Christus-Einung wird die Ich-Du-Relation so verdichtet, daß sich die Unterschiede von *Extra* und *Intra* auflösen. Calvin kann sagen, daß "Christus nicht außer uns [non extra nos]" ist, wenn wir fest an ihn glauben, sondern "in uns wohnt [in nobis habitat]: er bindet uns nicht nur durch ein unzerreißbares Band der Gemeinschaft an sich, sondern wächst durch eine wundersame Gemeinschaft [mirabili quadam communione] von Tag zu Tag mehr mit uns zusammen [in unum corpus nobiscum coalescit], bis er ganz mit uns eins wird [donec unum penitus nobiscum fiat]."[89] Es ist der Geist, der das "extra nos" überwindet, damit wir mit dem gegenwärtigen Jesus Christus über alle Distanzen hinweg zusammenwachsen.[90]

(2.) In der Christus-Einung sind wir getröstet und vergewissert; wir wissen, daß uns das Heil geschenkt ist. Der Mensch der sich in Christus verankert, muß das Gericht Gottes nicht fürchten, sein Gewissen erfährt "friedliche Ruhe und heitere Gelassenheit [serena tranquillitas]."[91] Dennoch oder gerade deshalb wird der Christ in die härtesten Konflikte verwickelt. Seine Existenz wird nun zum Kampfplatz des unversöhnlichen Streits zwischen Gnade und Sünde. Auch wenn er Christus gehört und in der Wiedergeburt das neue Leben geschenkt bekam, streiten in ihm die "Reste des Fleisches [reliquiae carnis]" gegen das Gebot Gottes.[92] Es gibt in den menschlichen Angelegenheiten keinen schärferen Konflikt als den zwischen Geist und Fleisch.[93] Und dieser Konflikt läßt sich weder versöhnen noch überbrücken, sein Antagonismus muß ausgehalten und ertragen werden. Er *kann* ertragen werden, indem wir uns durch Jesus Christus heiligen lassen. Durch die Kraft seines Geistes werden wir zur wahren Reinheit des Lebens geführt und sterben der alten Existenz des Fleisches immer mehr ab.[94]

Aber noch auf einer anderen Ebene wird der Christ in Konflikte gestürzt: in den Zerreißproben der Anfechtung, des Leidens, der Bedrängnis in der Kreuzesnachfolge. Es wird oft übersehen, daß Calvin den damit verbundenen existentiellen Nöten nicht weniger Aufmerksamkeit zugewendet hat als der Frage nach der—stärker ethisch orientierten—Heiligung des Menschen.[95] Das

---

[89] *Institutio* [1559] 3:2:24 (deutsche Übersetzung von O. Weber; vgl. OS 4:35, Z. 7-11).

[90] Vgl. *Institutio* [1559] 3:1:3 (OS 4:5, Z. 1ff.). Siehe auch OS 4:26, Z. 29-32: "Hic praecipuus fidei cardo vertitur, ne quas Dominus offert misericordiae promissiones, extra nos tantum veras esse arbitremur, in nobis minime: sed ut potius eas intus complectendo nostras faciamus."

[91] *Institutio* [1559] 3:13:1 (OS 4:215, Z. 22-23).

[92] *Kommentar zu Röm.* 7:14 (CO 49:128).

[93] Vgl. ebd.

[94] Vgl. *Institutio* [1559] 3:14:9 (OS 4:228, Z. 5ff.).

[95] In der *Institutio* handelt es sich vor allem um die Kapitel 3:6-10, in denen es in mehreren Schritten der Konkretion vornehmlich um die seelsorgerlichen Aspekte des neuen Lebens, seine Bewährung im Leiden und in der "tolerantia crucis" geht.

Tragen des Kreuzes ("tolerantia crucis") ist fester Bestandteil der Christusgemeinschaft. Auch in ihm erprobt und bewährt sich die Selbstverleugnung des Christen.[96]

> Für moderne protestantische Ohren formulierte Calvin wenig einladend, wenn er Jesu Wort vom Kreuztragen (Matth. 16:24) so kommentierte: "... wen der Herr zum Kind angenommen und der Gemeinschaft mit den Seinen gewürdigt hat, der muß sich auf ein hartes, mühseliges, unruhiges Leben gefaßt machen, das von gar vielen und vielartigen Übeln erfüllt ist."[97] Daraus ergibt sich aber mit Röm. 8:29 ein "hervorragender Trost": Wenn es uns nämlich hart und rauh ergeht und wir meinen, Unglück und Böses zu erleben, haben wir eigentlich Anteil an Christi Leiden ("nos Christi passionibus communicare").[98] Die hier in Erscheinung tretende Simultaneität von Leidenmüssen und Getröstetsein läßt sich nur in antithetischer Gedankenführung, also dialektisch, ausdrücken: "Die Schrift nämlich erteilt den Heiligen das Lob der Geduld [tolerantiae laudem] dann, wenn sie von der Härte der Not angefochten werden [afflictantur] und doch darüber nicht zerbrechen und zu Boden fallen, wenn die Bitterkeit sie quält und sie dennoch von geistlicher Freude [spirituali gaudio] erfüllt sind, wenn die Angst sie bedrückt, und sie dennoch aufatmen, weil Gottes Trost sie fröhlich macht [Dei consolatione exhilarati respirent]."[99]

In der Anfechtung des Leidens lernen wir es, uns zu Christus zu flüchten und alle stolze Selbstbehauptung fallen zu lassen. Die Schule des Leidens ist keine Spezialerfahrung der verfolgten Protestanten im Frankreich des 16. Jahrhunderts (obwohl Calvin sicher auch deren Situation vor Augen hatte, als er solche Sätze niederschrieb), sie gehört essentiell in die Christusrelation des Glaubens hinein und wird, wenn sie bestanden wird, die Gemeinschaft mit Christus in *dieser* Zeit vertiefen, um sich dann als eschatologische Gemeinschaft in *jener* "Zeit" des Reiches Gottes zu vollenden.

(3.) Die Frage nach einem Fortschreiten *(progressus)* im Glauben und in der Existenz im Glauben läßt sich klar bejahen. Calvin kann sogar in einer Kapitelüberschrift vom "initium iustificationis" und von einem kontinuierlichen Fortschreiten auf der Basis der Rechtfertigung sprechen.[100] Der Glaube ist nichts Starres. Er wächst und entwickelt sich. Das Fortschreiten in der Einung mit Christus ist mit einem Wachstum in der Erkenntnis des Glaubens verbunden: Wir werden—gezogen vom Heiligen Geist—"nach Verstand und Herz weit über das erhoben, was wir aus uns selber erfassen können."[101] Im

---

[96]Vgl. *Institutio* [1559] 3:8:1 (OS 4:161, Z. 17ff.).

[97]*Institutio* [1559] 3:8:1 (deutsche Übersetzung nach O. Weber; vgl. OS 4:168, Z. 29-33).

[98]Ebd. (OS 4:161-62).

[99]*Institutio* [1559] 3:8:10 (deutsche Übersetzung nach O. Weber; vgl. OS 4:168, Z. 29-33).

[100]*Institutio* [1559] 3:14: "Quale initium iustificationis et continui progressus" (OS 4:220, Z. 27).

[101]*Institutio* [1559] 3:2:34: "... ita ubi [Spiritu Dei] trahimur, mente et animo evehimur supra nostram intelligentiam" (OS 4:45, Z. 21-22).

Leiden in der Christusbindung werden wir zu tieferer Selbsterkenntnis geführt,[102] aber unser Glaube kann auch wieder ermatten und in den Konfrontationen mit dem Zweifel ermüden.[103] Wenn wir dann aber fortschreiten—Calvin beeilt sich, sofort hinzuzufügen: " ... nos assidue proficere decet"—, dann kommen wir im Weitergehen ("progressu") "mehr und mehr zu einem näheren und deshalb auch gewisseren Schauen seines Angesichts: so wird es uns gerade im Vorwärtsschreiten immer vertrauter."[104]

Und auch das im Glauben gelebte neue Leben wächst und entwickelt sich. Wer durch die Wiedergeburt geführt worden ist, wird verändert. Calvin hat das dialektische Arrangement mit der Sünde, das fromme Treten auf der Stelle, entschieden abgelehnt. Die Einung mit Christus führt auch zu einem von ihm gewirkten Fortschreiten in der Heiligung. Das ist niemals unser Verdienst! Aber der Dynamik unserer Erneuerung, der schrittweisen Abtötung des alten Menschen und der schrittweisen *vivificatio* seines neuen Seins, sollen wir nicht widerstreben. Wenn wir Christus gehören, hat die Sünde ihre Vormachtstellung über uns verloren—auch wenn wir weiterhin von ihr geplagt werden, hat sie doch aufgehört, über uns zu herrschen ("sed regnare tantum non etiam habitare desinit").[105]

> Calvin redet den Leser des Römerbriefkommentars direkt an: "Wenn du ein Christ bist, dann muß an dir das Zeichen deiner Gemeinschaft mit dem Tod Christi sichtbar werden, deren Frucht es ist, daß dein Fleisch mit allen seinen Begierden gekreuzigt wird. Im übrigen ist diese Gemeinschaft nicht deshalb als nicht vorhanden anzusehen, weil du spürst, daß sich die Reste des Fleisches in dir regen. Im Gegenteil: Es ist ständig auf ihr Wachstum zu achten, bis man das Ziel erreicht hat."[106]

Christ sein ist ein Weg zu einem Ziel. Wer diesen Weg beschreibt—und darin besteht eine wesentliche Aufgabe der Theologie—, muß den Schritten und Bewegungen, die auf diesem Weg vollzogen werden, folgen. Es ist oft darüber nachgedacht worden, weshalb sich Calvins Soteriologie so schwer systematisieren läßt. Rechtfertigung und Heiligung erscheinen bei ihm bekanntlich nicht in einer einfachen Ursache-Folge-Struktur. Man kann Rechtfertigung und Heiligung eher mit zwei sich gegenseitig stützenden und fördernden Strategien vergleichen, die Gott wählt, um uns zu seinen Kindern

---

[102] Vgl. *Institutio* [1559] 3:8:2 (OS 4:162, 35-36).

[103] Vgl. etwa *Institutio* [1559] 3:2:4 und 3:2:15.

[104] *Institutio* [1559] 3:2:19 (deutsche Übersetzung von O. Weber; vgl. OS 4:29, Z. 31-34).

[105] *Institutio* [1559] 3:3:11 (OS 4:66, Z. 26-27).

[106] *Kommentar zu Röm.* 6:7 (CO 49:108).

und zu Teilhabern an seiner Herrlichkeit zu machen.[107] Den orthodoxen *ordo salutis,* der dem intellektuellen Bedürfnis nach einer logischen Zuordnung der Stufen der Heilsapplikation entsprang, finden wir bei Calvin nicht.[108] Aus diesem Grund dürfen auch Worte wie "Wachstum" und "Prozeß" nicht naiv mit der Vorstellung einer kontinuierlichen Entwicklung verbunden werden. Denn bei *diesem* Prozeß kann es sehr abrupt zugehen, kommt es zu Turbulenzen und Sprüngen, kann man immer wieder auf die Anfänge zurückgeworfen werden. Deshalb kann man nicht scharf genug die Vollkommenheit der Rechtfertigung betonen: Deus "iustificat ... non ex parte."[109] Die Dynamiken geistlichen Wachstums lassen sich keinesfalls mit sanft ansteigenden Kurven vergleichen. Eher haben wir es mit konzentrischen Wellenbewegungen zu tun, die auf die *unio cum Christo* .

VI. Schlußbetrachtung

Calvin hat ein *spezifisches* Denken in Relationen praktiziert. Es ist ein Denken, das von der lebendigen Dynamik seines Gegenstandes erfaßt ist und dieser Dynamik in den Akten des Denkens unmittelbar gerecht zu werden versucht. Der eigentliche "Gegenstand" dieses Denkens—und hier wird zugleich die Tauglichkeit des Wortes "Gegenstand" zum Problem—ist der dreieine Gott, der in Jesus Christus den von ihm entfremdeten Menschen für sich zu gewinnen sucht. Das Denken engagiert sich für die Erkenntnis des dreieinen Gottes und für die unlöslich mit ihr verbundene Selbsterkenntnis des Menschen. Es gewinnt seine Einsichten im Dialog mit dem Zeugnis der Bibel, der sich als ein Dialog mit dem sich uns hier und jetzt zuwendenden Du Gottes herausstellt. Dieses Denken fixiert sich nicht auf "Standpunkte." Es involviert sich in Bewegungsabläufe. Es verharrt nicht in Strukturen, sondern bewegt sich in Relationen.

---

[107]Sehr klar bemerkt F. Wendel, daß zwischen Rechtfertigung und Heiligung bei Calvin weder eine kausale noch eine finale Verbindung bestehe: "Die Heiligung ist nicht das Ziel der Rechtfertigung. Sie entspringt derselben Quelle, bleibt aber unabhängig oder, genauer gesagt, logisch unterschieden von der Rechtfertigung. Calvin hat des öfteren großes Gewicht auf das Vorhandensein und die Art der Verbindung gelegt, die diese beiden aus der Einigung mit Christus hervorgehenden Wohltaten miteinander verknüpft ... In der Tat kann die Heiligung in diesem Leben nur einen Anfang machen; die Gläubigen bleiben trotz aller Fortschritte doch Sünder bis in den Tod. Die Rechtfertigung dagegen ist von Anfang an vollkommen, wie die Gerechtigkeit Christi vollkommen ist, mit der sie uns bekleidet. Im übrigen ist vom Standpunkt der Theologiegeschichte nicht diese Unterscheidung am interessantesten, sondern die Tatsache, daß für Calvin Rechtfertigung und Heiligung zwei gleichwertige Gnadengaben sind." (Wendel, *Calvin,* 225-26).

[108]Vgl. C. Graafland, "Hat Calvin einen Ordo salutis gelehrt?" in Neuser, hg., *Calvinus Ecclesiae Genevensis Custos,* 221-44.

[109]*Institutio* [1559] 3:11:11 (OS 4:193, Z. 36).

Wilhelm Neuser hebt hervor, daß für Calvins Menschenbild eine "dynamische Betrachtungsweise" kennzeichnend sei,[110] und fügt hinzu: "Die ontologische Darstellung der Scholastik sucht er durch akthafte Beschreibung zu überwinden."[111] In der Tat läßt sich gerade an der Anthropologie Calvins ablesen, daß das ontologische Denken versagt, wenn wir konsequent die radikale Erlösungsbedürftigkeit des Menschen und dann auch die innere Dramatik des Kampfes zwischen Gnade und Sünde zur Geltung bringen möchten. Ich habe zu zeigen versucht, daß die akthafte Beschreibung auch bei anderen zentralen Themen Calvins zum Vorschein kommt. Sie kommt um so deutlicher zum Vorschein, je stärker sich das Denken durch die Relationen bewegt weiß, die es gerade zu erläutern und zu interpretieren hat.

Die Affinität zu einem solchen Denken hat viele Ursachen. Für Calvin war es auf alle Fälle von Vorteil, daß er seine Theologie relativ unbeeinflußt von den Denkgewohnheiten und Fragestellungen der Scholastik entwickeln konnte. Er brauchte auf die Paradigmen dieser hochentwickelten Denktechnik keine Rücksicht zu nehmen und konnte daher deren Schwächen illusionslos erfassen. Eine andere Frage ist es, ob Calvin ein gerechtes Urteil für die intellektuelle Kapazität des scholastischen Denkens aufgebracht hat.

Unter den Autoritäten, die Calvins Bereitschaft zum relationalen Denken mindestens anregten, ist gewiß Augustinus zu nennen. Aber der entscheidende Impuls kam sicher aus der Schriftgebundenheit der Calvinschen Theologie. Seine Theologie basierte nicht auf a priori konzipierten Konstruktionsprinzipien, sondern auf Grundeinsichten, die im ständigen Gespräch mit biblischen Texten gewonnen wurden. Biblischen Texten eignet eine relationale Tiefengrammatik. Nicht jedes Denken (und ganz sicher auch nicht jede Hermeneutik) vermag diese Tiefengrammatik zu neuem Leben zu erwecken. Calvins Theologie war zweifellos dazu in der Lage. Die entscheidenden Relationen im Denken Calvins reproduzieren relationale Geflechte, wie sie durch die Textwelten der Bibel hindurchscheinen.

Der Calvin-Forschung hat es Calvin auf diese Weise nicht gerade leicht gemacht. Unser wissenschaftliches Verlangen nach logischer Folgerichtigkeit und systematischer Geschlossenheit wird durch den Stil seiner Theologie immer wieder irritiert und gestört. Man denke nur an die große Kontroverse um den kognitiven Status der Theologia naturalis bei Calvin. Man kann zeigen, daß er sie braucht. Man kann ebenso zeigen, daß er sie verwirft. Ähnliche Probleme entstehen, wenn man versucht, die Zuordnung von Rechtfertigung und Heiligung zu systematisieren, oder fragt, ob und wie der Sünder als *imago*

[110]W. Neuser, "Dogma und Bekenntnis in der Reformation: Von Zwingli und Calvin bis zur Synode von Westminster," in C. Andresen, A. M. Ritter, *Handbuch der Dogmen- und Theologiegeschichte II* (Göttingen: Vandenhoeck & Ruprecht, 21998), (167-352) 250.

[111]Ebd.

Dei zu bestimmen ist, oder ergründen will, wie Gottes Allwirksamkeit mit der Verantwortungsfähigkeit des menschlichen Geschöpfs zu verbinden ist.[112]

Calvins Denken in Relationen folgt den Dynamiken, die durch die Ich-Du-Relation zwischen Gott und dem Menschen erzeugt werden. Um ein Bild zu gebrauchen: Dieses Denken in Relationen agiert wie ein Maler, der den Vogel im Flug zeichnen soll.[113] Der Zeichenstift folgt der Flugbewegung des Vogels. Aber eigentlich kann der Vogel im Flug nicht gezeichnet werden, man erhält allenfalls Momentaufnahmen einer Flugbewegung. Tatsächlich muß man die Bewegung des Vogels stoppen, um ihn zeichen zu können. Man kann allerdings mehrere Punkte aus der Fluglinie herausgreifen, aber auch dann bekommt man bestenfalls eine Serie von Momentaufnahmen, die einzelne Flugpositionen wiedergeben. Die einzelnen Bilder, die bei diesem Verfahren entstehen, können zu widersprüchlichen Deutungen führen, und sie können—für sich betrachtet—einander sogar widersprechen. Vor einer analogen Schwierigkeit steht unser Denken. Wenn es Bewegungen folgt und einen Eindruck von ihrer Relationalität zu vermitteln versucht, muß es jeweils die Bewegung anhalten, um etwas über sie aussagen zu können. Es "stellt fest," will sagen: es hält einen Prozeß an, um ihn zu beschreiben. Sowohl das systematisch-ordnende Denken als auch das relationale Denken haben mit diesem Problem zu kämpfen. Auch das relationale Denken kommt ja über einzelne Bilder nicht hinaus. Aber es ist dem systematisch-ordnenden Denken darin überlegen, daß es seine Systematik nicht für den einzigen Schlüssel zu seinen Themen halten muß. Fasziniert von der Bewegung des Vogels im Fluge, nimmt es auch Widersprüche und Spannungen in Kauf. Es wäre übertrieben, wenn wir Calvin attestieren würden, daß er das immer beachtet habe. Gelegentlich hat wohl auch er etwas zuviel geordnet. Aber er war immerhin in der Lage, den Relationen in der Gott-Mensch-Beziehung den Vorrang vor ihrer systematischen Auflösung in lauter unbewegliche Einzelbilder einzuräumen.

---

[112]F. Wendel hat eine ganze Liste von—wie er sagt—"Paradoxen Calvins" benannt und damit einen an wesentlichen Punkten noch längst nicht eingelösten Forschungskatalog aufgestellt: Vor allem handele es sich "um die Einheit und Verschiedenheit der zwei Naturen in Christus ..., um die gleichbleibende Liebe Gottes zu seinen Geschöpfen und seinen Zorn über die gefallene Menschheit, um die Rechtfertigung, die den Menschen auch weiterhin Sünder bleiben läßt, um die vollkommene und unmittelbare Zurechnung der Gerechtigkeit Christi und die langsame und stets unvollkommene Erneuerung, um die Größe des Menschen und sein Elend, um die Abschaffung und die bleibende Gültigkeit des Gesetzes, um den Wert der irdischen Güter und ihre Verachtung, um die zugleich sichtbare und unvollkommene und unsichtbare und vollkommene Kirche, um die Gegenwart Christi im Sakrament und sein Sitzen zur Rechten Gottes. Die Reihe könnte ohne Mühe fortgesetzt werden" (Wendel, *Calvin,* 317). Ob es gelingt, mit Hilfe eines bipolaren Verständnisses von Dialektik über solche "Paradoxe" hinauszukommen, erscheint mir fraglich, denn auch damit könnten vorschnell unbewegliche Strukturen fixiert werden (vgl. dazu die—kontroversen—Voten von A. Ganoczy, *Le jeune Calvin. Genèse et évolution de sa vocation réformatrice* (Wiesbaden: Franz Steiner, 1966), 196ff.; Dowey, "Structure of Calvin's Thought," 146ff.; Butin, *Revelation, Redemption and Response,* 15ff.).

[113]Die Anregung zu diesem Bild verdanke ich einem Passus in der *ersten* Auflage von Barths Römerbriefkommentar: Vgl. K. Barth, *Der Römerbrief (Erste Fassung) 1919,* hg. H. Schmidt (Zürich: Theologischer Verlag, 1985), 384, 391.

New Sources and New Ideas on the Life and Career of Calvin, 1541-1557

William G. Naphy

There is a very real sense in which a more accurate title would be "New Approaches to Old Sources and New Twists on Old Ideas." That is, most of what will be discussed below is not necessarily "new." Rather, it is the result of a more integrated use of sources in Geneva and a shift of focus away from Calvin's life and career to the wider (albeit more "parochial") Genevan setting for that life and career. While this may seem likely to obscure "Calvin, the man" it is hoped that it will, in actuality, provide a deeper and fuller understanding of his ministry in Geneva in its broadest sense.

The most obvious place to begin is to examine the reasons for Calvin's recall to Geneva in 1541. If one takes the view that the Guillermin-Articulant crisis was, to a great degree, the result of a clash over religious policy and that the *Guillermins* were the ardent supporters of Calvin and Farel then the recall makes some logical sense.[1] The problem with this view is that Farel was not recalled and the city never showed any real enthusiasm for him. If, on the other hand, one takes the view, as this essay does, that Calvin and Farel were merely casualties in a Genevan debate over the city's relationship with Berne (and how best to maintain that crucial military alliance) then the recall of either man raises some other questions.[2] Namely, why then was either man recalled?

[1]W. Balke, *Calvin and the Anabaptist Radicals* (Grand Rapids: Eerdmans, 1981) is a particularly enthusiastic proponent of this interpretation (see esp. 84). He relies rather heavily on Beza's and Colladon's accounts of the disputes with the Anabaptists and a single case involving a number of local Genevans. Balke does admit (83) that this view, and its reliance upon Beza and Colladon, was not favoured by Kampschulte or Roget (see below, notes 6 & 21, for references to their work). Cf., W. J. Bouwsma, *John Calvin: A Sixteenth-Century Portrait* (Oxford: O.U.P., 1988), 20, where he follows Balke's view (*Anabaptist,* 73-96). The case mentioned, AEG, Procès Criminels [PC], 2e Série, 385 (11-14 Sep. 1537), involved Jacques Merauld from Lyon. Cf., M. Roset, *Chroniques de Genève* (Geneva: Georg, 1894), 255, 262, 265; T. Beza, "Life of Calvin," in H. Beveridge, ed. and trans., Tracts relating to the Reformation by Jean Calvin (Edinburgh: Calvin Translation Society, 1844), 32. Roset's account is reproduced in P. Geisendorf, "Les Annalistes," *Mémoires et documents publiés par la Société d'Histoire et d'Achéologie de Genève,* 37:481-94. Cf., P. E. Martin, *Histoire de Genève des Origines à 1798* (Geneva: A. Jullien, 1951), 235.

[2]This precarious and complex relationship is discussed in detail in my "Genevan Diplomacy & Foreign Policy, c. 1535-1560: Balancing on the Edge of the Confederacy," in W. Kaiser, C. Sieber-Lehmann, C. Windler, eds., *Eidgenössische «Grenzfälle»: Mülhausen und Genf/En Marge de la Confédération: Mulhouse et Genève* (Basel: Schwabe, 2001), 189-219.

A close examination of the events surrounding the expulsion of Calvin and Farel and the subsequent reign of the *Articulants* has produced some interesting points. First, Marcourt and Morand seem to have been as competent ministers as enthusiastically devoted to maintaining a high moral standard in the city as Calvin and Farel had been.[3] However, where they differed was their willingness to accept a "Zwinglian" state domination of ecclesiastical affairs. The *Guillermins,* opposed to the *Articulant* platform of appeasing Berne, focused their political opposition on the expulsion of the ministers.[4] On a number of levels this was a very astute move. It gave the *Guillermins* an opportunity to protest against state policy without coming into direct conflict with the state. Also, the *Guillermins* were able to portray their political protests as a compassionate attachment to the victims of *Articulant* viciousness. Marcourt and Morand became caught in the middle of this on-going political debate (as Calvin and Farel had been previously) and it became almost impossible to imagine their being able to work with the *Guillermins.*[5]

It is perhaps worth pausing for a moment to consider the work of Marcourt and Morand in Geneva. At their instigation, the Senate first discussed the establishment of a consistory in Geneva. Since Berne (Geneva's "protector") already had such bodies this was hardly surprising. More interestingly, they were also able to persuade the magistrates to consider creating deacons to handle the city's social welfare.[6] In the end, because of the political turmoil, these issues never moved beyond mere discussion. Two points are worth making though. First, two things near and dear to the Calvinist system were discussed in Geneva during Calvin's absence and, therefore, much of the groundwork laid for the later *Ecclesiastical Ordinances.* Second, neither Marcourt nor Calvin was ever able to persuade the city to introduce a diaconate. Indeed, it is worth recalling that Dutch magistrates often used Geneva as a model of a city where social welfare remained under magisterial not ministerial control—much to the consternation and annoyance of their Reformed ministers.[7]

[3]See my *Calvin and the Consolidation of the Genevan Reformation* (Louisville: Westminster John Knox Press, 2003), 31 [Henceforth, *Consolidation*]. See AEG [Archives d'État de Genève], RC [Registres du Conseil, vol.] 32, fol. 52r (10 May 1538) where Jacques Bernard complained about adultery. Also, AEG, RC32, fol. 149r (17 Sep. 1538); RC34, fols. 219r (30 Apr. 1540), 334v (16 Jul. 1540), where all the ministers complained of slanders against them. And also AEG, RC32, fol. 129v (23 Aug. 1538) and RC33, fol. 19r (19 Feb. 1539) for more ministerial complaints about immorality.

[4]For example, AEG, RC33, fol. 259v (25 Aug. 1539); RC34, fol. 185r (16 Apr. 1540); Roset, *Chroniques,* 266.

[5]For a slightly fuller treatment of their position vis-à-vis the *Guillermins* see *Consolidation,* 41-42.

[6]AEG, RC35, fol. 207r (17 May 1541). Reference to the original discussion is contained in F. W. Kampschulte, *Johann Calvin, seine Kirche und sein Staat in Genf* (Leipzig: Duncker & Humblot, 1869-99), 377. However, by the time it had passed through the hands of H. Höpfl, *The Christian Polity of John Calvin* (Cambridge: C.U.P., 1982), 95, A. McGrath, *A Life of John Calvin* (Oxford: Blackwell, 1990), 112 was led to say: "a prototype (Consistory) had actually been established."

[7]I am grateful to Prof. Andrew Pettegree (St Andrews) for this information.

With the publication of the *Articles* between Geneva and Berne, the *Guillermins* were able to mount a full-blown political protest and force the *Articulants* from power. The *Articulants* further undercut their position by an abortive coup. This gave the *Guillermins* almost complete power. However, it also left them with a problem. Their earlier, politically-motivated protests (of which Calvin disapproved), revolved around the expulsion of the old ministers and the hiring of Marcourt and Morand. This had created a legacy of bitterness and acrimony between Geneva's new rulers and the *Articulant*-appointed ministers. Although the *Guillermin* magistrates seemed willing to attempt to make the situation work, Marcourt and Morand came to the conclusion that no *modus vivendi* was likely and resigned. At this point, the magistrates began discussing Calvin's recall *because of* the resignation of these ministers.[8] In other words, Calvin was recalled because the *Guillermin* magistrates were left with no high-calibre ministers and a chaotic ecclesiastical situation. What they wanted was stability and quality. Calvin, the lawyer and theologian, offered both; Farel, whose style had been, and would remain, fiery, did not. Calvin's recall, therefore, made perfect sense in that situation, as did Farel's continuing "exile."

None of the above is "new," with the possible exception of the timing of the magisterial discussions to recall Calvin and the resignations of Marcourt and Morand. If there is any new idea it relates to the placing of the events in the context of a wider, yet very internal, Genevan debate about the best way to secure the alliance with Berne. In this scheme, Calvin, Farel and the ecclesiastical settlement were not the focus of the 1538-41 crisis. Rather, the modification to church practices was the first phase in the *Articulants'* appeasing of, and conforming to, Berne. Once the *Guillermins* settled that internal debate with the virtual rupture of relations with Berne, the major concern for the Genevan government became the re-establishment of order and stability within Geneva. Bereft of its two leading ministers, the city naturally turned to someone who knew the situation, who had counselled reconciliation throughout the crisis, and who had the training and skills necessary to stabilise Geneva's ecclesiastical situation.

A number of subsequent crises which involved Calvin are also open to a more nuanced interpretation. These are not meant to be exhaustive but rather illustrative of the way in which a more comprehensive use of sources coupled with a focus on Geneva rather than Calvin can produce some new interpretations of events in Calvin's life and career. Four key crises are most useful for this discussion: the Lect wedding, the "Slashed Breeches Affair," baptismal names, and excommunication.

---

[8]Morand departed 10 Aug. 1540 (AEG, RC34, fol. 376r), and Marcourt left on 20 Sep. 1540 (AEG, RC34, fol. 452r). The *Petit Conseil* acted the next day to recall Calvin (AEG, RC34, fol. 452v). This undercuts the idea that the Guillermins were ever enthusiastic partisans of Calvin and Farel, a view expressed in R. Guerdan, *Histoire de Genève* (Paris: Fayard, 1981), 80.

The Lect affair broke on 26 March 1546.[9] Antoine Lect celebrated the marriage of his daughter to Claude Philippe, son of the executed *Articulant*, Jean Philippe. As part of the festivities, dancing took place. The ministers were incensed. Even more so, they were angered because most of the participants were leading political figures. Worse, not only did the accused refuse to repent their actions, they even refused to admit they had danced at all. On the surface, this is simply a clash between the ministers, zealous for moral behaviour, and the magistrates, indulging in bit of traditional, but licentious, activity.

However, a close examination of all the records relating to this event, especially the criminal court records, highlighted some aspects not readily apparent. First, the marriage may have had considerable political significance if it was, as it would appear, part of an attempt to reconcile leading *Articulant* and *Guillermin* families (and, by proxy, the two factions). Second, Lect had extensive family ties with both Berne and Fribourg. That, coupled with the attendance of Urbain Guisard, a prominent figure from the Bernese-controlled Pays de Vaud, may imply that some aspects of the wedding involved an attempt to repair the breach with Geneva's neighbours in Berne and possibly even Fribourg.[10] Finally, Lect defended the dancing by presenting it as a feature of traditional Bernese practices.[11]

This is an important point. In effect, Lect argued that he and the other party-goers were simply being hospitable to their Bernese guests by indulging in a Bernese custom. There is every reason to dismiss this argument as spurious, which Calvin surely did when he preached that "the dancers were ruffians," but it is, nevertheless, interesting.[12] However, the complicated issues underlying this seemingly simple act of dancing are worth noting and considering. What comes through clearly is that Geneva's magistrates were very sensitive to the cultural and social aspects of their relations with their Swiss neighbours while Calvin seems to have been less aware of, or less willing to give value to, their significance.

---

[9]For a fuller discussion see *Consolidation*, 96-98.

[10]Guisard was also related to Ami Perrin. Cf., H. Vuilleumier, *Histoire de l'Eglise réformé du Pays de Vaud* (Lausanne: La Concorde, 1927); G. Baum, et al., *Calvini Opera* [henceforth CO] (Brunswick & Berlin: Schwetschke, 1863-1900), 13:26 (n. 11); and F. T. L. Grenus-Saladin, *Fragments biographiques et historiques* (Geneva: Manget et Cherbuliez, 1815), 14. Another Guisard, Pierre, married (in 1548) Françoise, daughter of Domaine d'Arlod—another politically prominent Genevan.

[11]AEG, *Registres de Consistoire*, vol. 2, fol. 44v (1 Apr. 1546): "que la coustume est rire Messieurs de Berne est de dancer."

[12]"Les danceurs estoyent ruffians." AEG, PC, 2e Série, 695 (29 Mar. 1546), 707 (31 Mar. 1546); RC41, fol. 59v (29 Mar. 1546). Pierre Alliod, who complained about the sermon, was forced to apologise, AEG, RC41, fol. 73r (15 Apr. 1546); cf., J. A. Gautier, *Histoire de Genève* (Geneva: Spon, 1898), 3:269. Treppereaux preached an offensive sermon as well, AEG, RC41, fol. 73r (15 Apr. 1546). Jean Favre was also entangled in the dispute and charged with blasphemy and slander, AEG, RC41, fol. 58r (26 Mar. 1546); PC, 1re Série, 424 (27 Mar. 1546).

Similar concerns and misunderstandings are apparent in even the most seemingly insignificant of events. For example, the "Slashed Breeches Affair" is often noted but rarely analysed. Although this is a single event it should not be dismissed as unimportant. Traditionally, this clash between Calvin and Perrin is mentioned only in passing as one small facet of the troubles which beset their relationship in the mid-1540s and which presaged the later rupture between the two. As with the Lect affair, in one sense this is an accurate portrayal and assessment of the event. However, there are features relating to this clash which can again inform our understanding of Calvin's work in Geneva.

In brief Perrin, as the city's military leader, suggested that the city guard be kitted out with "slashed breeches."[13] Calvin opposed this both as an unnecessary extravagance and an ostentatious display bordering on the immoral. Clearly it was both. The city records reveal that there was also the possibility of malfeasance at work; Perrin stood to benefit either directly or indirectly in the supply of the new uniforms. This, as much as Calvin's complaints, caused the city to halt the plan.

However, although Calvin decried the display, he may also have been aware of other motives underlying Perrin's suggestion. Genevans were known for indulging in political symbols and these slashed breeches may have been yet another example.[14] Swiss soldiers wore their breeches slashed; indeed, one can recognise Swiss troops in early modern woodcuts by their slashed breeches. Since Geneva was trying to gain admittance to the Confederacy at this time, Perrin might well have been trying to make a visible statement with the new uniforms. In other words, although he did not mention it, Calvin might well have been aware that the uniforms were part of the wider drive to bring Geneva into the Confederacy. Since Calvin's interests were directed more to France and he never seemed to have shared the Genevan enthusiasm for membership in the Confederacy, he may well have opposed the uniforms for additional, unstated reasons. In any case, it is hard to believe that he was unaware of the layers of coded meaning implied by Perrin's recommendation. Moreover, he was probably aware of the corruption which seems also to have motivated Perrin. None of this was mentioned explicitly at the time, certainly not by Calvin, yet it clearly informed the discussions in the Senate and its subsequent decision against the new uniforms.

Why, if Calvin was aware of the above, did he choose to focus solely on the issue of extravagance? Clearly, Calvin was aware that his sermons and even his letters were, to some degree, "public" property. It would hardly have been

[13]Such breeches were a normal feature of the "national" uniform of Swiss mercenaries. For a fuller discussion, see my "Genevan National Security & Defence Spending," *War in History* 5 (1998), 379-99.

[14]The use of symbols, especially those associated with the Confederacy, was a regular aspect of Genevan political debate. See *Consolidation,* 15.

politic to object to Perrin's proposals by accusing him of abusing his position for personal gain or by complaining that the symbolism would be "too Swiss." What becomes apparent through a careful reading of this affair is that nothing is as simple as it appears in Geneva and that, as with the Lect affair, there was often a subtext which pitted Genevan (and Swiss) sensibilities against the French-orientated interests of Calvin and his fellow, foreign ministers.

This is most obvious when one considers the long-running dispute about baptismal names.[15] Traditionally, this affair is mentioned twice. First, in 1546, Ami Chappuis objected to the surprise implementation of this new ministerial policy at the baptism of his son: the name "Claude" was put forth but the minister baptised the child "Abraham." Needless to say, the family was somewhat annoyed. The second outbreak of this dispute is known from Calvin's single mention of the issue, in a letter to Dryander in 1552.[16] Calvin related that there had been a tumult in the church when he supplied a name to his liking. Since the disturbance involved Philibert Berthelier, Calvin seems to have considered it worthy of comment. One might also take the view that he thought it politic to mention that Berthelier had been involved in a public riot during a baptismal service.

In any case, the one thing that is clear is that the importance of this affair has been woefully underestimated. Indeed from 1546 onwards, the issue of baptismal names was a constant source of friction between the ministers and the magistrates and, more importantly, between the French ministers and many local Genevans. It became the focus of complaints against the French in general and the ministers in particular. As with the *Articulant* crisis in the late 1530s, political and ethnic opposition to the growing power of the French in Geneva could focus on this policy without having to resist "authority" directly.

Basically, the ministers objected to a number of names. Some, for example Emmanuel, were obviously ones which Protestants would oppose. These seem to have caused no trouble in the city. However, the ministers also tried to proscribe other names such as those of the Magi (Balthasar, Gaspard, Melchior) and Claude. The latter name was the focus of most riots. Calvin and the ministers reasoned that this name, rare in France, must be common in Geneva because of the proximity of St Claude's shrine. Undoubtedly this was the original explanation. Most Genevans took the view that they had chosen this name for their sons (it was the most common boy's name) or their daughters (it was the third most common girl's name) for family reasons. In other words, Ami Chappuis wanted to name his son Claude because it was a family name, not because of a nearby shrine. There is a very real sense in which both explanations for this name's popularity were correct. However, they were also incompatible.

[15]For a fuller discussion, see my *Consolidation,* 144-53 and "Baptisms, Church Riots, and Social Unrest in Calvin's Geneva," *Sixteenth Century Journal 26* (1995), 85-95.

[16]CO 14:434 (Dec. 1552).

In an effort to guarantee stability, the magistrates accepted the ministers' views but insisted that a single list be published. The ministers were more than willing to publish such a list but seemed inclined to reserve for themselves the power to add to it on an *ad hoc* basis at the font. This made a certain amount of sense. Someone might well provide a name which was totally unacceptable but also completely unanticipated. It also meant that there was the constant possibility of parents having their children given surprise, spontaneous names at the moment of a (public) baptism. The list promised stability and predictability; the ministerial reservation guaranteed offence and rioting.

A similar reservation of power to the ministers led to problems in the area of excommunication.[17] As is commonly known, the original (1542) draft of the *Ecclesiastical Ordinances* drawn up by a committee led by Calvin, proposed a scheme which would have left excommunication wholly in the hands of the consistory. Since the consistory was made up of ministers and elders (all of whom were also elected councillors) this, in theory, had a significant magisterial check built in. Even this was insufficient for the secular authorities who insisted on a wording which was considerably less clear. Obviously, this set the stage for possible clashes between the state and the church in the form of the consistory. Calvin took the view that, although the state had insisted on a watered-down wording, the Ordinances still left the consistory with the power both to admonish and to excommunicate. The state believed that the new wording had ensured that any excommunication would have to be approved by the Senate. That is, the consistory could admonish a sinner and, when necessary, recommend to the Senate that a person be excommunicated.

However, by focusing on the Ordinances and Calvin's complaints about his clashes with the state over excommunication, one might conclude that the issue remained in dispute, unclear and debatable. This is most certainly not the case. On three separate occasions, the Senate made it explicitly clear that ministers could only admonish and had no power to excommunicate.[18] That is, the magistrates made the Ordinances perfectly clear and tried to implement a system in keeping with that which prevailed throughout Protestant Switzerland. In the light of these rulings it becomes clear that Calvin not only refused to accept the magisterial interpretation but also explicitly ignored the Senate's commands. In effect, his behaviour forced the state either to manage the situation or to sack him (and the other ministers) outright. In no way do the most commonly available sources for Genevan history ever make it clear how explicit was the state's view on the issue of excommunication and the "correct"

[17] A lengthier treatment of the key debates over excommunication can be found at *Consolidation*, 181-87.

[18] E.g., see AEG, RC37, fol. 37v (19 Mar. 1543) for the most explicit ruling by the Senate: "le consistoyre ne aye nulle jurid[iti]on ny puissance de deffendre synon seulement admonester et puys fere Relation en conseyl affin que le seyg[neu]r[i]e advise de juger sus les delinquans selon leur demerites."

(Zwinglian) relationship between the state and the church. Also, Calvin at no time even hints that he is taking a stance completely opposed to the explicit views of the Senate.

Do any of the above involve new sources? No, not at all. Rather, they utilise sources which are primarily in manuscript to interpret the published sources. Also, it is well worth remembering that the published sources are those which reflect the views and concerns of the ministers: Calvin's letters, sermons and commentaries as well as the records of the Company of Pastors and the Consistory. There is no need to assume intentional bias to realise that these sources, by their very nature, are unlikely to give the full context for Calvin's life and career in Geneva.

Are there any new ideas which arise from this use of all the available primary documentation? Perhaps. Calvin and the ministers appear to be much less in tune with, or sympathetic to, the social and cultural distinctiveness of Geneva. Also, the ministers seem to be very astute political manipulators. On more than one occasion they use the security of their positions to force their views upon an unwilling state. Does this make them bullies? No, I think not. Instead, what comes through is the absolute determination of Calvin and his colleagues to realise in Geneva their view of a truly reformed Christian commonwealth. Also, one begins to see that the conflict and tensions, which are so well known from the years around 1555, were in fact common to most of the period under discussion. That is, Calvin's life and career was considerably more contentious and difficult than might otherwise be thought.

If we leave aside these specific and admittedly isolated cases, is there value in a new approach to the sources for studying Geneva and Calvin's career there? This essay argues that heretofore there has been too great an emphasis on an approach to Calvin which is primarily biographical. At its worst, biography can tend to either character assassination or hagiography. Even at its best, biography is still a form of history much more in keeping with the "great men" approach than an integrated historiography which considers society, culture, economy, politics, religion, elites and "the common folk." Surely the increase in this sort of history, if nothing else, should warn against centring a study wholly on an individual—or sources largely produced by him (and his close friends).

Also, as said above, the types of sources for studying Calvin have become available to a wider audience in a peculiar fashion. Because of the interest in Calvin, Calvinism and Geneva as an ecclesiastical model, publication of sources has centred on letters, sermons, commentaries, and the minutes of the Company and the Consistory. Publication of these sources is laudable but they should not be used as the sole, or even the primary, sources for the study of Calvin's life and career.

In fact, Geneva is extremely rich in documentary material for this period. The Senate met almost daily and its minutes survive intact. Also there are many criminal court cases complete with depositions, verbatim record of interrogations, legal opinions (often by Calvin or other prominent refugees) and even medical reports. Finally, much of the state's diplomatic correspondence has survived. Coupled with these "official" records are over 30 volumes of notarial records containing wills, rental agreements, business partnerships, sales, wedding contracts and loans. Taken together, these records, with those already published, allow one to reconstruct much of the society, culture, economy, politics and religion of Geneva, in some cases, by use of the actual words of individuals. Indeed, through the criminal records and consistory minutes one can (over)hear the words, conversations, and personal opinions of senators, refugees, wealthy merchants, poor workers, fishwives, children, young girls, and a host of others drawn from every stratum of society.

One might think that, at least with reference to Calvin, the *Annales* in the *Calvini Opera* provide this wider context. In fact, they do exactly the opposite. These represent the attempt of an earlier generation of scholars to collect every reference to Calvin from every Genevan record. The very attempt highlights priorities and presuppositions about the importance of "great men" to these editors. What they have done is useful but it is without context. Reading an extract from the Senate's minutes in which Calvin is mentioned gives no idea of what the Senate discussed before or after. Nor does it always follow the issue to its conclusion unless Calvin is mentioned in the final entry.

More importantly, the *Calvini Opera* is not without errors. Mostly these are minor in nature; for example, Calvin witnesses some notarial documents and these have not been noted in the Annales. However, I would give one example which, although isolated and minor, could lead to some profoundly incorrect interpretations.

A careful search of the Genevan records shows that in 1554 there were two criminal cases for sodomy.[19] In March, Lambert Le Blanc, the son of the French royal controller of finances, was arrested, tried and, eventually, burned at the stake. In September, five schoolboys were also arrested. There survives a legal advice to the Senate signed by Calvin, Germain Colladon, François Chevallier and Abel Poupin. In this opinion they discuss the difficult question of the age of accountability. It is clear that, in their view, the two youngest should be punished by their relatives in private. They go on argue that the three older defendants should face the full rigour of the law. However, they then imply that they expect the state to be lenient and, if so, suggest that the three oldest boys should be publicly beaten and burned in effigy.

[19]The manuscript advice offered by Calvin is preserved in PC, 1re Série, 502 (7-16 Mar. 1554)—Lambert Le Blanc's actual case. The ascription (in CO 15:69—where the printed, published version of the advice is located) to the March date is simply based on the advice being located in the Le Blanc dossier. For what survives about the five youths, see AEG, RC48, fols. 167r-v (21 Dec. 1554); 168r-v (24 Dec. 1554) & 169r-v (27 Sep. 1554) as well as Roset, *Chroniques,* 363. PC, 2e Série: 1078 (26 Dec. 1554) contains a single sheet relating to evidence given by Gabriel Patru, one of the younger boys, against Jean Levet, one of the older boys.

According to the *Calvini Opera*, this advice relates to the case of Le Blanc. If so, then the suggestion of magisterial leniency would seem to imply that Calvin and the others expected the state to be merciful in a sodomy case which involved foreign refugees. This leniency, surprising in and of itself, could then be explained either as evidence of moral laxity on the part of the magistrates or an unwillingness to punish someone from a politically prominent French family. In either case, the magistrates' behaviour could be seen as "libertine" and quite unexpected. Now, it is worth remembering that the legal advice is undated and its only connection to the Le Blanc case is its inclusion in his trial's dossier at some later date.

However, a close reading of the Le Blanc dossier reveals that he alone was tried for sodomy. Only two other people are even mentioned in the course of the investigation and neither is apprehended. The Senate's minutes and Michel Roset's contemporary history show that the case of the schoolboys began in September and ended in December with the two younger children being beaten by their relatives in private and the three older boys being publicly beaten and burned in effigy in front of the assembled schoolchildren. In other words, this legal advice relates to this later case. If this is so, the state's leniency results from two primary concerns. First, the age of the defendants. Calvin and the others accept without discussion that the two youngest cannot be held fully accountable. They argue that the three oldest can be, but intimate that they expect the Senate to err on the side of mercy. The second consideration, which may explain other assumptions in the legal advice, is that the accused boys were almost certainly the children of prominent local families.[20]

Why should we assume the boys' social and political prominence and why has the advice been mis-attributed? No criminal dossier survives for their trial. Indeed, there is no evidence a formal trial took place. This still leaves the question of the attribution of the opinion to the Le Blanc case. Originally, criminal records, opinions, diplomatic papers, etc., would have been kept with the minutes for that year. In the course of the nineteenth century, these loose sheets were separated from the minutes and organised into distinct files. It is quite easy to imagine that someone, presented with a lengthy sodomy case and a single legal opinion for 1554, would assume that they went together. The mention of the youths' case in the minutes and in Roset simply did not attract sufficient attention to avert this mistaken connection.

The result is that Calvin's major statement on sodomy has been connected to a case supposedly involving Lambert Le Blanc, a refugee of prominent background, and four other unnamed individuals, all presumed to be refugees as

[20]In all of the deliberations and sources (pace the single sheet in the criminal dossiers) the children are named only once—AEG, RC48, fols. 169r-v (27 Dec. 1554)—when their sentence was announced. They were: Paule (son of Paul Tares), Gabriel-Daniel (son of Thivent Patru), Jean (son of Jean Levet), Jehan (son of Henry Goula), and Daniel (son of François Rigot).

well. This would naturally lead one to view Calvin and the others as staunch upholders of morality since they advise death for the three older defendants who, in this interpretation, would be fellow refugees. The Senate appears to be overly lenient in wanting to let all five of the accused live.

Once one shifts the advice to the case of the five local, and socially prominent, schoolboys the interpretation of this key document on sexual deviance changes dramatically. Here, Calvin and the others are suggesting that three school children be executed for what the state clearly felt was youthful experimentation. The magistrates are not defending immorality *per se* but are protecting their own children and possibly their own reputations. If there is anything to question about the state's approach it is its unwillingness to name the youths until the very last moment. Moreover, they were named only in the Senate's minutes and only after their relatives had made personal appearances on their behalf. Indeed, the advice specifically demands that everything should be recorded. The implied criticism in the advice is, therefore, not that the state is overly lenient to sodomites but that the magistrates are trying to protect their children and that the real question is whether or not these children were "adult" enough to die at the stake.

Admittedly, this is a minor affair but it again highlights the importance of a careful examination of all the remaining records. Further, it stresses the need for an integrated use of the Genevan sources. There is, however, one major area of Calvin's life and career in Geneva which has been almost wholly neglected. Calvin was, for most of 1541-1564, more than just Geneva's chief minister, he was also the city's main legal advisor. Chevallier and Colladon (once he arrived in Geneva) were also used regularly but the reality is that on most important legal questions, Calvin was consulted.

This aspect of Calvin's career in Geneva cannot be overestimated. He was as intimately involved in the drafting of the 1542 political constitution as he was in the drawing up of the *Ecclesiastical Ordinances*. [21] Also, he was in charge of the committee selected to re-draft the state's constitution in the 1560s.[22] However, there was more to this part of Calvin's work than grand projects like new constitutions—though this on its own is extremely important. Calvin was also often asked to give advice on specific legal cases. Moreover, he was asked by the city

---

[21]Cf., A. Roget, *Histoire du Peuple de Genève* (Geneva: Jullien, 1870-87), 2:65-68. M. E. Chenevière, *La Pensée politique de Calvin* (Geneva: Slatkine, 1970), 205-207, stressed that Calvin was perhaps rather more than just a redactor, as Roget argued. Those slight changes Calvin made tended to strengthen the aristocratic elements of the Genevan constitution.

[22]Calvin's role continued until his death. While it is fair to say that Calvin's position as the city's premier lawyer has been undervalued by historians, it has certainly not been unknown. Cf., P. Schaff, *History of the Christian Church. Modern Christianity: The Swiss Reformation* (Grand Rapids: Eerdmans, 1994), 7:284: "The [constitution] was revised with the aid of Calvin by his friend, Germain Colladon... The revised code was begun in 1560, and published in 1568."

to cast a legal eye over the wording of treaties including the one designed to heal the breach which opened between Geneva and Berne after 1555.[23] Indeed, Calvin was even asked to look at a draft law on customs charges.[24] After 1555 it is clear that Calvin actually drafted legislation before it was put to the city's electorate. On one memorable occasion proposed laws were rejected as "too severe" during a particularly stormy meeting of the General Assembly of citizens and bourgeois.[25]

As said above, Calvin's importance to Geneva's rulers, whether Perrinists or Calvinists, should not be underestimated or discounted. Calvin was a useful man to have around. He was an international figure, a "star" to use modern terminology. He "put Geneva on the map." He had grouped around himself one of the greatest collection of ministers ever assembled. His presence in Geneva had made it a centre for an entire industry: French-language religious literature. Because of him, the city had become a Mecca for men of like mind from across Europe. Despite all this, he was still unpopular in the city and disliked by a significant section of Geneva's ruling elite. This leads to that great question, how was Calvin able to survive in the city after 1541 and why, ultimately, was he able to triumph?

Basically, the answer is rather simple. The two main groupings in Geneva had different goals. Perrin and his supporters never seem to have contemplated defeating Calvin. That is, they never undertook to rid the city of him and his fellow ministers. Rather, their goal throughout seems to have been controlling and containing the ministers within an ecclesiastical settlement which was both Swiss and Zwinglian. They wanted Calvin to behave, to toe the line, to accept magisterial authority and control. Fundamentally, they accepted that the city needed him and the other ministers for all the reasons listed above. Calvin was useful and Calvin was entrenched. After 1546 and the arrival of a united body of ministers, the city must have realised that any attempt to remove Calvin would mean the loss of the entire Company of Pastors.[26] Not only would this have been internally disastrous, it would have destroyed Geneva's external image. In other words, Calvin survived in Geneva in large part because there was never any real chance that he would be expelled. His position was secure since there was no viable alternative.

---

[23]AEG, RC50, fol. 29v (7 Nov. 1555). Even before the complete overthrow of the Perrinists but, significantly, immediately after the victory of Calvin's local political supporters he was involved in discussions with Berne. See AEG, RC49, fols. 29r-33r *passim* (14-21 Mar. 1555).

[24]I am grateful to Prof. Francis Higman (director-emeritus, Institut d'Histoire de la Réformation, Geneva) for this information.

[25]"Trop rudes," AEG, RC52, fol. 96v (15 Nov. 1556).

[26]For more on the process of creating a strong, united Company of Pastors, see my "Renovation of the Genevan Ministry," in A. D. M. Pettegree, ed., *The Reformation of the Parishes: The Ministry in Town and County* (Manchester: Manchester University Press, 1993), 113-32.

In a sense then, the Perrinists were fighting a defensive battle against Calvin and his supporters. Although the Perrinists never sought to remove Calvin, it is clear that Calvin's political supporters were intent on removing the Perrinists from political power. Why? First, they were convinced that the Perrinists were lax on morals. Second, the Perrinists were fixated on Switzerland and joining the Confederacy but not overly interested in France. Third, the Perrinists were obviously unable to contain the Company of Pastors and, if something was not done, the clashes between church and state were only likely to worsen. In other words, although the Perrinists were unwilling to do what was necessary to win (oust Calvin), their opponents were quite willing to win (oust the Perrinists).

It does seem that the Perrinists were a little less than ruthless. This was not because they did not want to solve the problems between the magistracy and the ministry but because Calvin's position was all but unassailable. It is also true that the Perrinists seemed as a group to be "anti-French."[27] They were willing to assist the refugees but were determined to limit their impact and influence on the city. The Perrinists were convinced that membership in the Confederation was the best safeguard of Genevan independence and that greater involvement in France or greater power for the French was likely to hamper or preclude the realisation of this goal. The Perrinists identified socially and culturally with the Swiss. Also, they were more comfortable with the religious settlements they saw throughout Protestant Switzerland. They wanted Geneva to "turn Swiss" because, in their minds, it was Swiss.[28]

Were they morally lax though? This evaluation of the Perrinists is understandable but unfair. Many of the clashes with the church are commonly traced to the issue of excommunication. In Calvin's interpretation, the magistrates were unwilling to excommunicate sinners. Superficially, this is true but the reality is much more complex. In the overwhelming majority of cases, the Senate allowed the Consistory to admonish and excommunicate. The magistrates seemed to have considered their veto over excommunication to be a power exercised only occasionally and reactively. That is, they did not seek to review every excommunication but were content to rely on the wisdom of the ministers and, more importantly, the elected magistrates on the Consistory. Occasionally however, they felt that the Senate itself should deal with the person under threat of excommunication.

Was this moral laxity? The result at times was. Primarily, the Senate was interested in adjudicating in some cases for social and political reasons. Geneva was a small town where family and faction were often interchangeable. The government was always concerned to contain the damage when a senior member of the ruling elite got into trouble. Although unpleasant, this is not exactly the same as moral laxity. It is corrupt but not unexpected or extraordinary. Basically, the

---

[27] *Consolidation,* 121-43.

[28] Again, for a fuller discussion, see my essay "Genevan Diplomacy & Foreign Policy."

Perrinists wanted to protect important Genevans, especially of their own faction, from social humiliation. One must hasten to add that the Calvinists after 1555 were more than willing and able to do the same to protect the reputations and family names of leading Genevan Calvinists.[29]Also, when one looks behind the excommunication crises one often discovers that the issue is actually baptismal names. For example, the original dispute which set Berthelier against Calvin was a clash on this point. Berthelier, the Septs and the Favres constantly protested at baptismal services and before the Senate about this ministerial policy which they considered insulting and arrogant. Who were these foreigners to tell Genevans which names to use? Or, as Gaspard Favre put it, "since his name could not be given he would present no child for baptism."[30] Gaspard and Balthasar Sept even asked the Senate to declare that their names were "acceptable" or, failing that, to give them new names which were.[31] The fury, hurt and embarrassment occasioned by this policy were at the root of much of the discord between the ministers and leading Genevans. The Senate often moved to contain the crisis by avoiding direct confrontation or public punishment. This frequently involved refusing to punish the malcontents. To Calvin and the ministers this was wilful perversion. The state was clearly unwilling to uphold the church's views and was, therefore, morally lax. The logic is sound and, on one level, perfectly correct. However, the reality was much more complex.

This seems a logical point at which to conclude. By using the whole panoply of Genevan documents it is possible to produce an evaluation of Calvin's life and work in Geneva which is more complex, better contextualised and, arguably, more accurate. In its individual parts, this new interpretation may not be "new"—at some point just about anything that happened in Geneva has been mentioned in some history. However, the sum of these re-interpretations and the integration of sources do provide a new and more nuanced history. More importantly, it draws the focus of the discussion from Calvin, the individual, to an examination of Calvin as but one person, albeit a prominent person, in Geneva. Isolated from Geneva and its history Calvin's life and work make for fascinating, even inspirational, reading but the result is not as clear and as detailed as it could be.

---

[29]Genevans noticed this even at the time. Pierre Pape was admonished for pointing out official hypocrisy in the ruling elite, AEG, PC, 1re, Série, 635 (3-9 Apr. 1557). For specific examples of both criminal immorality and official malfeasance amongst the Calvinists see *Consolidation,* 217-18.

[30]AEG, *Consistoire,* vol. 5, fol. 74r (16 Oct. 1550)

[31]AEG, RC46, fol. 144v (4 Feb. 1552). The Senate relented and allowed the use of the names of the Magi but Calvin protested and the matter was referred to the larger council, the *Deux Cents,* where the matter lapsed with the approach of the elections the following week. See also Roget, *Histoire,* 3:224-25.

Calvin and Calvinists on Resistance to Government

Robert McCune Kingdon

It is a special pleasure for me to speak today in this country and on this subject. I am happy to speak in this country because it is the land of my mother's birth, yet this is the first time I have visited it. I am happy to speak on this subject for two reasons. Calvinist resistance theory interests me very much and I have done research on it off and on for decades. But I have another and more personal reason. My grandfather, George Shannon McCune, a Presbyterian missionary and educator, was dismissed from his positions and forced to leave Korea in 1936 by the Japanese military government because of his resistance to its requirement that he participate in rites that he felt involved pagan forms of worship. To a rare degree, therefore, this lecture combines personal with scholarly interests.

When we speak of resistance we must first distinguish among types. We must distinguish between passive resistance, the refusal to obey certain commands of a government, and active resistance, the attempt to overthrow a government and replace it with another. We must also distinguish between individual resistance, as exercised by any single member of a society, and collective resistance, as organized on behalf of a society, most probably by its natural leaders. Passive resistance can be displayed by an individual or by a group. It can then lead to punishment, which traditionally had to be patiently accepted. Active resistance can also be displayed by an individual, for example one who tries to assassinate a tyrant, or by a group, for example one which tries to organize an army to force a tyrant out of power. It necessarily involves violence.

Passive resistance, it can be argued, is of the very essence of Christianity. Christ himself, some would say, was arrested, tried, and crucified for resistance to both the political and religious authorities of his day, climaxing with his provocation of a riot in the great Temple of the Jews when he drove out the money-changers and sellers of animals for sacrifice. And the earliest followers of Christ were explicit in their support of passive resistance. When the Apostle Peter was called before the Sanhedrin, and ordered to explain why he and other apostles were openly violating orders to stop teaching in the name of Christ and blaming the temple authorities for Jesus' death, he answered simply,

"We must obey God rather than men" (Acts 5:29). That short verse in Scripture becomes the most important single justification for all Christian resistance.

Resistance, even when it led to death, became common in the earliest Christian churches. It is displayed in many of the martyrdoms in which the early church gloried and which it publicized widely. Tertullian, the great early Church Father, was only describing a historical fact when he observed that the blood of martyrs had become seed, seed for the church. One story of an early collective martyrdom that may have been familiar to people in Calvin's Geneva was that of the Theban Legion. This legion was an all-Christian contingent within the Roman army in the days before the empire itself had become Christian under Constantine. Its members, while stationed in the valley of the Rhone near Geneva on the eve of an important campaign, refused to accept an imperial command, apparently to attend a rite of solemn sacrifices to the pagan gods thought to be patrons of the army. The infuriated commander of the army twice ordered that this legion be decimated—every tenth soldier, selected by lot, would be beaten and decapitated in front of his comrades. When that brought no change, he ordered that the entire legion be put to death. The Christian members of the Theban Legion remained steadfast in their refusal to join in a pagan religious ceremony; they also refused to fight back and meekly accepted this terrible death.[1]

Active resistance has a much less glorious history. Early Christians had been reluctant to adopt it, even in the face of savage persecution by governments of the most odious character. They usually agreed with the Apostle Paul, when he said in Romans 13:1-2, "Every person must submit to the supreme authorities. There is no authority but by act of God, and the existing authorities are instituted by him; consequently anyone who rebels against authority is resisting a divine institution." It can be argued that early Christianity survived precisely because it did not practice active resistance. Jewish sects like the Zealots or Sicarii that did promote active resistance to Roman authority were completely crushed. Christianity, beginning as a Jewish sect but accepting the authority of the pagan Roman imperial government in areas not involving religious practice, was persecuted only sporadically. It managed to survive and prosper. In the sixteenth century, Christian advocates of active resistance, including many Calvinists, had to argue their way around the obvious meaning of the Pauline injunctions in Romans 13, and the extensive tradition built upon them, in order to make their case.

[1]For a full account of this story, known only from martyrologies written centuries later but widely circulated throughout Europe, no doubt exaggerated for dramatic effect, see H. Leclercq, "Maurice d'Agaune (Saint)" in F. Cabrol and H. Leclercq, eds., *Dictionnaire d'archéologie chrétienne et liturgie,* 10/2 (Paris: Letouzey & Ané, 1932), cols. 2699-2729.

In general Calvin taught passive resistance, by all individuals and groups committed to true Christianity. Toward the end of his life he also accepted active resistance, but only when led by governmental leaders of the rank of princes of the blood royal, with a reasonable chance of success. His conversion to active resistance, in fact, can be dated with some precision. It is not to be found in either his publications or his sermons. It is rather to be found in his letters and records of advice he tendered to government leaders in Geneva and elsewhere. As late as 1560, he was still discouraging proposals for overthrow of the French monarchy by young Protestant noblemen like La Renaudie. In 1562, however, he supported strongly the revolt against the French crown led by Louis I de Bourbon, the prince of Condé, of the French blood royal.[2] This attitude reflected, it seems to me, considerable political shrewdness. He discouraged active resistance that was doomed to failure; he accepted active resistance that had a reasonable chance of success. Calvin's successors, especially in France, elaborated in some detail arguments for active armed resistance, but only when led by "inferior magistrates," agents with a legal if subordinate position within a government, never by individuals alone. These basic conclusions, it seems to me, are still supported by the consensus of scholars in the field, although with more and more nuances as the political ideas of individuals are analyzed more closely. Most of my work on Calvinist resistance theory has concentrated on the arguments of Calvin's successors, particularly Theodore Beza, as developed in his tract, *Du droit des magistrats.* Today I want to offer a fresh examination of Calvin's own ideas.

What, in Calvin's mind, justified resistance? One can sum up his answer in just one word: idolatry. If a government permits or even commands idolatry, it must be resisted. If a government misbehaves in other ways, it normally cannot be resisted. Calvin despised idolatry with a passion that deserves examination and reflection. It can be justly labeled an expression of the emotion of hate, as I argued in a recent research seminar at the Institute for Advanced Studies of the Hebrew University in Jerusalem on the "historicity of emotions" in early modern Europe. It can also be labeled an expression of the emotion of fear, as participants in that seminar pointed out to me. It might even be labeled as including a variant of the emotion of love, reflecting an honest desire to save the deluded. Human emotions are rarely pure types. They almost always come in bundles.

Calvin justified his dislike for idolatry by a close reading of the Hebrew Scriptures, as they are recorded in the Old Testament of the Christian Bible. In this, as in many other fields, Calvin and his followers were deliberately returning to the Jewish roots of Christianity. Those Scriptures make a repeated point

[2]See Robert M. Kingdon, *Geneva and the Coming of the Wars of Religion in France* (Geneva: Droz, 1956), chs. 7 and 11.

that the Almighty God despises and discourages the worship of any material objects as representations or substitutes for God himself, particularly if they are manmade objects, even if they be constructed of the most precious materials available to man, like gold and silver, as in the golden calf described in Exodus 32. These Scriptures go further and make the point that God threatens with punishment and destruction any community that permits the worship of these objects. In his *Institutes of the Christian Religion* (especially 1:11), Calvin denounces idolatry at some length, using as his proof-texts citations from Scripture, including from the Ten Commandments, "You shall not make for yourself a graven image, nor any likeness..."(Exodus 20:4, quoted in *Institutes,* 1:11:1). These passages he uses to denounce both Catholic and Orthodox dependence on images and icons as a help to worship. The very word "idolator" becomes in the writing of Calvinist polemicists a code term for "Roman Catholic."

For some even more striking statements of Calvin's views on idolatry and their implications for political resistance, we can turn to his sermons, including those that only now are coming to light as a result of work leading to their edition for the *Supplementa Calviniana.* I think particuarly of a number of examples brought to my attention by Max Engammare, as a result of his current work as an editor of the sermons on Genesis. He has uncovered about a dozen of these statements, some of them in sermons already published, some in sermons assembled for publication in the near future, some noticed by earlier students of the problem, many of them overlooked. Let me quote from just two of them:

(1) In 1550, in his sermons on Acts, Calvin says that if princes "wish to turn us from the honor of God, if they wish to force us to idolatries and superstitions, they then have no more authority over us than frogs and lice."[3]

(2) In 1560, in his sermons on Genesis, Calvin says, "if kings wish to force their subjects to follow their superstitions and idolatries ... they are no longer kings" and their subjects must be prepared to "die a hundred times rather than abandon the true service of God. They must render to God that which belongs to him and denounce all edicts and menaces, all commandments and all traditions, holding them all for filth and dirt produced by earthworms in the face of him to whom alone obedience belongs."[4]

This is rather strong language. It may not technically reveal full endorsement of active resistance, but it certainly was a step in that direction. In a period when rulers, particularly kings, were regarded as agents of God, who some would say ruled by divine right, who were to be treated with the greatest defer-

[3]Jean Calvin, *La servante chassée: sermon inédit sur l'histoire d'Agar (23 mars 1560),* ed. Max Engammare (Geneva: Minizoé, 1995), 43-44, from Sermon 41 on Acts, as edited by Willem Balke and Wilhelmus Moehn.

[4]Ibid., 28-29.

ence and described only with the most obsequious language, Calvin is now calling them frogs, lice, and earthworms, deserving no respect or obedience if they stoop to idolatry. Those epithets in themselves would have gotten Calvin into serious trouble in many of the monarchies of his day. They remind us of how passionate and involved Calvin could become when in the pulpit. They clearly shocked at least some of the people in his audience. Max Engammare has brought to our attention one striking example. Antoine Cathelan, who spent eighteen months in Geneva from 1554 to 1555 before returning to Catholicism, reported with evident horror in a pamphlet he published in 1556, that he had regularly heard in Protestant sermons preached in Geneva atrocious insults thrown at the pope, the emperor, and all Christian kings and princes, without any attempt by the local government to control this. [5]

These denunciations of idolatry in themselves, replicated in other parts of Europe by dozens of Reformed preachers in sermons and by dozens of Reformed polemicists in pamphlets, generated in the public arena intense emotions. They inspired Protestant mobs to storm into Catholic churches and religious houses, and smash images and altars. Chronicles of the period, even those composed by Protestants, record dozens of examples. Sometimes the mobs were disciplined, making careful inventories of every object removed; sometimes they ran amok, simply destroying every object of idolatry in sight. This violence, in turn, generated equally intense counter emotions, as mobs of Catholics attacked Protestant iconoclasts for breaking the bonds of community, for pollution and desecration, often killing them.

Even more upsetting to Catholics and government authorities were Calvinist applications of these strictures on idolatry to the central Christian sacrament of the eucharist, as celebrated in the Catholic mass. The argument that the mass is a form of idolatry was stated early by Calvin himself (*Institutes,* 4:17:35-37). It was then developed with more vehemence and popularized in a cruder and more provocative form by the preachers and pamphleteers to whom I have already alluded.[6] Both routinely spoke of "the idol of the mass."

Let me explain more fully the targets of these particular attacks on idolatry. Since approximately the thirteenth century, Catholic theologians had developed and then promulgated officially an explanation of what happens in the eucharistic sacrament, which they called transubstantiation. This doctrine holds that when an ordained priest in good standing celebrates a mass in the proper way, using the proper words, the elements of the sacrament, the bread and the wine, actually become the body and blood of Jesus Christ. This mirac-

[5]Max Engammare, "Calvin monarchomaque? Du soupçon à l'argument," *Archiv für Reformationsgeschichte* 89 (1998), 6-7, n. 22.

[6]French examples of these pamphlets have been explored with particular care in Christopher Elwood, *The Body Broken: the Calvinist Doctrine of the Eucharist and the Symbolization of Power in Sixteenth-century France* (New York and Oxford: Oxford University Press, 1999).

ulous change, to be sure, does not occur in the "accidents" of the elements, in the properties of bread and wine that we can see, touch, and taste. But it does occur in the "substance," or inner essence of the elements. And since Jesus is a part of the divine Trinity, that means these consecrated elements become in a very real sense God himself. The devout Christian who is receiving these elements, thus, is actually eating and drinking God, absorbing into his own body the divine principle that creates and rules the entire universe.

Corollary to this doctrine of transubstantiation is the practice of the reservation of the sacrament. If, after the celebration of the mass, there remain consecrated communion wafers, we must not forget that they are now God. They must be protected with special care from falling to the ground, from perhaps being eaten by dogs or other animals. They must be treated with the special reverence we reserve for God. It became traditional for the consecrated elements to be put in a special locked container called a pyx, usually made of precious metal or ivory, often beautifully decorated, sometimes in the shape of a dove. With increasing frequency, a pyx would be put for safe-keeping within a special decorated box called a tabernacle, placed on the main altar in a church, with a light burning perpetually above it as a reminder that God is present here. In the fifteenth century, another type of container for the consecrated host came into common use. This was the monstrance. It was designed to make the consecrated host visible, by placing it in a special transparent container between layers of glass. It was portable, and could be carried about, within a church, even outside a church, for display to the general public. Monstrances became more and more elaborate, works of real art assembled with loving care, made out of precious metals like gold and silver, studded with jewels. People were encouraged to worship before these objects, to fall to their knees and to repeat prayers, often led by a priest or religious.

Reservation of the sacrament in turn led to a festival that came to be of central importance in the Catholic liturgical year. This was the festival of *Corpus Christi*. It involved a special mass, usually followed by a procession, in which the body of Christ in the form of a consecrated host would be carried throughout a city, generally in a monstrance under a highly decorated canopy. The procession would include the priests who had been responsible for the miracle of bringing God to the community in this form, some of them carrying the monstrance. They would be accompanied by the political leaders of the community, wearing their insignia of office, some of them often helping to carry the canopy over the monstrance. People owning houses along the route of the procession were expected to decorate with appropriate tapestries or other hangings the buildings in which they lived. All the population would be urged, even required, to line the streets as the procession passed, showing due reverence for the God among them. The festival became an occasion for visibly demonstrating the piety and unity of the entire community. The practice of holding *Corpus Christi* processions began in the thirteenth century, apparently in Belgium, and spread rapidly throughout western Europe.[7] Indeed it continues down to the present, if in vestigial form. In many Catholic countries the day of *Corpus Christi* remains a public holiday.

It was these practices that most fully triggered early Protestants' hate and fear of idolatry. It was bad enough from their perspective that Catholic priests were everywhere claiming to create God on the high altar, of insisting that the pieces of bread and wine that they were distributing to the faithful were in fact God, of requiring worship of a material manmade object, of what Calvinist polemicists routinely called a "dieu de pâté," or "God of bread." One could always, after all, refuse to go to church, refuse to attend mass, refuse to receive communion elements from a priest. It was far worse that this belief and the accompanying practices could be forced upon an entire community, that during a *Corpus Christi* procession those Protestants whose houses lay along a processional route might find themselves required to decorate them, sometimes at considerable personal expense, probably with pictures that in themselves could be regarded as objects of idolatry, and that all Protestants would be expected to join their neighbors in lining the route and show proper reverence when the monstrance passed.

Some of the nastiest riots of the early Protestant Reformation were provoked by *Corpus Christi* processions. In 1560, for example, in Rouen, the second largest city in France, members of the growing Protestant community refused to "tapissé devant leurs maisons," to erect the usual *Corpus Christi* decorations in front of their houses. This so enraged local Catholics that mobs of them, led by priests, broke into several of these houses, smashed them up and killed a number of people whom they found in them—as many as eighteen according to one contemporary reporter.[8] In other communities, Protestant zealots seem to have been even more provocative, grabbing hold of monstrances, smashing them open, throwing consecrated hosts into the mud and trampling upon them; Catholic reaction was likewise violent.

Both sides in these bloody riots were displaying fear as well as hate. They were trying to protect the entire community against divine vengeance. Protestants were afraid God's vengeance would be provoked by idolatry; Catholics were afraid it would be provoked by desecration. This fear of divine vengeance is so pronounced, indeed, that it can be argued that fear rather than hate is the primitive emotion most evident in these displays of violence. It may also be the primary difference between Christians in the sixteenth century and today. Few Calvinists in Seoul, I suspect, really believe that the celebration of idolatrous

---

[7]For a full study of the early development and shape of this festival, see Miri Rubin, *Corpus Christi: the Eucharist in Late Medieval Culture* (Cambridge: Cambridge University Press, 1991).

[8]See the accounts in *Histoire ecclésiastique des églises reformées au royaume de France...* (1580), 1:309-10, and in the notes attached to the Baum-Cunitz-Reuss edition of this chronicle (1883-1889), later reprinted (Nieuwkoop: de Graaf, 1974), 1:352-53.

rites in Catholic churches now is likely to bring down divine vengeance on your city, perhaps in the form of a tsunami, or an earthquake, or some other natural disaster. And few Catholics in Seoul today, I suspect, really believe that Protestant failure to adore the consecrated hosts as displayed in Catholic churches would provoke a similar disaster.

The primary target of Calvinist fear of idolatry was clearly Roman Catholic eucharistic practice. A secondary target, however, came to be Lutheran eucharistic practice. Lutherans continued to accept a variant of the doctrine of transubstantiation, although they would not use the word. Luther and his followers believed that in the eucharistic sacrament, when an ordained minister pronounces the required words, the elements of bread and wine really do become the body and blood of Christ, inasmuch as Christ really is present "in, with, and under" the elements, to use proper Lutheran terminology. For Lutherans, however, the miraculous change is only temporary. While Christ really is present in the elements during a communion service, when the service is over he departs. The consecrated bread becomes ordinary bread again. The consecrated wine becomes ordinary wine again. Luther himself developed a striking metaphor to explain the process. Consider what happens when a smith puts a bar of iron into a fire. It turns color, becomes red and then white. It grows hot, emitting intense heat. It is manifestly something different. But withdraw the bar from the fire, and it becomes plain iron again. It becomes gray instead of brightly colored. It becomes cold instead of hot.

To someone adopting this understanding of the eucharist, there would be no point in reserving the elements after the communion service, or adoring them in a ceremony like a *Corpus Christi* procession. For Calvinists, however, this version of eucharistic theology still retained an element of idolatry. Lutherans, like Catholics, are still worshipping a God of manmade bread, even if they limit their worship to the period of a communion service. This led to ferocious polemics in the later part of the sixteenth century, particularly in Germany where tensions between Lutherans and Calvinists became explosive. Jakob Andreae, superintendent of the Lutheran Church in the duchy of Württemberg, led the polemical charge for the "Evangelical" Lutherans. Theodore Beza, Calvin's successor in Geneva, led the charge for the "Reformed," including Calvinists. [9] The controversy reached a climax in 1577, when a coalition of Lutherans led by Andreae developed an official summary of theology called the Formula of Concord, a summary that explicitly and formally excludes Calvinists from the community of true Christians, and then asked every Protestant government in the Holy Roman Empire of the German Nation to endorse this statement.

In the Calvinist polemics that accompany this controversy, Lutherans are often accused of advocating cannibalism. Do they not claim that Christians are

[9]For more on Andreae's role in this controversy, see the works of Robert A. Kolb, Irene Dingel, et al. For more on Beza's role, see the succeeding volumes of Alain Dufour, Béatrice Nicollier, Reinhard Bodenmann, et al., eds., *Correspondance de Théodore de Bèze* (Geneva: Droz, 1960ff.).

actually eating the body of Christ? And since Christ was in part a human being, does this not mean they are eating human flesh, thus becoming cannibals? To drive the point home, these Calvinist polemicists then consider some of the corollaries of such a point of view. If Christians eat the actual body of Christ, does that not mean that they digest the divine body? And if they digest the body of Christ, does that not mean that the remnants of that body, like all food, must be excreted? So what these Lutherans are actually advocating is not only the eating of God but also the excreting of God. This version of the argument, naturally enough, enraged Lutherans. A striking example of their anger can be found in an oration drafted by Andreae for repeated delivery in a tour of Germany at the height of the controversy over the Formula of Concord. At the point in which, according to the rules devised (by Cicero) for the drafting of an oration, the speaker is advised to attack his enemy, he named Theodore Beza. Then he claimed that Beza had said that, if we adopt the view of Lutheran theologians, we must conclude that the bread in the holy sacrament becomes "excrementum Satanae," satanic excrement. We can imagine the gasp of horror that statement must have provoked every time Andreae repeated it among his audiences of pious ministers and lawyers.

The tensions between Calvinists and Lutherans never reached the intensity of tensions between Calvinists and Catholics. They seldom led to riots and killings. But they did lead to wholesale dismissals of clergymen and teachers, as they were forced out of jobs by governments that had adopted one version of Protestantism and felt they had to eliminate all traces of the other. This in turn provoked substantial migrations of intellectuals from one country to another during the later sixteenth century, and many kinds of related human distress. It left Protestantism hopelessly split into two main camps, of two groups of churches, both of which call themselves heirs of the Reformation. In our own century ecumenical initiatives like the Leuenberg Konkordie are finally seeking to escape from these polemics and bring our churches back together.

Let me now sum up my argument: Calvin and his followers hated and feared idolatry, and they were convinced that Roman Catholic practices, particularly those surrounding celebration of the eucharistic sacrament, constituted blatant forms of idolatry. They also thought that their Lutheran brethren had not gone far enough in ridding worship of all traces of idolatry. They were convinced, furthermore, that continuation of these practices, even after the preaching of the pure gospel made clear their idolatrous nature, created a real threat that divine punishments of the most terrifying sort would soon be visited upon their communities. They insisted that no Christian government should permit these expressions of idolatry. They were prepared to resist any government that persisted in trying to force them to participate in idolatry. In the beginning that resistance was expected to take a passive form, even if it led to martyrdom. Later on, however, specifically after 1562 in France, it was permitted to take an active form, although only if led by "inferior magistrates," authorities who themselves held legal positions within government.

Let me now pass on to what seems to me a more recent example of the same problem of resistance. In the 1930s, here in Korea, the Japanese military government then in control of the peninsula tried to impose rituals of state Shinto on the entire population. They required that students at all the schools in the country regularly attend services at *jinja* or shrines, and perform a ritual of obeisance or bowing. They required that the teachers and administrators of these schools attend the shrine services as well, doing obeisance themselves to set a good example for the students. In the beginning these requirements were not imposed upon all the many Christian schools set up and partially staffed by foreign missionaries. In 1935, however, these requirements were imposed upon the Christian schools as well. When Christian leaders protested, the Japanese authorities claimed that these shrine services were not religious, that they were simply patriotic. In one official statement, a Warning tendered to my grandfather, it was asserted "*Jinja* (shrines) are dedicated to the memory of our Imperial Ancestors and to ancestors of the people who have contributed distinguished services to the nation, and are public institutions through which the people of the nation display the sincerity of their veneration." They insisted that these ceremonies would teach children the respect and obedience that they must show to the government which now reigns over them, that by visiting a shrine and making the required *Keirei* or obeisance, students would be doing nothing more than displaying "their spirit of patriotism and allegiance." Americans will think of the parallel of the pledge of allegiance to the flag which many American schools still require of their students at the beginning of a school day. Christians all over Korea and Japan had to make a decision on this requirement. Was participation in the rites at state Shinto shrines simply an expression of political loyalty? Or did it contain a religious content that was incompatible with Christianity? Did the Christian faith require its supporters to accept or to resist this requirement?

Many Christian leaders of the period accepted the assurances of the Japanese government that the rites were purely political, and instructed their followers to obey its orders to attend services at state shrines. Among them was the *Congregatio de Propaganda Fide* in Rome, which sets general religious policy for Roman Catholics throughout the world. Among them also was the National Christian Council of the Protestant Churches in Japan.[10] Among them also, I understand, were a number of missionaries here in Korea and a number of executives of bodies in the United States and elsewhere sponsoring missionary work here.

Other Christian leaders, however, flatly refused to accept these assurances. They insisted that the rites celebrated at state Shinto shrines were in fact religious, that participation in them would involve a betrayal of basic Christian principles, that this was a requirement that must be resisted. Among them was

[10]See Joseph M. Kitagawa, "Japanese Religion: An Overview," in M. Eliade, ed., *Encyclopedia of Religion* (New York: Macmillan, 1986), 7:535.

my grandfather, George Shannon McCune (in Korean, "Yun San-on"), then principal of the Soongsil Boys' Academy and president of the Union Christian College in Pyongyang. He was led to this conclusion by his understanding of the nature of these shrines and of the rites that occurred within them. He understood that in each state shrine in Korea the Sun-Goddess, Amaterasu-omi-kami, the first ancestress of the household of the Emperor of Japan, was enshrined, and that each of these shrines was ritually purified to drive off any influences or spirits from other religions. He further understood that the ceremonies held at these shrines involved, (1) an invocation of spirits to descend into the shrine and then to ascend after the ceremony; (2) prayers for forgiveness of sins, bountiful harvests, victories in war, and other goals; (3) offerings to the spirits of gifts of grain, wine, and other objects.[11] These ceremonies, furthermore, were tied into the Japanese war effort then underway. A part of many of these services was special prayers and offerings to the spirits of Japanese soldiers who had recently died in the wars of aggression against Manchuria and China. This political dimension of Shinto services became even more apparent after my grandfather left Korea. In September of 1937, for example, all schools in this country were ordered to send their students and teachers to state shrines in order to pray to the Sun Goddess for victory for the Japanese armies in China.[12]

It was my grandfather's conclusion that these rituals were obviously religious and that the shrines were obviously houses of worship. He felt that most of the Korean people would agree with him and find the Japanese claim that the rituals were purely political to be ridiculous. For this he was disciplined by the Japanese. In a meeting held on December 31, 1935, the Honorable Watanabe, Educational Director of the Japanese Government General in Korea, and a number of other representatives of the government, confronted my grandfather and representatives of the Northern Presbyterian Mission's Executive Committee. The Japanese representatives presented my grandfather with the formal Warning from which I have already quoted. In this Warning he was informed that he must himself go to a shrine to make ritual obeisance and that he must agree to send his students to the shrine for the same purpose, or face serious consequences. On January 16, 1936, my grandfather submitted a formal reply to the Japanese, which I gather was not printed at the time in either Korea or Japan, but copies of which are in my possession. In that document, my grandfather stated: "I am a Christian and the Government statements have failed to meet my conscientious objections to the act of doing obeisance at the Shrine. I greatly regret the necessity of informing your Excellency [the Japanese Governor of the South Heian Province] that (1) because these ceremonies held at Shrines dedicated as they are and conducted as they are, seem to me to con-

[11]From a printed set of "Notes on the Warning to Dr. McCune," in my possession.

[12]George S. McCune, "The Korean Shrine Question," *The Presbyterian Tribune*, January 20, 1938.

tain definite religious significance; (2) because large portions of the populace believe that spirits are actually worshipped there; (3) because Christians believe ancestor worship, as distinguished from filial piety, is a sin against God; and (4) because I also believe such to be forbidden to Christians by the Word of God (the Bible), I am therefore unable conscientiously to perform the act which you have required of me as a school principal." He then reported that, to avoid embarrassment, he had submitted his resignation as Principal of Soongsil Academy, but that the Board of Directors of the Academy had decided that he had done nothing wrong and refused to accept his resignation.

In retort to this defiance, the Japanese suspended my grandfather from his functions and placed him under house arrest. Several weeks later he and his family were forced out of the country and returned by ship to the United States of America. Even though I was only eight years old at the time, I still retain vivid memories of his visit to our family home in Hawaii on that return voyage. To the end of his life he retained a deep affection for the Korean people among whom he had lived most of his life, and real regret at having been forced to leave them. But he never wavered in his belief that he had done the right thing: that the Japanese had been demanding all Christians within their empire to compromise essential elements of the Christian faith and that they had to be resisted. In a letter he sent to his many friends soon after his departure he quoted these words from the Bible, 2 Timothy 4:17: "The Lord stood with me and strengthened me, that by me the preaching might be fully known and that all the Gentiles might hear, and I was delivered out of the mouth of the Lion."

This leads me to a final question which I would like to put to you, particularly those of you who are Korean. Was my grandfather faithful to the Christian tradition of resistance as understood by Calvinists? I think I know that body of thought pretty well as it was first developed by Calvin and his immediate followers. But parallels between different countries and different times can never be exact. Calvin lived in countries with governments that claimed to be Christian, even if he felt that many of them had betrayed the essentials of Christianity. My grandfather lived under a government that did not pretend to be Christian. In some ways his position was more like the earliest Christians in pre-Constantinian Rome, like the members of the Theban Legion and their Christian contemporaries, than like Calvinists in sixteenth-century Europe. Still the Christian obligation to resist idolatry and all forms of false religion continues through all historical periods and in all places.

I cannot pretend to be a specialist on the recent history of Korea, including its religious history. I have never before visited this country. I do not know your language. So I must leave a final verdict on my grandfather's behavior to those of you who are specialists in Korean history. I hope very much that you decide he was in his way faithful to the Calvinist tradition of resistance, and to the even older Christian tradition of resistance of which it is an illustrious part, that he, along with John Calvin and the Apostle Peter put into practice the belief that "We must obey God rather than men."

Why Was Calvin So Severe a Critic of Nicodemism?

David Wright

Nicodemism continues to attract the attention of sixteenth-century studies, even though the lack of Nicodemite texts frustrates researchers and leaves the origins of Nicodemism, or what might be called its pre-Calvinian phase, inscrutable. The two most significant documents to be published in recent years are a letter of Antoine Fumée written probably in Paris in the early 1540s to Martin Bucer and his fellow-pastors in Strasbourg, edited by Jean Rott in 1983,[1] and Bucer's own *Consilium Theologicum,* written perhaps in late 1540 or early 1541, published in full by Pierre Fraenkel in 1988.[2] The first part of it had been published by Carlo Ginzburg in *Il Nicodemismo* (1970), where it was attributed to Wolfgang Capito as an exponent of Nicodemism, whose theoretical roots Ginzburg claimed to trace to the ferment of reformist religion a decade earlier in Strasbourg.[3]

It may be too much to hope for the discovery of writings by professed Nicodemites—which might be a contradiction in terms. A published Nicodemite, certainly a self-published one, would presumably thereby have ceased to be so describable.[4] Nevertheless, Fumée's letter, part of a *literarum colloquium* with Bucer of which it is the sole surviving relic, is surely from a Nicodemite's pen, as Calvin would undoubtedly have regarded him. Fumée

[1]Jean Rott and Olivier Millet, "Miettes historiques Strasbourgeoises," in Pierre Barthel et al., eds., *Actes du Colloque Guillaume Farel, Neuchâtel 29 septembre—1er octobre 1980,* 2 vols, Cahiers de la Revue de théologie et de philosophie 9 (Geneva, Lausanne, Neuchâtel: Revue de théologie et de philosophie, 1983), 1:253-77, at 262-67. Cf. Heiko A. Oberman, *The Impact of the Reformation* (Grand Rapids: Eerdmans, 1994), 190-94.

[2]Pierre Fraenkel, ed., *Consilium Theologicum Privatim Conscriptum,* Martini Buceri Opera Latina 4 = Studies in Medieval and Reformation Thought 42 (Leiden: E. J. Brill, 1988).

[3]Carlo Ginzburg, *Il Nicodemismo. Simulazione e dissimulazione religiosa nell'Europa del '500* (Turin: Giulio Einaudi, 1970), 139-46, 207-13. Cf. P. Fraenkel, "Bucer's Memorandum of 1541 and a 'Lettera Nicodemitica' of Capito's," Bibliothèque d'Humanisme et Renaissance 36 (1974), 575-87.

[4]Francis M. Higman, "The Question of Nicodemism," in Wilhelm H. Neuser, ed., *Calvinus Ecclesiae Genevensis Custos. Die Referate des Congrès International des Recherches Calviniennes ... Vom 6. bis 9. September 1982 in Genf* (Frankfurt am Main: Peter Lang, 1984), 165-70, at 166.

writes from within a Catholic Church in France whose progress in reform Bucer had partly commended and partly found inadequate. Fumée laments that the sacraments are not explained in the vernacular to worshippers and that in *nostris missarum sacris* the Gospel and Epistle lections are not expounded. Bucer and his colleagues had approved of *nostram de justificatione opinionem*, but demanded from Fumée and his fellows *parem ... integritatem* in public profession and proclamation. "You must realize, brethren [Fumée replies], that we are not free, whether out of impotence (whose force we recognize in ourselves) or from the relentless calumnies of opponents, clearly and explicitly to teach that justification comes solely from the grace of God, not from works."[5]

Yet Fumée protests the faithfulness of their beliefs to Scripture and the Fathers, nor is the letter's tone shamefaced or apologetic. Fumée is bold enough to criticize the low view of the Lord's supper current in Strasbourg and to rebuke Bucer for the scolding offensiveness of his letters. Fumée represents here a robust evangelical faith operating within a limiting but reforming Catholic setting and urgently soliciting diplomatic pressure on the French king to secure a greater measure of freedom.

This recently published letter by Fumée is not alone. It joins others by him to Calvin which voice the plaintive anguish of reformist French believers who know that Calvin's *Petit traicté* (1543) and *Excuse* (1544) were addressed directly to the likes of themselves.[6]

In default of other Nicodemite texts, a number of scholars have turned their attention instead to extant texts, mostly published (with one significant exception), which have not hitherto been recognized as Nicodemite but whose teaching or ethos stands in continuity with the stance or demeanour Calvin (later) attacked. At the Third International Congress on Calvin Research at Geneva in 1982, Francis Higman listed some ten texts from evangelical Gallican Catholics, as they would fairly be called. They doctrinally agreed with most of what Luther (but not yet Calvin) taught and held it to be the true teaching of the Catholic Church. They rejected papal authority, but were committed to reforming the Church from within and opposed schismatic separation. The most substantive of these witnesses to a kind of proto-Nicodemism was Gérard Roussel's still unpublished *Familière Exposition* (c. 1548-49), proposed for our consideration as "the definitive Nicodemite text?"[7]

Without reference to Higman's programmatic essay, two articles in the *Bulletin de la Société de l'Histoire du Protestantisme Français* in 1985 by Maurice

---

[5]Rott, "Miettes historiques Strasbourgeoises," 264.

[6]See Fumée's letters to Calvin of Nov.-Dec. 1543 (CO 11:645-46, no. 516 = A. L. Herminjard, ed., *Correspondence des Réformateurs dans les Pays de Langue Francaise*, 9 vols (Geneva: H. Georg, 1866-97), 9:126-28, no. 1316) and of late 1544 (CO 11:825-30, no. 600 = Herminjard 9:444-48, no. 1430).

[7]Higman, "The Question," 167-70.

Causse expound the thesis that the moderate evangelical reformism set forth in Roussel's *Familière Exposition* and espoused by Marguerite de Navarre was the initial phase of what Calvin would call Nicodemism.[8] Causse's argument probably survives the correction of the several errors and the discounting of the more hazardous hypotheses in his two-part study.

A slight variation on the common theme of Higman and Causse is sketched in Thierry Wanegffelen's recently published thesis *Ni Rome ni Genève,* subtitled *Des fidèles entre deux chaires en France au XVIe siècle.* All three writers reject the appropriateness of clear distinctions between Catholic and Protestant in France in the 1530s and 1540s, and perhaps later still. For Wanegffelen, Nicodemism emerged among "non-confessional" practitioners of a "religion du privé" who trod an uncomfortable "third way" in France between Catholicism or Lutheranism (or Protestantism), and indeed elsewhere also. For this was a Europe-wide phenomenon, this disenchantment with an unreforming Catholic Church accompanied by rejection of any open rupture. Wanegffelen argues for the principled "non-confessionalism" of such evangelical Catholics, which he distinguishes from the "temporizers" (cf. Wolfgang Musculus's *Proscaerus* of 1549, translated into French the next year by Valérand Poullain as *Le Temporiseur*). These were the crypto-Protestants who had worked out a religious praxis based on a deliberate tactic of simulation.[9]

This subtle distinction between "temporizers" and "non-confessional" Nicodemites who were *ex animo* "neither Lutherans nor papists" illustrates the complexity or perhaps elusiveness that recent scholarship generally recognizes in Nicodemism. Carlo Ginzburg's ambitious thesis of a coherent, homogeneous pan-European movement, inspired by Otto Brunfels' *Pandectae* of 1527 and disseminated from Strasbourg as a ready-made theoretical construct, finds little favour nowadays.[10] Nicodemism is to be identified neither with spiritualism—interiorized piety disinterested in externals—nor with libertinism.[11] The chapter on "Calvin and Nicodemism" in Perez Zagorin's *Ways of Lying. Dissimulation, Persecution, and Conformity in Early Modern Europe* (1990) benefits from viewing the role claimed for Brunfels by Ginzburg against the backcloth of cen-

---

[8]Maurice Causse, "La 'Familière Exposition' de Gerard Roussel et l'aventure 'Nicodémite' en Guyenne," BSHPF 131 (1985), 5-33, and "Les dissimulations de Marguerite de Navarre et l'Aventure Nicodémite," ibid., 347-89.

[9]Thierry Wanegffelen, *Ni Rome ni Genève. Des fidèles entre deux chaires en France au XVIe siècle,* Bibliothèque littéraire de la Renaissance ser. 3, 36 (Paris: Honoré Champion, 1997), 35-74. On Musculus's work see now Marc van Winjkoop Lüthi's "Druckwerkverzeichwis des Wolfgang Musculus," in Rudolf Dellsperger *et al.*, eds., *Wolfgang Musculus (1497-1563) und die oberdeutsche Reformation,* Colloquia Augustana 6 (Berlin: Akademie Verlag, 1997), 395-98; cf. Eugénie Droz, Chemins de l'hérésie. Textes et documents, 4 vols. (Geneva: Slatkine Reprints, 1970-76), 1:173-271.

[10]Perez Zagorin, *Ways of Lying. Dissimulation, Persecution, and Conformity in Early Modern Europe* (Cambridge, MA: Harvard University Press, 1990), 63-82, at 68-70.

[11]As Causse, "La 'Familière Exposition'," 11-22 argues.

turies of earlier discussion of the case for dissimulation and lying in the light of biblical precedents. Brunfels' supposed originality rapidly dissolves, and Zagorin suggests that Lefèvre d'Etaples may have instructed Brunfels in this subject and not the reverse.[12] What unifies the diversity of Nicodemism, which even Calvin attests can be little more than residence in Catholic territory where one's evangelical or Protestant convictions cannot, to a significant degree, acceptably be given overt expression and where non-participation in Catholic rites and ceremonies exposes one to disabilities of varying severity? Within the generous embrace of this approach towards a definition we encounter a wide variety of both practice and motivation, from the settled acquiescent conformism which has made a virtue out of pretence and mastered the skills of non-identification, to the restless agonizing of well-instructed consciences over insufferable tensions which can be resolved only by a choice between equally painful and costly challenges. Calvin's anti-Nicodemite writings display not a little awareness of such differences, but the impression they give of unparalleled harshness on his part arises in good measure from his refusal to make significant allowances for these differences.

For there appears to be agreement at least on this aspect of the study of Nicodemism—that Calvin's hostility to it was sharper than that of other leading Reformers, except perhaps for Heinrich Bullinger. Yet the confidence with which one makes comparative statements of this kind wavers when one reckons with the lack of analyses of most other Reformers' attitudes to Nicodemism. The obvious candidates for investigation include Guillaume Farel and Pierre Viret, Melanchthon, Bullinger, Bucer, Capito and Peter Martyr Vermigli. On Bucer my former colleague Peter Matheson has written a learned and perceptive article "Martyrdom or Mission? A Protestant Debate?", which is often overlooked. It is largely based on his reading of Bucer's *Consilium* in advance of Fraenkel's edition in the *Opera Latina,* in which Fraenkel in turn had time merely to note Matheson's forthcoming essay and to dissent from the main lines of his interpretation.[13] The debate is not yet settled. Francis Higman's "Bucer et les nicodémites" focusses chiefly on the *Consilium,* apparently unaware of Matheson's essay.[14]

Carlo Ginzburg, of course, devotes a handful of pages to all the Reformers I have mentioned and to others also, which remind us of the continuing value of his *Il Nicodemismo* despite the weakness of its main thesis. Capito receives most

[12]Carlos M. N. Eire, War *Against the Idols. The Reformation of Worship from Erasmus to Calvin* (Cambridge: Cambridge University Press, 1986), 250-53; Oberman, *Impact,* 192-93.

[13]Peter Matheson, "Martyrdom or Mission? A Protestant Debate," ARG 80 (1989), 154-72; Fraenkel, ed., *Consilium,* xxxii. See also my review of the latter in *JTS* n.s. 42 (1991), 769-70.

[14]Francis Higman, "Bucer et les nicodémites," in Christian Krieger and Marc Lienhard, eds., *Martin Bucer and Sixteenth Century Europe. Actes du colloque de Strasbourg (28-31 août 1991),* 2 vols, Studies in Medieval and Reformation Thought 52-53 (Leiden: E. J. Brill, 1993), 2:645-58.

extended notice, resting in part on Ginzburg's mistaken attribution to him of a fragment of Bucer's *Consilium,* as we have already noted. Yet Capito's Nicodemite leanings are not in doubt, as is clear from a letter of early 1542 from a Frisian preacher, Johannes von Bekensteyn, who had been so alarmed by a letter bearing Capito's name (which "openly taught that the papist church is [a/the] true church of God") that he travelled to Strasbourg to ascertain the truth. It was as he feared, and Bekensteyn's letter summarized Capito's views in terms of lamentation. Bekensteyn attached to his letter copies of letters by Bullinger, Sebastian Franck and Calvin. This letter by Calvin, of late 1541 to an unidentified recipient, directly addresses the heart of the Nicodemite problem. It has the distinction of having been published (with Bullinger's) in an English translation in the 1540s but in the original Latin not until 1906, having escaped the *Corpus Reformatorum* editors. Jacques Pollet discussed the Bekensteyn material in 1985, still unaware not only of the early translation, but also, it seems, of Ginzburg's lengthy examination of the Bekensteyn dossier.[15]

More recently, summary assessments have been advanced from time to time about this or that Reformer. Thus Pierre Viret, the author of several pertinent treatises, is briefly portrayed by Higman and Bernard Cottret as more moderate than Calvin. Viret held that the mass was reformable rather than meriting only replacement, and could talk of "genuine Nicodemites" as well as "false" ones.[16] But the gap between Calvin and Viret was narrow enough for the latter, in the preface to his *Epistre envoyée aux fideles conversans entre les chrestiens papistiques* (1543), to regard Calvin's *Petit traicté,* of the same year and the same printer, as having made his own labour redundant. Calvin had "so well analysed the issue and so clearly proved and confirmed it by arguments and scriptural authorities as to be beyond all possible contradiction—except by any who want openly to resist the clear Word of God".[17]

Among recent literature concentrating on Calvin himself, reference must be made to the publication in 1997, in Korean, of a doctoral dissertation from Chongshin University by Dr. Kyong Lim Kang (now Professor of Church

---

[15]Ginzburg, *Il Nicodemismo,* 136-54: J.V. Pollet, *Martin Bucer. Études sur les relations de Bucer avec les Pays-Bas, l'Electorat de Cologne et L'Allemagne du Nord,* 2 vols, Studies in Medieval and Reformation Thought 33-34 (Leiden: E. J. Brill, 1985), 1:293-320; Calvin's letter: Alfred Hegler, ed., *Beiträge zur Geschichte der Mystik in der Reformationszeit,* Walther Köhler, ed., ARG Ergänzungsband I; (Berlin: C. A. Schwetschke, 1906), 32-41, at 36-41. For the early English translation see *Bibliotheca Calviniana* 1:144-46 (no. 44/1), 254-55 (no. 48/2). On Capito's Nicodemite proclivities see also Millet in Rott and Millet, "Miettes historique Strasbourgeoises," 268-75. See now the introduction to Calvin's 1541 letter with translation by Robert White, "Calvin and the Nicodemite Controversy: An Overlooked Text of 1541," CTJ 35 (2000), 282-96.

[16]Higman, "The Question," 166; Bernard Cottret, Calvin. *Biographie* (Paris: J. C. Lattès, 1995), 277-78. Cf. also on Viret, Zagorin, *Ways of Lying,* 103-107; Matheson, "Martyrdom or Mission?", 165; Droz, *Chemins* 1:165-66.

[17]See *Bibliotheca Calviniana* 1:134.

History at Anyang University), entitled *The Identity of Nicodemism and Calvin's Anti-Nicodemite Controversy.*[18] I am grateful to the author for a copy of an abstract of his work in English. Professor Kang emphasizes the central theological inspiration of Calvin's controversy with Nicodemism in his rejection of idolatry. He is disposed to retain some space for Ginzburg's account of Otto Brunfels' catalytic influence, and he pays some regard to the differences between Calvin and other Reformers in their evaluation of Nicodemism.

Carlos Eire's *War Against the Idols. The Reformation of Worship from Erasmus to Calvin,* first published in 1986, remains the single most satisfactory treatment of Calvin's teaching in a European language.[19] This monograph and preliminary articles have been influential in their critique of Ginzburg, but in turn it would be a mistake to assume too easily that Nicodemism is fully understood when viewed in the light of Calvin's "war against simulation".[20]

A literary and rhetorical analysis of most of Calvin's major anti-Nicodemite writings has been provided in Olivier Millet's immense volume *Calvin et la dynamique de la parole. Étude de rhétorique réformée* (1992). The two "open letters" written in Italy in 1536, each to an unnamed but easily identified friend, were furnished with a revealing preface when they were made available to a wider readership the following year from Geneva under the title *Two Letters on Matters Supremely Necessary for This Age to Take Cognizance of (Epistolae Duae)*.[21] The title page quotes Elijah's challenge to Israel in 1 Kings 18:21, "How long will you waver between two opinions? If the Lord is God, follow him, but if Baal is God, follow him." This prophetic solemnity sets the tone for the preface, in which Calvin explains that he was moved to publish the letters on learning that friends and others who had read them, though agreeing with him *verbotenus,* had not taken them very seriously because (so they complained in excuse) he imposed on them an exceedingly hard and severe condition. He now besought all persons of good will *per tremendum illud Dei nomen* to receive what he had written not like a poetic tale or rhetorical declamation but as *vitae doctrinam* which

---

[18]Published by the Christian Literature Crusade, Seoul, 1997. The author also assesses Calvin's "Nicodemites" in the light of New Testament scholarship on Nicodemus. Most of Calvin's writings against Nicodemism have now been translated, in all cases from the French, by Seth Skolnitsky, *Come Out From Among Them: "Anti-Nicodemite" Writings of John Calvin* (Dallas: Protestant Heritage Press, 2001).

[19]See earlier Eire, "Calvin and Nicodemism; A Reappraisal," Sixteenth Century Journal 10 (1979), 45-69; "Prelude to Sedition? Calvin's Attack on Nicodemism and Religious Compromise," ARG 76 (1985), 120-45.

[20]Eire, *War Against the Idols,* 240; Wanegffelen, *Ni Rome ni Genève,* 71.

[21]Millet, *Calvin et la dynamique de la parole. Étude de rhétorique réformée,* Bibliothèque littéraire de la Renaissance ser. 3, 28 (Paris: Librairie Honoré Champion, 1992), 480-504. For the *Epistolae Duae, see Bibliotheca Calviniana,* 1:40-43 (no. 37/1); text in OS 1:287-362 (and CO 5:233-312). There is an English translation of the first letter, *De fugiendis impiorum illicitis sacris,* by Henry Beveridge, *Tracts and Treatises,* 3 vols. (Edinburgh: Calvin Translation Society, 1844-51), 3:359-411.

was God's Word to be approved only by obedience. To cut matters short, Calvin will quote Ezekiel 33:31-33, where the Lord says to the prophet: "They come to you in crowds, they sit before you and hear your words but do not carry them out ... You have become to them like the entertaining song of a sweet-sounding voice ... But when the time has come (which indeed is already at hand) they will know that a prophet has been among them."[22]

By the time this introduction to the reader was written, Calvin had become, as the title page identifies him, "Professor of Sacred Scripture in the Church of Geneva". In the letters themselves, Millet finds Calvin writing not as a theologian-reformer or minister, and without appeal to his vocation or special calling, but more as a moralist, partly in a Senecan mould, and as a spiritual director. Only the citation of Revelation 3:1-2, 15-16 at the end of the second letter hints at "the sharpness and forcefulness, which will never subsequently be equalled", with which in 1537 Calvin assumes the magisterium of the prophet.[23]

Millet links this imperious preface with the beginning of the fourth of Calvin's anti-Nicodemite treatises, the Excuse, of 1544, his *Defence ... to the Nicodemites on their Complaint of his Excessive Rigour.* Again the title page cites an Old Testament prophet, Amos 5:10, "they have hated the one who delivers rebuke in the gate, and they have loathed the one who speaks the right". Above this, in the middle of the page, the device of a right hand holding a sword vertically, is surrounded by the words of Jesus, "I have come to bring not peace but a sword." The verso of the title page quotes Isaiah 30:9-10, "This people is a rebellious people, they are hypocrites, folk who refuse to listen to the law of the Lord. They say to those who see, 'Don't see anything,' and to those who consider, Don't consider anything of what is right,' but speak of things which please us, and see illusions."[24]

Almost immediately Calvin launches into as brutally authoritarian an exordium as one finds in his corpus.

> I have written a treatise [the *Petit traicté* of 1543] in which I show that a believer living among the papists cannot take part in their superstitions without offending God. This doctrine is clear. I have proved it by testimonies of Scripture, and by arguments so certain that they cannot be contradicted. What is more, there is a categorical argument which closes the issue in one word. [Calvin proceeds to declare that our bodies no less than our souls belong to God.]...

[22]OS 1:287-88.

[23]Millet, *Calvin,* 492, 497, 503.

[24]For the Excuse, see CO 6:589-614, and Francis M. Higman, ed., *Three French Treatises* (London: Athlone Press, 1970), 21-26, 131-53, 166-68. It is translated by Eric Kayayan, "Apology of John Calvin, To Messrs. The Nicodemites ...," CTJ 29 (1994), 346-63. For the title page, *Bibliotheca Calviniana* 1:164 (no. 44/9). Translation also in Skolnitsky, *Come Out From Among Them,* 97-125.

> There are always some people who find me too rigorous and, what is more, complain of me for treating them too inhumanely. If one asks the cause of their discontent, it is because they cannot bear to be scratched where they itch *(on leur gratte leur rongne)*. What semblance of a self-defence do they have, as if I were wrongly condemning them? [More on the soul-body relationship.] ... So as I said at the outset, as far as the doctrine is concerned, it is clear and easily decided, if one wants to abide by the truth. And the proofs are so obvious that it would be impudent to hold out for the contrary.[25]

A few lines later, Calvin compares his critics who advance flabby excuses to cesspool cleaners *(maistres Fifiz)* who, by dint of long exposure, have lost their sense of smell. Thus after again casting himself in the role of a prophet whether the people will pay heed or not, Calvin bursts into his initial paragraphs with a truly exceptional bluntness.[26]

Olivier Millet also furnishes an illuminating comparison of the *Petit traicté* of 1543 with the first letter of 1536/37, *De fugiendis impiorum illicitis sacris,* of which it is a reworking into the French vernacular. More significant than the change of language is the change in Calvin's position, from a humanist orator using a letter in arguing a case of conscience, with some intemperance and doctrinaire rigour, to a pastor and biblical theologian composing a treatise no less stringent in its demands, but more direct and accessible in its didactic edification, involving Calvin himself in the first person more prominently in engagement with his readers, somewhat softer in tone and even marginally more moderate in its counsels, as befits the work of a pastor of souls.[27]

Such a comparison, although at base literary in its interests, invites us to a differentiated reading of Calvin's anti-Nicodemite works according to their setting in the course of his career. This must be insisted upon even though virtually the whole essence of his refutation of Nicodemite theory is contained already in the letter to Duchemin of 1536. Furthermore, a comprehensive study of Calvin's opposition to Nicodemism will not isolate this handful of writings—even though together they constitute the most sustained and influential of sixteenth-century Protestant discussions of the subject—from others of his works. In addition to several with obviously overlapping concerns, such as *On Scandals, the Reply to Sadoleto* and his responses to Trent and the Interim, a search of his biblical expositions is likely to reveal how instinctively Calvin's mind turned in an anti-Nicodemite direction.

Some half-a-dozen passages in his commentaries name the Nicodemites, but they are reinforced by numerous other applications of biblical texts where they

---

[25]Higman, 133-34; Kayayan, 346-47 (adapted).

[26]Millet, *Calvin,* 449, 453.

[27]Millet, *Calvin,* 809-28. Jean-François Gilmont implies some doubt on the use of "traduction," *Bibliotheca Calviniana* 1:133.

are not named.[28] Benoît Girardin has drawn attention to verses in Romans where Calvin's preoccupation with this target distinguishes him from other prominent Reformation commentators.[29] Paul may exhort his readers to "live peaceably with all" (Romans 12:18), but Calvin's commentary picks up the two qualifications "if it is possible" and "as far as it depends on you", warns against conciliation degenerating into compliance in others' sins and (in the 1556 revision) denies that Christ's soldiers can enjoy lasting peace in a world ruled by Satan. When Paul predicts that before the judgement seat every knee shall bow and every tongue confess (Romans 14:11), Calvin's anti-Nicodemite bias fastens not only on confession by the mouth but also literally on "the outward gesture of the body which he has designated by the bowing of the knee". If Romans 10:10 is a gift for an anti-Nicodemite expositor, Calvin is careful to debar a Nicodemite appeal to Romans 11:4 (the seven thousand who had not bowed to Baal indicated "only those who did not prostitute their body to the worship of idols, even by an outward act of pretence", *ne externa quidem simulatione*), and 14:22, where having a conscience clear before God did not make attendance at "foolish superstitious ceremonies" an adiaphoron. Calvin comments pithily: "Ceremonies ... are also a part of our confession. Those who separate faith from confession rob the sun of its heat." These two sentences were added to the commentary in the 1551 edition.[30]

One might expect fewer explicit references to Nicodemism in Calvin's sermons, and certainly the literature has so far assembled very few. The lack of indexed editions and translations prevents convenient searching. The editors of the sermons on Acts 1-7 published in 1994 are a notable exception and have indexed a handful of unmistakeable rebukes of Nicodemite behaviour, including one explicit naming of "ces nicodemites".[31]

Not to be forgotten, of course, are *Quatre Sermons* Calvin preached in 1549 and revised and issued in 1552 which form part of his anti-Nicodemite dossier proper.[32] He explains his purpose in a preface. Despite having written two trea-

---

[28]For the references to "Nicodemites," see commentaries on Psalm 16:4 (CO 31:153), Jeremiah 10:11 (CO 38:74), Hosea 4:15 (CO 42:290), John 7:50 (CO 47:186-87), 19:38 (CO 47:424), Acts 21:26 (CO 48:486).

[29]Benoît Girardin, *Rhétorique et théologie. Calvin: Le Commentaire de l'Épître aux Romains, Théologie Historique* 54 (Paris: Éditions Beauchesne, 1979), 123-29.

[30]See T. H. L. Parker's edition, *Iohannis Calvini Commentarius in Epistolam Pauli ad Romanos,* Studies in the History of Christian Thought 22 (Leiden: E. J. Brill, 1981), ad loc; COR II/13, ad loc.

[31]Willem Balke and Wilhelmus H. Th. Moehn, eds., *Sermons on the Acts of the Apostles,* SC 8 (Neukirchen-Vluyn: Neukirchener Verlag des Erziehungsvereins, 1994), 224-25 (on Acts 6:11-15), and for allusions of varying clarity, 106, 240-41.

[32]CO 8:369-452; *Bibliotheca Calviniana* 1:463-66 (no. 52/9), and for an early English translation of the first two, ibid., 469-71 (no. 53/1). Cf. T. H. L. Parker, *Calvin's Preaching* (Edinburgh: T&T Clark, 1992), 60-61. Translation now in Skolnitsky, *Come Out From Among Them,* 127-237.

tises "assez amples" to demonstrate the unacceptability when living "en la Papaulté", of giving any appearance of consent or adherence to its regnant abuses, superstitions and idolatries, he is asked almost daily for fresh counsel—as though he had never spoken. He is also aware of others who incessantly advance rebuttals and evasions of what he has written.[33] The first sermon calls for the shunning of all idolatry, including the mass, even in a partially reformed observance—with no adoration of the elements, omission of the canon and distribution in both kinds to all present.[34] This sermon's text is Psalm 16:4 ("I will take no part in their blood sacrifices, and their names will I never take on my lips")—a verse on which Calvin refers openly to "demented Nicodemites" in his Psalms commentary. (He does likewise in his lectures on Jeremiah 10:11, which is cited in this first sermon, as too is 1 Kings 18:21, which was printed on the title page of *Petit traicté* in 1543. Thus one can assemble Calvin's anti-Nicodemite scriptural arsenal.) The second sermon is a summons to suffer persecution for Christ, based on Hebrews 13:13, "Let us follow Christ outside the camp ..." The third and fourth sermons hold out the inestimable goal of liberty to worship God in a properly ordered church. All four sermons are replete with the tough, exacting pastoral casuistry that characterizes Calvin's anti-Nicodemite writings from the outset. Always there were objections to parry, excuses to explode, pathetic pleas to disarm, but Calvin's stomach was equal to the task.

He had faced stringent criticism, not least from well-disposed friends, ever since the two letters of 1536 began to circulate privately. The diagnosis might be sound, but the prescription was fearsome—*duram asperamque nimium conditionem.*[35] The response of Antoine Fumée and his fellow-evangelicals in Paris to the Petit traicté of 1543 was surely only typical, and yet from a trusted companion from student days it had to be taken seriously. "Most people think that your message is utterly depressing *(miserrimum)*. They complain of your heartlessness and severity to those under pressure. It is easy for you to preach and admonish where you are; if you were here, you would perhaps have a different attitude."[36] When the *Excuse* followed in 1544, Fumée protested the integrity of his community, which did not merit—or appreciate—its scolding reproaches. "The Lord knows that we are prepared for his sake to leave [everything] and move promptly and smartly wherever he calls—provided that, through you and other trusted souls whom you know, namely Luther, Melanchthon and Bucer, the Lord shall declare to us what once he did to faithful Abraham, 'Depart from your land and your kinsfolk.'" Fumée stresses the magnitude and diffi-

---

[33]CO 8:373-74.

[34]CO 8:387.

[35]OS 1:288, from the preface to the *Epistolae Duae* of 1537.

[36]CO 11:646, no. 516 (Herminjard 9:126, no. 1316).

culty of such a migration, but pledges his people to undertake it once "the Lord makes his divine mind plain to us through you".[37]

The request Calvin acted upon was to consult Luther, Melanchthon and Bucer on several specific questions Fumée listed. The three should receive both his letter and one from Calvin. The Parisian brethren were not unaware of what these venerable men had written on these issues, but a nagging doubt persisted which Calvin's *Excuse* reinforced rather than resolved. They had been deeply disturbed to hear that on this question *non satis adhuc inter vos omnes convenire.* The nub of this momentous matter was this:

> Must we so strictly shun our opponents' church *(ecclesiam alienorum),* which nonetheless you all admit in your writings is a church in some sense *(esse aliquam),* that we cannot attend their services, most of all the mass, without defiling ourselves with plain, naked idolatry—which must not be done even to save life?

Fumée impresses on Calvin in this deeply serious, forthright and poignant letter the precise terms in which the consultation was to be carried out.[38]

The results of the exercise were published in mid-1546 as an appendix (translated into French as needed) to the 1545 reprint of the *Petit traicté* and *Excuse* together. (Very few copies survive, one without the appendix.) For the purpose of the consultation, Calvin translated these two works into Latin, "word for word", which version was issued in 1549 under the title *De vitandis superstitionibus* (the title in reality of the *Petit traicté* translation only), together with the supplement now in Latin.[39] Some scholars refer to this as the first printing of the responses, but Fumée's importunity would have brooked no such delay.

Claude de Senarclens was Calvin's envoy for the consultation. He carried to Melanchthon both his own letter and the one for Luther, which, as Calvin both allowed for and no doubt expected and even welcomed, Melanchthon judged it unwise to pass on to "Pericles". Senarclens took Melanchthon's response to Strasbourg, with the result that Bucer's *consilium* is partly a comment on Melanchthon's as well as on the original enquiry, and Peter Martyr's in turn on both Melanchthon's and Bucer's. Calvin published these three judgements with his own *Consilium et Conclusio* and two of his letters, one to an unknown friend and the other to Valérand Poullain, who took closely to do with the Nicodemite debate, acted as a distribution agent for Calvin's *Petit traicté* and *Excuse* and had himself been asked by brethren in France to consult Luther, Melanchthon and Bucer in the hope of tempering Calvin's "severity". Finally,

---

[37]CO 11:826, 827, no. 600 (Herminjard 9:445, 446, no. 1430).

[38]CO 11:828, no. 600 (Herminjard 9:447-48, no. 1430).

[39]*Bibliotheca Calviniana* 1:195-98 (no. 45/9), 303-306 (no. 49/5). Although Calvin describes his Latin version as *ad verbum* (CO 12:26) it is not scrupulously close to the French and might repay detailed comparison.

an approbation of Calvin's *De vitandis superstitionibus* arrived from Zurich in late autumn 1549 and was added to the 1550 reprint of the work and to some copies of the 1549 printing.[40]

A comparison of these *consilia* should help one to understand the distinctiveness of Calvin's position. Since this has never, to my knowledge, been undertaken (Eire states limply that "Calvin's position was defended by" Bucer, Melanchthon, Martyr and Bullinger),[41] to this we now turn.

Melanchthon's *consilium* is the most difficult to characterize or sum up.[42] It approaches the issue in more general terms, beginning and ending with the First Commandment, which requires "all rational creatures" to flee idols, whether *ethnica, mahometica, haeretica et quarumcunque sectarum portenta.* "Heretics" is the nearest Melanchthon gets to "papists", he twice mentions living "among Turks", he lists the errors of the Anabaptists and warns against the appeal of Schwenckfeld and other radical leaders. This warning appears in the midst of his urging any who do go into exile to join a properly ordered congregation. Is it too subtle to discern here on Melanchthon's part a hint that a root-and-branch rejection of the Old Church and its worship landed one in the same camp as the radicals in their pursuit of a totally new church?[43]

Yet when Melanchthon comes to details it is obvious that he has not forgotten the question. Some elements remind one immediately of Calvin, such as the necessity for "external ... confession or profession" as well as inward worship, and the recommendation of exile for the weak. *Infirmi, infirmitas* recur throughout the *consilium,* confirming the general impression that Melanchthon knows what has to be said but shrinks from insisting on it without reservation. He distinguishes between the *regula,* which teaches what is to be done, and the doing *(factum)* itself. He is sensitive to the human frailty that will not be able to sustain *supplicium* (he warns those who choose this path to be sure of their *patientia* or *constantia,* lest, having begun boldly, their nerve snaps as danger approaches) and yet cannot face exile.

> To these, as to invalids, I can say only that they acknowledge their weakness and lament it, and gradually build up their strength, and give a progressively more clearcut witness of confession. I know it is a difficult business, making a start on confession *(haec exordia confessionis).* But it is a matter of departing or else awaiting death.[44]

---

[40]*Bibliotheca Calviniana* 1:356-58 (no. 50/11). The details of the exercise are largely given by Gilmont, ibid., 197. The *consilia,* Calvin's two letters and the Zurich response are in CO 6:621-44 (all in Latin).

[41]Eire, *War Against the Idols,* 247, n. 51.

[42]CO 6:621-24.

[43]Cf. Matheson, "Martyrdom or Mission?," 159 with n. 27, for a parallel in Bucer. The reference should be to *Consilium* para. 795 (Fraenkel, ed., 176).

[44]CO 6:623.

Several times Melanchthon urges that "confession of some kind" *(aliqua)* should be made. Here Nicodemus, like the apostle John, was *imbecillis.* "Many in court circles call themselves Nicodemuses, and weak *(infirmos),* when they are really prevaricators."

So the flow of thought moves like a swinging pendulum. He is conscious that his task is *recte docere, non blandiri infirmitati,* but immediately softens his tone: "Although indulgence *(venia)* may be granted for a moderate period of time, especially for neophytes, in major cases in fear of public disorder, yet dissimulation should not be unending."[45]

Melanchthon found confusion in Jerusalem near the birth of Jesus. "The true church" of Zacharias, Elizabeth and Mary gathered in the temple for all its vitiated worship and perverse beliefs. All, strong as well as weak, should bring their babies for baptism, and should observe *ritus adiaphoros,* e.g. vespers, despite an admixture of corruption, for the assembly will include some elect children, and some adults of sound conviction but weak, members of Christ who need to be gradually led forward. Nevertheless there are *manifesti cultus idolorum* to be shunned, and mass, it seems, must not be attended, although the only aspects of it that the *consilium* mentions as objectionable are the adoration of the bread and its processional display.

Calvin acknowledged receipt of Melanchthon's reply and gave God unceasing thanks that on the essence of the question they were of one mind, despite a little difference in certain details.[46] In his own *Consilium et Conclusio* which rounds off the file, Calvin notes that, without responding seriatim to excuses advanced, Melanchthon discounted them all at one go by affirming that nothing warranted permitting a Christian *idololatriae professionem, etiam obscuram.*[47]

Martin Bucer began by assenting briefly to Dominus Philippus's statement (and also appended his approval to Peter Martyr's).[48] He then set off on quite a different track and not until the last third of his *consilium* (two columns, a full page, in *Corpus Reformatorum*) did he get round to the standard items on Calvin's agenda. His first two substantive sentences deserve to be quoted at length.

> I want the brethren held in Babylonian captivity to take most careful precautions not to incur, by inopportunely and wantonly denigrating the ordinary services of worship *(vulgatas caeremonias),* a reputation for impiety with the elect of God whom they ought to win *(lucrifacere)* for the Lord, and thereby render themselves useless in bringing *(adducant)* them to the Lord. I want the following to be held for certain among the brethren: whatever

---

[45]Ibid.

[46]CO 12:100, no. 657.

[47]CO 6:632.

[48]CO 6:625-26. This is discussed by Higman, "Bucer et les nicodémites" (n. 14 above), 652-54.

> there is from God and Christ that survives in the ordinary *(vulgatis)* lections, sermons and other transactions in church cannot be corrupted, whether by the ministers' impiety, an unholy admixture of man-made fabrications or superstitious misuse, to such a degree that the godly are unable to hear and sense the Lord speaking and acting in them, and to use them for the increase of godliness.[49]

This was the situation in Jerusalem after Christ's crucifixion, but the apostles took part in worship and applied to Christ the Lord the elements surviving from divine appointment, and exposed and condemned human intrusions. They made use of a *dispensatio,* both in teaching and in "ceremonies". They were weak with the weak, they were Jewish with Jews, using Jewish ceremonies in order to call away from them those who used them superstitiously. *Nihil dissimulabant, aut simulabant.*

As appropriate *(in loco),* they did keep quiet about certain things, but in order to impart more conveniently and effectively the teaching whereby they might prepare people's minds to grasp also what they still withheld from them—withheld, that is, for the reason that they could not yet fruitfully transmit it.

Bucer at last comes to the mass with a critique that bites more sharply than Melanchthon's, and is then extended to processions, relics and images. "These must be shunned, exposed and anathematized, and people summoned away from them with utmost care." Bucer too addresses the *infirmiores;* they must not deck out their weakness in the guise of prudence or *dispensatio,* but pray for strength. "The more resolute should revive and strengthen the weaker in a gentle spirit and not reject or crush them." "Crushing them" was not far from what Fumée accused Calvin of doing.

Bucer's *consilium* ends with a short prayer: "May the Lord Jesus himself gather and feed his sheep." Distinctively undergirding his whole declaration is a theological utterance of typically Buceran length and solidity:

> Since we have been created and redeemed in order to invoke, confess and celebrate our God and Father through our Lord Jesus Christ everywhere and in all our doings with the utmost devotion, liberty and confidence, and to neglect no opportunity to proclaim his kingdom and to draw to him and to his flock any sheep still straying from his fold, it is essential that all Christians seek to bring this about with total commitment in sacred assemblies and services *(caeremoniis),* that is, in the presence of the Lord himself *(coram ipso Domino)* and in the very profession of invoking, confessing and proclaiming our God and Saviour and in thanksgiving.[50]

---

[49] CO 6:625.

[50] Ibid.

No acknowledgement of Bucer's *consilium* has survived from Calvin's pen. He cannot have been comfortable with it, but he probably expected nothing better. The inclusion of Bucer, perhaps even more than Luther, in the French demand helps to explain Calvin's marked lack of enthusiasm for the exercise.[51] We must assume that Calvin knew nothing of the *Consilium Theologicum Privatim Conscriptum,* which Pierre Fraenkel has placed in the context of work on the Regensburg Book in late 1540 and early 1541. Fraenkel has argued that a major part of this *Consilium* is so direct a polemic against Calvin's first anti-Nicodemite writing, *De fugiendis impiorum illicitis sacris* of 1536/37, that it merited being so titled in his critical edition.[52] Bucer of course does not name Calvin and never cites his text, nor did Calvin often name Bucer in letters of these years in which the debate about Nicodemism continued. This has been shown by Peter Matheson in his valuable article "Martyrdom or Mission? A Protestant Debate", where he proposes that Bullinger is the likely target of much of Bucer's *Consilium.*[53] Strasbourg's position as the chief forum for the ongoing debate is clear.[54]

The points of contact between our one-page *consilium* and Fraenkel's edited text are undeniable and important, but missing from the former is the key role that vocation plays in the latter. But Calvin could not have failed to notice Bucer's silence on both exile and martyrdom, his extended appeal to apostolic practice in support of being economical with the truth, his clear sense of the objective God-givenness of much in the Old Church (Melanchthon had mentioned only the continuing presence within it of some of God's elect), and, as the overriding burden of Bucer's counsel in its total concentration on making the most of the situation, the priority of mission. This note sounds throughout the *Consilium ... Privatim Conscriptum,* which follows its title with 1 Corinthians 9:19-22, "Since I was free from all, I made myself a slave to all, in order to win (*lucrifacerem*—as in our *consilium*) the more", and ends with the prayer "May our Lord Jesus Christ, the one Good Shepherd, grant us to minister faithfully, prudently, steadfastly and successfully to encompass the salvation of his sheep."[55]

Winning souls to Christ was scarcely a concern that Calvin could entertain in this context. It does not surface at all in 1536/37 in *De fugiendis,* while in the *Excuse* in 1544 he is contemptuously dismissive of those who claim to dissimulate

> in order to win our neighbours and raise new seed by the day. By this way the Church is preserved and grows. Otherwise it would perish. Is that how they

---

[51]Calvin told Viret on February 2, 1545, that the consultation was not his choice or undertaken in expectation of a good outcome, but the French had determined on it: CO 12:27, no. 611.

[52]Fraenkel, *Consilium,* 129-67, cf. xvi, xxiv. Higman, "Bucer et les nicodémites," 647-52, agrees with Fraenkel in seeing Calvin as a main target of Bucer's.

[53]Matheson, "Martyrdom or Mission?," 164-69. He views Bucer also as in debate with Calvin.

[54]Oberman, *Impact,* 192.

[55]Fraenkel, *Consilium,* 1, 177.

> esteem God [Calvin retorts], as if he could not preserve his Church if they did not help him with their sham, which he condemns and rejects so strongly? ... Can they boast of having ever set up a Church of ten people in one village, with their so great discretion and their so cautious wisdom? On the contrary, the whole world was won by the mere preaching of the Gospel.[56]

By the time of the *Quatre Sermons* in 1549/1552, especially the third and fourth, Calvin's focus is on the freedom of opportunity in a reformed church far from the papists' reach.

Peter Martyr's brief *consilium* endorses those of Melanchthon and Bucer, but that was no more than proper form.[57] His contribution will merely add explanation, not guidance. Correcting Melanchthon, he points out that even infant baptism and evening and morning prayers are not free of perversions like intercessions for the dead, and that the example of "holy Jews" participating in the temple before the coming of Christ is irrelevant to the question at hand. Correcting Bucer, he construes the precedent of Naaman less encouragingly, and recalls that the apostles not only took part in Jewish worship in the temple but had their own Lord's supper and met also for their own prayer and ministry of God's Word. The brethren in Babylonian captivity should hold some such assembly if possible. As one whose flight from Italy in 1542 marked a break with Nicodemism, Vermigli was one of Calvin's most reliable allies.[58]

The *Response of the Pastors of the Zurich Church,* although added a little later, should be treated at this stage.[59] Bullinger's covering note explains that it was written to obviate any uncertainty that they were of one mind with Calvin, who others were alleging stood alone. The *Response* itself is typically Bullinger in its apocalypticism, framing the dilemmas of French evangelicals in the harsh light of "the immense evils and perils of the last time" when God forbids any yoking of Christ and Belial, orders his servants to strive against Satan, and threatens the timid who desert Christ with eternal punishment, alongside dogs, pigs, liars, idolaters and murderers (Revelation 21:8). "A simple and open confession of God's name and truth" is what God requires. The path to life is through a narrow gate and by a narrow way.[60]

---

[56]Higman, ed., 144; Kayayan, tr., 356 (amended).

[57]CO 6:627-28.

[58]Cf. Joseph C. McLelland's introduction in *Early Writings. Creed Scripture Church,* Peter Martyr Library 1, Sixteenth Century Essays & Studies 30 (Kirksville, MO: Sixteenth Century Journal Publishers, 1994), 19-23, with a brief mention of this consilium. Cf. too Zagorin, *Ways of Lying,* 109-11.

[59]CO 6:641-44.

[60]CO 6:642-43.

Bullinger adds a catena of scriptural verses and a catalogue of "great and illustrious examples" from the martyrs and confessors of the early church.[61] The Zurich response never gets close to the messy confusions of the reformed in France, but we understand immediately why Calvin was happy to insert it when *De Vitandis Superstitionibus* was reprinted in 1549/50.

When we turn back to Calvin's *Consilium et Conclusio* from such solemn generalities, the stark contrast is inescapable, as it is no less when it is set alongside Melanchthon's sinuous ruminations or Bucer's bullish advocacy of critical solidarity. Calvin responds to five objections or questions with the deadly accuracy of the sharpest six-shooter in Protestantism. In less than a page and a half not a word is wasted, no bolt-hole is left for compromise of any kind, and Fumée and his brethren are served ice-cold comfort.[62]

Calvin will not rehearse again the incompatibility of a total lack of confession and of a pretence of idolatry with being a Christian. This is taken as read. First, then, should the godly migrate and abandon their vocations rather than take part in masses and suchlike corruptions? All those, replies Calvin, who cannot offer to God where they live all that he demands as essential from all Christians must realize that "Depart from your land and your kinsfolk" (Genesis 12:1) is their instruction no less than Abraham's—unless, that is, they possess the fortitude to meet death unflinchingly. But surely a lawful vocation from God should not be forsaken on one's own initiative? On the contrary, states Calvin, where God cannot be rendered his due, nothing must or can detain us. The first table of the law takes precedence over the second, and everything is subservient to the pure worship of God. But what if (the third question) the common good and edification of others make it expedient for someone to reap many benefits *modica, et quoad in se erit sobria simulatione?* It is for us to fulfil God's commands, for God to determine advantageous outcomes. "The obligation to keep ourselves for God unpolluted in spirit and body is not open to change by any circumstantial factors." A similar rejoinder awaits the fourth objection: what if our leaving incites the harshness of the ungodly, enervates the weak, causes damaging offence? Our duty is to follow whither the Lord calls without disputing, and to commit the consequences to him. To us, all is uncertainty, and our departure may conceivably wound the conscience of the heedless, humble the arrogant and invigorate the shaky. Does this mean, finally, that if we leave, we do nothing more to assist brethren already under duress for their witness to Christ? Again, the relentless response is immediate and curt: no better counsel can be given than to risk one's life to vindicate Christ's glory, but for those who lack the spirit for this fight, no duty of the second table gives an excuse for idolatry.

---

[61]CO 6:643-44.

[62]CO 6:629-32.

How then should we explain the exceptional, if not truly unique, severity of Calvin's position? From one angle the question can be rephrased as follows: how did Calvin come to such a severe position as early as 1536? For this is indeed the case, that *De Fugiendis Impiorum Illicitis Sacris* written in 1536 and published presumably without revision, in 1537, contains the permanent core of Calvin's anti-Nicodemite argument.[63] Its adaptation in *Petit traicté* for 1543 can still be called translation (by Olivier Millet), and the French treatise in turn was translated by Calvin himself "word for word" as *De Vitandis Superstitionibus* in 1549. So one key question has to delve into the antecedents in Calvin's formation to his writing in 1536.

This is not to deny that Calvin's standpoint underwent some elaboration—but this may be the appropriate term rather than development or evolution. One of the few mentions of the topic in Bouwsma's portrait states that Calvin's "insistence on the church as a functioning community was closely related to his rejection of what he called 'Nicodemism'", with the implication that the latter flowed from the former.[64] Perhaps the movement ran in the reverse direction, but, whatever the sequence, the importance of Christians belonging to a publicly and regularly ordered church in which its proper activities could proceed without hindrance was, for reasons that are not hard to seek, not an element in 1536/37. It barely surfaces in the Excuse in 1544 (which Bouwsma refers to as Calvin's broadest onslaught) and comes into its own only in the *Quatre Sermons* of 1549/1552.[65]

Somewhat similarly, Eugénie Droz argues that Calvin's opposition was not theologically inspired but fired by the need for hordes of French refugees of unflinching commitment to build the new Jerusalem in Geneva. Thus the Petit traicté of 1543 was his first appeal to the French to incite them to come to live in Geneva in great numbers.[66] Whether this is a plausible characterization of *Petit traicté*, the claim cannot stand up if applied to 1536/37 when the main lines of Calvin's case are set in concrete. Droz is restricted to the briefest reference to historical and political realities in Geneva in 1537-38[67]. It is surely impossible to believe that the publication of the *Epistolae Duae*, whose preface is dated January 10, 1537, really had in mind the personnel requirements of Calvin's allegedly theocratic project in Geneva.

---

[63]The possibility that Calvin revised the 1536 letters before publication in 1537 is considered and rejected by E. Doumergue, *Jean Calvin. Les hommes et les choses de son temps*, 7 vols. (Lausanne: Georges Bridel, 1899-1927), 2:27, n. 6.

[64]William J. Bouwsma, *John Calvin. A Sixteenth Century Portrait* (New York: Oxford University Press, 1988), 216.

[65]Ibid., 240, n. 29; 289, n. 20.

[66]Droz, *Chemins*, 1:156-57.

[67]Ibid., 155-56.

Nevertheless, the last paragraph prompts a fresh form of the main question. Why was it that Calvin *persisted in* such stalwart opposition to religious dissimulation and simulation? (Calvin, by the way, distinguished clearly between the two in *Petit traicté:* "Dissimulation is committed by concealing what one has in one's mind. Simulation goes further, in giving appearance and pretence of what is not the case. In short, simulation by action is the equivalent of lying with the mouth." Calvin says at this point that his enquiry is restricted to whether simulation is acceptable, but his incessant demand that inward faith must be accompanied by external confession made dissimulation no less problematic.)[68] It may well be that Calvin's persistence owed something to both the needs and the attractions of Geneva. Millet comments that "the struggle against 'Nicodemism', which would take a decisive turn with the *Excuse* of 1544, must serve *(devait servir)* to reinforce, by an influx of refugees, the reformed citadel that the Reformers sought to erect in the city of Geneva",[69] but how do we distinguish between intention and effect? That the outflow from France enormously benefited Calvin's endeavours in Geneva goes without saying, but at what stage, if ever, may we validly claim that Calvin's anti-Nicodemite propaganda had immigration into Geneva among its aims? Substantiating this calls for particular sensitivity to textual evidence.

By the time of the third of the *Quatre Sermons* of 1549/1552, Calvin knew of common talk that "people were not Christians at all unless they trotted off to Geneva to have their ears steeped *(confictes)* in sermons and to use the ceremonies they observe there. Can one not read and pray to God well enough on one's own? Does one have to enter a temple to be taught when each of us has a Bible at home?"[70] Once exile has been flagged up as a live option, of course Calvin was concerned that the refugees make their new home in a faithfully reformed congregation—and where better than Geneva? After all, most pastors are mini-imperialists at heart! But how may we satisfactorily disentangle Calvin's concern for pure religion in France from his alleged overriding interest in peopling Geneva with reliable supporters of the reform? Since the preoccupation with the French mission among the Geneva pastors became so important, was the counsel of exile geared towards "reculer pour mieux sauter"?

When, to be sure, did exile first emerge as a possible line of action in Calvin's anti-Nicodemite writings? Eire's discussion rests almost entirely on the *Quatre Sermons*[71]. Flight is not raised in the first letter of 1536/37, although martyrdom is commended.[72] But departure if possible is the first recommendation Calvin

[68]*Petit traicté,* CO 6:546. Eire, *War Against the Idols,* 256, reads Calvin here as treating dissimulation as acceptable, but he was already condemning it in *De Fugiendis* in 1536/37, OS 1:294.

[69]Millet, *Calvin,* 810, followed by Cottret, *Calvin,* 278.

[70]CO 8:412. Cf. Eire, *War,* 263.

[71]*War,* 260-63.

[72]OS 1:328.

makes in the *Petit traicté* of 1543 to the questioner who asks for guidance for "the alien sojourning in such an Egypt or held prisoner in such a Babylon".

> I would advise that he should betake himself to a place where he would not be forced to defile himself with this filth, listen to blasphemy of the name of God and his Word, keeping quiet and dissimulating as if he consented, but on the contrary where he would be free to make profession of his Christianity in the assembly of Christians, share in the holy teaching of the gospel, enjoy the pure and complete use of the sacraments, and participate in public prayer. This in my view is the best thing to do.[73]

In letters of October 1543 Calvin advises Monsieur and Madame de Falais to leave France. "It is to us also that these words are addressed, 'Leave your country and your kinsfolk *(nativité)*' [Genesis 12:1], when there we are constrained to act contrary to our conscience, and cannot live to the glory of God."[74] How much earlier than late 1543 was exile being commended by Calvin? The *sententia* of Calvin which accompanied Johannes von Bekensteyn's letter of January 1542 homed in with typical rigour on the virtual impossibility of conducting oneself faithfully under the papacy. "What then will you say? Must one therefore either migrate or despair? I do not press the issue so categorically *(Non ita praecise urgeo)*." Yet Calvin would have the recipient cease never to lament his "captivity" and to plead for God to restore his people's "liberty". God would not abandon such humility, and would surely come to its aid, if not to open up some *exitum*.[75]

Published together with the *Petit traicté* in 1543 was a letter of Calvin's to an unknown addressee in France written from Strasbourg in September 1540. It is no less forthright, no less unqualified in its condemnation of the mass, but markedly less explicit in urging escape.

> I am not of such extreme severity as to condemn all Christians who do not abandon their country when they are detained in such servitude, as though I totally despaired of their salvation.[76]

Yet he goes on to make this outcome the focus of prayer and aspiration, that God will indeed redeem his captive people. Whether Calvin counselled migration from France openly before the date of this letter I do not know. Between it and the *Petit traicté* of 1543 lay not only his return to Geneva but also further experience of the pastorate of the congregation of French refugees in Strasbourg. Perhaps it was the latter that convinced him that exile should be more vigorously promoted as the preferred release from the irreconcilable

---

[73]CO 6:576.

[74]CO 11:630 (no. 508), 632 (no. 509). Cf. Françoise Bonali-Fiquet, ed., *Lettres à Monsieur et Madame de Falais,* Textes Littéraires Français (Geneva: Librairie Droz, 1991), 22-23, 38-39, 42.

[75]Hegler, ed., *Beiträge zur Geschichte,* 40-41.

[76]CO 6:586; Herminjard 6:304, no. 888.

demands of living under the papacy. A difference of tone is certainly discernible between these earlier counsels and the directness of the *Petit traicté* and the *Consilium et Conclusio* of 1545. The former are more inclined to leave the exodus to divine initiative, the latter inculcate escape as the plain path of duty.

It seems inevitable that Calvin's personal and professional history, if not his personality, should be brought into play to help explain the harshness of his anti-Nicodemism. What part should we attribute to his own experience of flight and his lifelong status as an exile? Does this pen-portrait of François Hotman by Donald Kelley fit Calvin also?

> Being a fugitive brought out the best and the worst in Hotman. If he displayed courage, he acquired also a kind of intolerance that was coming to be a distinguishing mark of Calvinist exiles... How could he feel sympathy for those who stayed behind? Bridges burned, he had no use for hesitancy; uprooted, he scorned other men's need for security; forced to make the ugliest of choices, that between his family and his faith, he scorned too their tendency to compromise. One of the most derogatory words in his (as in Calvin's) vocabulary was "nicodemite".[77]

Having taken the courageous route of exile no doubt qualified Calvin to urge the same path on others without risking the charge of hypocrisy. But trapped in a Catch 22 situation, he demanded "No compromise!" from a position of relative safety that provoked Fumée and others to cry, "There you can easily preach and admonish, but if you were here you would perhaps feel differently."[78] Calvin never to my knowledge appealed to his own abandonment of his motherland as giving him the right to speak, but he came quite close to it a passage in the *Excuse* of 1544 that addresses the cavil "Since Calvin is so brave, why does he not come here to see how he would cope? He behaves like captains who thrust their own troops into the breach to receive the onslaught while they remain far from danger." Calvin cited the example of the apostles but this in turn was contested.

> To this I reply that each of the apostles often exhorted to patience and constancy a church from which he had fled because of danger... As for me, I will not boast of having endured much. But I can well say that it is not my failing that I have not several times exposed myself to dangers... In fact they make a mistake in placing me so far from dangers. For while persecution is not near and pressing on me today, I do not know what could happen tomorrow. So much so that I would be very stupid not to be preparing myself this very hour to avoid being caught by surprise. When it must come to that, I hope strongly

[77]Donald R. Kelley, *François Hotman. A Revolutionary's Ordeal* (Princeton: Princeton University Press, 1973), 45. I owe this reference to Bouwsma, *John Calvin,* 240, n. 29.

[78] *Petit traicté,* CO 6:573 *(extra teli iactum in De vitandis superstitionibus);* Fumée, CO 11:645, no. 516 (Herminjard 9:126, no. 1316).

> in my God that he will grant me the grace of glorifying his name by my blood, as much as I do now by tongue and pen, and with no more hesitation.[79]

What remains tantalizingly obscure is what lies behind Calvin's first exercise in anti-Nicodemism, the letter to Duchemin in 1536. It was written in Italy on his visit to Renée of Ferrara, together with the other open letter to Gerard Roussel. Eugénie Droz's judgment has been adopted by other scholars:

> From the violence and brutality of these texts, we can conclude that the author of the *Institutio* was transformed into a revolutionary propagandist spirit by the sight of evangelicals disguising *(dissimulant)* their faith and following the papist mass.[80]

Perhaps Calvin had even, she speculates, dissimulated himself and gone to confession and mass.[81] Was his burst into print driven even to a minor degree by self-revulsion? Eire has drawn attention to a small biographical fragment in one of Calvin's sermons on 2 Samuel preached in 1562-63, speaking of the vulnerability of the church in France.

> And I may say that twenty years ago, nearly thirty, I was in such distressing circumstances that I would almost have preferred to have been dead, and remove all this anguish from my sight. At the least, I would have desired to have had my tongue cut out, so as never to say a word *(pour ne point dire le mot)*... It would have taken only a word of confession by me to have stamped out the whole doctrine of our salvation.[82]

We have no need of speculation to be certain that for Calvin in 1536 the memory of the trials of the brethren in France was painfully fresh. He writes to Duchemin of the slippery slope to ruin:

> Within our own memory it has happened that people have reversed tack and been wrecked on the very rocks from which they had escaped. At first, when the great risk of making a candid profession of their convictions as they should was fully in view, they reckoned it a minor matter if they trifled a little to gratify the populace... They accordingly played their part in godless ceremonies with others. Then, when even this failed to exempt them from general suspicion, they advanced another step further, judging it sufficient if men of quality were aware of their faith; the opinion of others, deceived by some stratagem, was harmless. So, when Christ's enemies twittered on against sound doctrine, they expressed assent by a look, a nod, a gesture of the whole body, eventually by voice also. Realizing that not even this tactic

---

[79]Higman, ed., 146-47; Kayayan, tr., 357-58 (adapted).

[80]Droz, *Chemins,* 1:136; cf. Millet, *Calvin,* 480.

[81]Droz, *Chemins,* 1:132.

[82]Eire, *War,* 238, n. 15; *Predigten über das 2. Buch Samuelis,* ed. Hanns Rückert, SC 1 (Neukirchen: Neukirchener Verlag, 1961), 122, Douglas Kelly, tr., *Sermons on 2 Samuel Chapters 1-13* (Edinburgh: Banner of Truth Trust, 1992), 211.

> succeeded as intended, they began to be content with a conscience kept secret from all human assessment. To achieve this, they studiously guarded against giving any indication of Christian commitment... At last, blind and forgetful of themselves, they hurled themselves headlong into destruction... This was the final act in their drama: not only did they allow no ear or eye to witness their true heart, as previously, but they strove to the very utmost to have everyone witness in them things which should be as remote from the Christian as possible, and openly to abhor and detest what earlier they at least adhered to privately.[83]

Thus stretched the ever-widening path from mild *dissimulatio* to blatant *simulatio*. We must allow that what crystallized for Calvin in Italy or previously was the conviction that in the strictest opposition to both lay the only route to salvation for the evangelical church in France.

We should not exaggerate the surprising or exceptional character of *De Fugiendis* among Calvin's early writings. In it he refers readers to the *Institutio* for the sacrileges of the mass. There, no less starkly than to Duchemin, Calvin declares the mass to be not the corruption of the Lord's supper but its "removal, destruction and abolition". "The mass, taken in the highest, most refined integrity it can claim, ignoring its appurtenances, from root to tip swarms with every sort of impiety, blasphemy, idolatry and sacrilege."[84] This was of course one of the most fundamental elements in Calvin's anti-Nicodemite polemic. The mass was ripe not for reform but for replacement. The influence of Zwingli or the Bucer of *Grund und Ursach* (1524) may here be visible.

Two other possible factors may be mentioned more speculatively. Was *De Fugiendis* influenced at all by a concern to distance himself from Seneca's late medieval reputation as a follower of Nicodemus? From the twelfth century the revival of interest in Seneca depended in part on acceptance of the apocryphal Paul-Seneca letters and consequent recognition of him by Jerome and Lactantius.[85] So Seneca became a secret Christian and protector of Christians, especially in the life by Gasparino Barzizza in the early fifteenth century, who likened him to Joseph of Arimathea and Nicodemus, both hidden disciples of Christ for fear of the Jews. Barzizza's presentation fell into disfavour (there are reports of debates in the court of Ferrara in the mid-fifteenth century), and Erasmus fiercely attacked both the apocryphal correspondence and the claim of Christians that Seneca was one of their own: "I do not agree with those who

---

[83]OS 1:290-91; Beveridge, tr., 3:361-62 (adapted).

[84]OS 1:306; *Institutio,* (1536), OS 1:155, 157 (cf. F. L. Battles, tr., *Institutes of the Christian Religion* [1536 edition] (Grand Rapids: Eerdmans, 1975), 117, 119).

[85]See Letizia A. Panizza, "Gasparino Barzizza's Commentaries on Seneca's Letters," *Traditio* 33 (1977), 297-358, especially 305-341. I owe this reference to Charles Trinkaus, *The Scope of Renaissance Humanism* (Ann Arbor, MI: University of Michigan Press, 1983), 436, n.12.

strive to make Seneca a Christian, like Nicodemus."[86] Among those Erasmus had in mind may well have been Lefèvre d'Etaples who included the Seneca letters in his commentary on the Pauline epistles (editions from 1512 to 1533), with no doubt as to their authenticity but without holding to Seneca's ultimate conversion and so not calling him a Nicodemus. But Lefèvre's interest in religious dissimulation is undoubted, and through his links with Brunfels he plays a key role in Ginzburg's thesis.[87] Calvin had devoted his first publication to Seneca. He must prior to the 1536 letters have known of the attitudes of Erasmus and Lefèvre, but did he encounter something in Ferrara that made worrying connexions in his mind?[88] There is a footnote in Battles and Hugo's edition of the Seneca commentary on the verdict of Erasmus quoted shortly above. It merely asks, "Was this perhaps the origin of Calvin's usage of the term Nicodemitae or Pseudo-Nicodemi?"[89]

This line of speculation runs athwart Olivier Millet's analysis of *De Fugiendis,* which specifically finds Senecan echoes in the *Epistolae Duae.* One in particular caught my attention, concerning *De Fugiendis:*

> La grande idée sans cesse reprise, selon laquelle l'assistance au rite catholique comme à un spectacle suffit à souiller l'âme, est elle-même peut-être un echo de l'Epître de Sénèque sur les spectacles...[90]

On reading this, I immediately asked myself, why not Tertullian rather than Seneca (whose cited letter turns out to be a dissuasive against crowds)? Calvin the anti-Nicodemite rigorist reminds me of no-one so much as Tertullian, the rigorist among the Fathers par excellence. The parallels are almost uncanny, from a treatise *De Spectaculis* (which does target the immoral and irreligious content of the shows) to another *De Idololatria,* with its maximizing interpretation of the prohibition of idolatry and its pastoral tough-mindedness in countering objections, and an insistence that outward demeanour must match inward attitude. Evidence of Calvin's early knowledge of Tertullian is limited, and of his knowledge of his moral-disciplinary works scanty throughout his cor-

---

[86]From the preface to his second edition of Seneca (1529), P. S. Allen and H. M. Allen, eds., Opus Epistolarum, 11 vols (Oxford: Clarendon Press, 1906-47), 8:30.

[87]Eugene F. Rice, Jr., ed., *The Prefatory Epistles of Jacques Lefèvre d'Etaples and Related Texts* (New York: Columbia University Press, 1972), 301; Ginzburg, *Il Nicodemismo,* 85-90.

[88]Lefèvre died early in 1536. Farel reported that before his death he was full of remorse and foreboding for having failed earlier to give explicit confession of his convictions: cf. Herminjard 3:400, nn. 6-7; Zagorin, *Ways of Lying,* 36-37; Guy Bedouelle, *Lefèvre d'Étaples et l'Intelligence des Ecritures,* Travaux d'Humanisme et Renaissance 152 (Geneva: Librairie Droz, 1976), 133-34. Whatever its basis in fact, the report's currency could itself have carried weight.

[89]F. L. Battles and A. M. Hugo, ed. and transl., *Calvin's Commentary on Seneca's De Clementia,* Renaissance Text Series 3; (Leiden: E. J. Brill, 1969), 58*, n. 2.

[90]Millet, *Calvin, 491; Seneca, Epistulae Morales* 7, Richard M. Gummere, ed., Loeb Classical Library, 1:28-37.

pus. Twice at least he criticized Tertullian's opposition to flight in order to escape persecution, and once in defending his rejection of images he cited *De Idololatria.*[91] Tertullian came into his own in more than one of Calvin's dogmatic controversies, and we should remember that he was a fan of Seneca—*saepe noster,* as he called him. Evidence that Calvin read Tertullian seriously early on will be gratefully received.[92]

The explanation for Calvin's rigorous stance to Duchemin and Roussel is likely to by multi-factorial. Whether Calvin had previously insisted that true piety must be manifested by *externa professio, vera confessio* is unclear. Moreover, although, as we have seen, the 1536 *Institutio* condemns the mass as idolatry, the work as a whole, e.g. in its consideration of the First Commandment, does not prepare us for the hermeneutical advance in *De Fugiendis* that scriptural injunctions against pagan idolatry apply no less to papal abominations.[93] Here reform begins with the worship of God. This open letter introduces us to the heart of the dominant concerns of Calvin throughout his career—the honour and glory due to God in purity of worship. A passion for true worship provides a consistent core to Calvin's anti-Nicodemism, from the detailed casuistry of the *Epistolae Duae* to the rebuttal of internalized spiritualism in *Response à un Certain Holandois* of 1562.[94]

---

[91]Comm. on John 10:12 (CO 47:242) and Acts 8:1 (CO 48:174) on flight to avoid persecution. *De Idololatria* cited CO 10/I:194, from a *consilium* of 1562 (?); Mary Beaty and Benjamin W. Farley, tr., *Calvin's Ecclesiastical Advice* (Louisville, KY: Westminster/John Knox, 1991), 72. Johannes van Oort, "John Calvin and the Church Fathers," in Irena Backus, ed., *The Reception of the Church Fathers in the West. From the Carolingians to the Maurists,* 2 vols (Leiden: E. J. Brill, 1997), 2:661-700, at 686, confuses "lapsing" in persecution with flight to escape it—very different in both Tertullian's and Calvin's book. Also ibid., 686, n. 51 Calvin's reference (CO 20:38) is to *sermo Tertulliani.*

[92]Cf. *Institutio* (1536), OS 1:152 (Tertullian, *De Resurrectione*); Lausanne Disputation (1536), CO 9:879 *(Adv. Marcionem)*. For an account of Calvin's use of Tertullian, cf. A. N. S. Lane, 'Tertullianus Totus Noster? Calvin's Use of Tertullian,' *Reformation & Renaissance Review* 4:1 (2002), 9-34.

[93]Cf. OS 1:302-303, 312-13: whom is Calvin criticizing here? The Genevan *Instruction et Confession de la Foy* of 1536/37 condemns the papal mass as diabolical and idolatrous (para. 16, OS 1:423).

[94]CO 9:581-628. Translations by Rob Roy McGregor, "Response to a Certain Dutchman ...," CTJ 34 (1999), 291-326, and in Skolnitsky, *Come Out From Among Them,* 239-306. The Dutchman in question was Coornhert; see Gerrit Voogt, *Constraint on Trial: Dirck Volckertsz Coornhert and Religious Freedom,* Sixteenth Century Essays and Studies 52 (Kirksville. MO: Truman State University Press, 2000), 10-17; Mirjam G. K. van Veen, "Sursum Corda: Calvijns polemiek tegen nicodemieten, in het bijzonder tegen Coornhert," *Nederlands Archief voor Kerkgeschiedenis* 79 (1999), 177-203.

Toward the Recovery of the Historical Calvin: Redrawing the Map of Reformation Europe[1]

Heiko Oberman

I. Calvin's Vanishing Act

Ne preschez plus la Vérité,
Maistre Michel!
Contenüe en l'Evangille,
Il y a trop grand danger
D'estre mené
Dans la Conciergerie.
Lire, Lire, Lironfa.
(*Chanson Nouvelle,* c. December 1525)

At the beginning of the twentieth century, John Calvin filled a significant chapter in any history of Europe. Considerable attention was paid to the resiliency of Calvinism in withstanding the alliance of pope, Spain and—after some hesitations—the Most Christian King of France; and ironically the Calvinist pirate See-Beggars, the *Geuzen,* were more widely known than the powerful French noble House of the *Guises.* While the spread of Calvinism was highlighted in its impressive outreach to the Seven Provinces and the Kingdom of Scotland and along the intellectual axis from Heidelberg to Harvard, its organic center was clearly placed in Geneva; and in Geneva ruled the uncontested, dominant figure of John Calvin.

This interpretation is not merely the product of those who are today decried as Whig historians. Quite generally, the St. Bartholomew's Day Massacre (24 August 1572) was treated as a more significant event than the slaughter of the German peasants in 1525, nearly fifty years before. When Stefan Zweig moved from *Die Welt von Gestern* to the travail of modern Europe, he cast Calvin vis-à-vis Servetus in the role of towering tyrant, foreshadowing the terror of Nazi Germany. Indeed, the very fact that, among the many thousands of sixteenth-century martyrs, Calvin's execution of Michael Servetus (d. 1553), and his con-

[1]The present chapter contains the paper given by Professor Oberman at the Congress and is published by permission of his widow. It was subsequently published, with endnotes, in his *The Two Reformations: the Journey from the Last Days to the New World,* ed. Donald Weinstein (New Haven and London: Yale University Press, 2003), 97-115, 214-20.

demnation of Sebastian Castellio (d. 1563) as well, can be singled out for such special treatment is the unintended confirmation of the consensus between disciples and opponents concerning the uncontested stature of Geneva's Reformer.

Calvin's stature, however, has diminished. If we want to assess this reversal—what one might call John Calvin's vanishing act—we are forced to leave the safe protection of our geographically-defined areas of specialization. We will not only have to paint on a larger canvas, but will also have to redraw the map of Reformation Europe in order to account for the emergence of international Calvinism. This larger work must precede consideration of Calvin's vanishing act. As a first step, we will turn to six factors which together tend to block our access to the historical Calvin, in every case, curiously enough, not because of misguided scholarship but exactly because of the invariably distorting impact of singular advances on isolated fronts.

(1) The founding of the French journal *Annales d'histoire économique et sociale* in 1929 is often invoked to document the shift from cultural to economic history, from personal agency to impersonal causation. It should not be overlooked, however, that its founding fathers, Marc Bloch and Lucien Febvre, urged the cultural historian, Johan Huizinga, to join the first editorial board. The decisive stumbling block preventing the formation of this eminent triumvirate was Huizinga's rejection of the assumption that an analysis of long-term developments would yield processes which one must regard as historical laws, or to put it in the words of Lucien Febvre, that the multitude of details would yield general laws *(des lois se dégageront)*. Huizinga's answer was uncompromising:—sheer illusion *(ijdel illusie!)*; in the field of history, causality has only a "limited validity." Sadly, his warning has gone unheeded. In the succeeding decades the pursuit of long-term processes was intensified even to the point that the demise of biography seemed a foregone conclusion: Why study a person such as John Calvin when individuals are merely leaves swept along on the powerful currents of processes beyond their ken and control?!

Yet the prison of conditions in which every generation is born should not negate the factors of contingent human initiatives and unpredictable responses. The blind force of material conditions is not to be underestimated, of course. It shapes our social history. As the eminent Czech scholar Frantiek Graus pointed out, it is exactly a characteristic of early modern times that political and economic hardship, formerly suffered simply as an act of God, was increasingly interpreted in terms of human responsibility and culpability. The impact of such a programmatic leader as Calvin is directly related to the formation of a new social consciousness which questions the status quo by widening the gap between the divine doom of disaster and the human perpetration of evil. It has frequently been noted that the providence of God plays an extraordinary role in Calvin's thought. For him, this providence is not the modern necessary process but the reliable expectation of unforeseen and unpredictable consequences. Above all, it provides the rationale for transferring the ills of church and society from the realm of doom and destiny to that of challenge and responsible action.

(2) No historian today takes pride in being identified with *Historismus*, or historicism, since it is a defamatory designation associated with a naive objectivism; we no longer share the nineteenth-century confidence that the meaning of history waits to be discovered in the documents. Yet we owe to this much-maligned *Historismus* a veritable explosion of critical editions which set the modern standard for medieval, Renaissance, and Reformation studies with patient and painstaking editions, all the way from the *Monumenta Germaniae Historica* and the *Corpus Reformatorum* to the *Bulletin de la Société de l'Histoire du Protestantisme Français* and the *Corpus Catholicorum*.

Against the backdrop of this mighty arsenal, we cannot fail to discern the stark narrowing of historical horizon initiated by the twentieth-century issue-driven reaction. The field of sixteenth-century studies was particularly hard hit when Luther scholarship first reduced its original broad grasp of Reformation history to the life and work of Martin Luther and then, since the mid-1950s, drew the best minds to the young Luther and his Reformation breakthrough. The initially promising pursuit of printing, preaching, and politics in the City Reformation remained preoccupied with the twenties and thirties of the sixteenth century. Historians of the Reformation in line with the ill-conceived notion of a *"Lutherische Engführung,"* the tunneling towards Luther, no longer seem interested in continuing the German story to the epochal events of the division of the Hapsburg Empire, the impact of the Schmalkaldic War, and the abdication of Emperor Charles V. These sad developments go quite a way towards explaining the breathtaking conclusion reached by Thomas A. Brady, Jr., in his reconstruction of the politics of the Reformation in Germany: "the decisive force in making Luther's movement into the German Reformation was not his message's content." It is exactly the parochial study of church history which engenders such marginalization of the impact of theology.

(3) Too often treated as an appendix to German Reformation history, Calvin studies have suffered a similar atrophy. The much hailed Calvin Renaissance of the 1930s was the result of the intensive theological debate about the anthropology of Calvin between Karl Barth and Emil Brunner, enriched after World War II by Otto Weber and Ernst Wolf in their search for the Reformed roots of the resistance against Hitler. When the learned Gottfried W. Locher opened the first Calvin Research Congress on September 16, 1974, he not only initiated a program consciously geared towards the theology of Calvin, but also explicitly addressed the participants as fellow-believers, united by the common vision of continuing Calvin's Reformation today. A careful perusal of the conference volumes produced over the next twenty years shows that these same characteristics continue to be seen: systematic-theological issues are pursued by grateful disciples who present their research with the assumption of Calvin's revelatory relevance. In this regards, the most significant contribution of William J. Bouwsma's *John Calvin* goes well beyond its merits as a sensitive, cultural history of the sixteenth century: for Bouwsma renewed the quest for the historical Calvin by moving away from the icon of the *Doctor Ecclesiae* to a historical person subject to

inconsistency, doubt, pain, pleasure—and as I have come to see, political opportunism. In bemoaning the hegemony of theology in Calvin studies, I do not doubt that the decisive force in Calvin's influence on the French Reformation is to be found in his "message's content," to use Brady's words. But at the same time, I feel equally confident that the discovery of Calvin's actual role in its reception will only be made if we follow the iconoclastic course set out by William Bouswma. The very titles of our conference volumes document a pre-critical stage, through which apparently all such single-person societies have to go, but true maturation spells critical emancipation.

As we will have good reason to note, the social and political history of Calvinism is thriving, significantly advanced by the work of William Monter, Robert Kingdon, Francis Higman, Henry Heller, Bernard Roussel, Harro Höpfl, and Philip Benedict. Yet Huguenot research will not be able to profit from Calvin studies as long as the chasm between Calvin's thought and Calvin's impact is not bridged but, rather, widened by historians of theology who allow their agenda to be set by contemporary relevance and modern spiritual trends.

(4) Ironically, the very riches of the Genevan archives prove to be a barrier as well as a boon. The preserved records of the city council, the *Compagnie des Pasteurs* and the *Consistoire* contain detailed data about the ebb and flow of Calvin's faction, the disruptive impact of the endless stream of refugees, and the Consistory's concerted effort to establish some form of social control over private and public life in Geneva. And of course historians have to go where the sources are. Yet, in this case the advance in knowledge hinders a more balanced assessment of Calvin's actual place and function. For such a concentration on the local archives gives us a much better grasp of actual conditions and daily life, yet tends to consolidate the traditional view of the intimate identification of Calvin with Geneva.

As a matter of fact, this symbiosis is only part of the total picture. When Calvin first took up his station in Geneva in July 1536, he served as lector and right-hand man of the French reformer, Guillaume Farel. Thrown out by the city council two years later, Calvin decided never to return. He reversed his decision in September 1541, moved only by the argument that Geneva was close to his beloved France, thus providing the most opportune staging area for the introduction of the Reformation into his own homeland. Calvin did not accept citizenship in Geneva until 1559, five years before his death. His biographers have paid little attention to this striking lack of identification with Geneva, but thanks to the research of Charlotte C. Wells we can now discern what it would have meant for Calvin officially to legalize his exile by giving up citizenship in France in terms of rights, duties, and loyalties. In the same year, 1559, the Genevan Academy was established to take over the task of its Lausanne predecessor in training missionaries who could provide leadership for the rapidly emerging French Reformed churches. True enough, Calvin was concerned that the Reformation be carried through in Geneva. But this reform was held up as a model—and where deficient, as an obstructive scandal—for the growth of the Kingdom of Christ in France and elsewhere in

Europe. In brief, Calvin the City Reformer is not sufficiently understood without stressing Calvin the Territorial Reformer who exploited the Genevan connection for his Reformation of the Refugees in France and Europe at large.

(5) The fifth factor responsible for Calvin's vanishing act has a name, an area, and country-code. It is called "confessionalization," hails from Bielefeld and Freiburg, and is now firmly established in German historiography. One of its founding fathers, Heinz Schilling, is a broad-ranging early modern historian with a far wider horizon than the trend associated with his name. With a firm grasp on the social, political, and cultural history of the young Dutch Republic in the seventeenth century, he has made a major contribution to our understanding of civic Calvinism, the impact of Calvinism on the Netherlands and northern Germany. In his coalition with Wolfgang Reinhard, however, the confessionalization thesis has been advanced to characterize the parallel shift from church to state control in the Lutheran, Catholic, and Reformed territories of the late sixteenth- and seventeenth-century Empire. This form of Big History has a number of advantages, not the least of which is the inter-confessional approach which can integrate related fields of interest, long-divided in religious, social, and political history. As often with Grand Theories, however, the concentrated pursuit of a particular theme functions as a searchlight which casts deep shadows over the surrounding areas. For our quest, three drawbacks are to be noted.

In the first place, though efforts are underway to test the pan-European applicability of the confessionalization theory, its origin and design are firmly grounded in German soil and post-Reformation developments in the Empire. The characterization of Calvinism as "the Second Reformation" is particularly revealing since this term only applies to a limited number of territories in Germany. For the majority of Europe, Calvinism spelled the first advent of the Reformation and above all marked the dramatic transition from religious ideas to social and political institutions that challenged the establishment outside the Empire.

As Martin Heckel has shown, the Peace of Augsburg of 1555 legalized the fiction of the one, undivided Church, a territorial *itio in partes,* each with a limited form of religious self-determination. This legal solution is fully in keeping with Luther's catholic conviction that reformed and unreformed Christians continue to be attached to one another in the one body of the Church vying for the birth right, as the twins in Rebecca's womb. When Calvinism hits Europe as the first Reformation, it demands not only a withdrawal from Roman obedience, but also the establishment of independent local congregations charged to ban the "Nicodemites" who do not want to join the visible church. Henceforth, two clearly separated churches are vying for the same birthright.

A secondary drawback pertains to the problematic assumption of confessionalization as a necessary process. This secularization of the formerly religious concept of divine destiny has, to be sure, a limited explanatory potential in trying to understand Germany's reconstruction and state building after the disaster of the Thirty Years War. The overarching era of early Calvinism, however, the century from about 1550 to 1650, confronts us with a network of short-term processes constantly interrupted and dislodged by unforeseen events. Its war-torn path is marked by battles which by definition are uncertain in outcome.

The good historian is the guardian of contingency, soundly aware that it is difficult to understand what actually did happen if one is not prepared to ponder what could have happened as well. For example, the reformist cardinal Reginald Pole lost out by one vote in the 1549 papal election of Pope Julius III. But what, we might well ask, would have happened to the curial Counter Reformation had the outcome of that vote been different? Again, a victory for the Spanish Armada would have profoundly affected the balance of power in 1588, threatening the precarious Elizabethan settlement. Of course as we now know, the Spanish naval tactics were not suited for the stormy weather, and, perhaps even more importantly, the English ships were more efficiently gunned. These are surely more convincing explanations than either the religious legend of God's direct intervention or the secular reference to the "Dutch courage" of the continental pirates. The point is, however, that all extant sources describe the outcome as a close call.

Historical contingency can also be seen in the unpredictable ascendancy of Henry of Navarre as King of France in 1589. After his coronation as Henry IV, he initiated a successful summer campaign in 1590 with victories at Arques and Ivry which nearly gained him access to Paris, where the anti-Huguenot leadership "had unleashed a reign of terror." On August 30 the Parisians expected him to enter victoriously, but Henry withdrew to cover his lines of communication. When he finally entered Paris four years later (March 22, 1594), the former Huguenot had returned to the Catholic fold.

The dissolution of the Edict of Nantes (1685) may well appear as a necessary process in light of the ascendancy of absolutism in France. Yet, the events leading up to the Edict are rife with contingent, unpredictable events. The phenomenon of French absolutism can no more easily be harmonized with the process of confessionalization than confessionalization can be invoked to explain the rise and near-victory of the Huguenots.

(6) One of the most formidable factors in Calvin's vanishing act is not located in the realm of the philosophy of history, but in developments within religious history, directly related to what one might call today's ecumenical spirit. The modern impatience with confessional polemics feeds into the trend towards silencing the sounds of battle, even those which occurred in the past. The Counter Reformation has become its most conspicuous victim. Significantly, the editors of *The Oxford Encyclopedia of the Reformation* decided to delete the Counter Reformation as a separate entry. The three traditional pillars of the Counter Reformation—the Inquisition, the Jesuit order, and the Council of Trent—are in a process of significant scholarly revision. The Inquisition is transformed into an administrative institution with a proto-modern respect for due process. The Jesuits are portrayed as eager recipients of the educational

ideals of Renaissance humanism as well as spiritually rejuvenated carriers of global missions. Finally, only those decrees of the Council of Trent which initiated the Catholic Reformation are highlighted. To top it off, scholars who question any or all of these revisionist trends as apologetic devices are assailed as Whig-historians, nineteenth-century spokesmen for the myth that parliamentary democracy and societal emancipation had to be wrested from the hands of an aggressive, empire-building papacy.

Whatever else may be wrong (or right) in this anti-Whig sentiment, it blocks the clear perception of the historical reality of that Counter Reformation as the conservative coalition of a Rome-oriented Europe with which early Calvinism was confronted and with which it had to contend and compete for hegemony in shaping the course of post-medieval Europe. True enough, in 1580 the Jesuit Luca Pinelli could still pay a personal visit to Theodore Beza at his house in Geneva. But as Scott Manetsch has shown in his extensive analysis of Beza's European-wide correspondence, towards the end of the century, the reports arriving in Geneva from the persecuted Reformed churches in France do not leave him in any doubt that the early Calvinist lead on the contested front of education and information is meeting with increasingly fierce competition from all kinds of new orders, but especially from the Jesuits. Well before the Jesuits gained access to Versailles as confessors to Louis XIII and XIV, they supported the Catholic League's Counter Reformation platform, and the French Jesuit Provincial was their go-between as fund-raiser at the Court of Philip II.

The competition between the Jesuits and Calvinists on the book market and the intellectual marketplace was so fierce that their agreement on certain issues, such as their criticism of medieval episcopacy and the mendicant orders, appears quite striking. But as Dale Van Kley shrewdly observes, as similar as they were in dedicating themselves to the honor and glory of God, "for the Jesuits, glory and honor did not remain confined to the heavens but rather cascaded downward on to the heads of kings and noblemen, making the social hierarchy a reflection of the Divine." Yet even before the Jesuits became the pillars of royal absolutism, they formed already the vanguard of the conservative establishment in the battle for the recatholicization of Protestant Europe, which in France meant a head-on contest with Calvinism.

Luther's Reformation, which lacked this context of competition, can be more readily understood than Calvin's. When Luther returned from the Wartburg and confronted his own radical, revolutionary wing in March 1522, he formulated his non-violent program in words too long overlooked: "Our battle is not with the Pope or a bishop but with the Devil." Significantly, Calvin was never given to making such a distinction: he confronted the Devil in the very rule of popes and bishops and their *suppôts*, that is, hit men. If it is Whig history to regard the Inquisition, Jesuits, and Council of Trent as the tripod of the conservative, backwards-oriented Roman Catholic counter offensive, then John Calvin himself was the first Whig historian. More importantly, however, even if Calvin's vision stands in need of correction and the concept Counter

Reformation of more precise definition, the demise of both within contemporary scholarship blocks our access to the world of John Calvin.

II. Toward a New Map of Reformation Europe

Nous prions donc le Roi du Ciel
Par sa bonté
Qu'il nous envoye sa lumière
Et qu'il nous escrive au coeur
Par la douceur
Le contenu en l'évangille
Lire, Lire, Lironfa.
(*Chanson Nouvelle,* c. December 1525)

The myth of the ideological and structural weakness of the late medieval church, propagated in ecumenical unison by Protestant and Catholic historians alike, has long misled us to ask the wrong question. The puzzle is not why and where the Reformation failed, but where and why it succeeded. The financial power invested in the much maligned, perhaps wasteful but functional, benefice system was heavily weighted against systemic change as were the political authority of precedent in canon and secular law and the prevailing conservative mentality which viewed innovation of almost any kind as a fearful prospect. In retrospect, it is clear that beyond the old dream of true reform initiated by the papacy there were two novel, systemic and realistic options for the reform of late-medieval Christendom from within. In the first place, there was the conciliar program along the lines of the Councils of Constance and Basel. We are indebted to Brian Tierney's *Foundations of the Conciliar Theory* for having established the traditional, canonistic roots of the seemingly revolutionary decree *Haec Sancta* with its declaration of the supremacy of the council above all other levels of authority in the Church including the papacy. As Tierney puts it pointedly in his Introduction to the new enlarged edition, "all conciliarists were papalists." At the same time, and in effect more important, a decreasing number of papalists were conciliarists. The curial fear for the explosive potential of conciliarism made for a twenty-five-year interim between the Edict of Worms and the beginning of the Council of Trent. This proved to be the window of opportunity for the Protestant Reformation—it was exactly the time needed to shift from a settlement-hungry Lutheranism in Germany to a dynamic, pan-European Reformation.

A second real option for the reconstruction of late-medieval Christendom is related to conciliarism. Though the effort at the Council of Basel to enforce *Haec Sancta* failed, it did provide the cradle for the birth of the *Ecclesia Gallicana.* The full story of the emancipation of the Eldest Daughter of Rome has not yet been told. The emergence of a Gallican church on French soil nationalized papal jurisdiction. Without questioning the spiritual authority of the See of St. Peter, the "Gallican Liberties" nullified the papal claim to the plenitude of power. The papal concordat of 1516 granted the French king extensive power over the Gallican church; in 1516 Gallicanism was centralized, but by no means terminated. With the support of the king's sister, Marguerite d'Alençon, the later queen of Navarre, a mixture of Gallicanism and biblical humanism produced a climate favorable to the spread of the Reformation, well beyond the Affair of the Placards of 1534. Calvin was to assail those who continued to adhere to the platform of the Gallican church as Nicodemites, but there can be no doubt that the Gallican independence from Rome favored the search for a *via media* throughout the Wars of Religion. The parallel development in the English realm did not take place until twenty years later when the king's Great Matter initiated the establishment of the *Ecclesia Anglicana*. A recent *Feminist Reinterpretation of the Wives of Henry VIII* makes a good case for Henry VIII's "monstrous ego" but then reduces the politics of dynasty to bedroom dynamics. The author may well be right in regarding Henry as "not capable of love," but to argue this with reference to "his treatment of Catherine [of Aragon] and of Thomas More" is to ignore the wider constitutional setting of Tudor politics.

A comparable drive towards ecclesiastical territorialization also brought about the emergence of the *Ecclesia Teutonica*. Based on a consensus of all imperial estates, including the Prince Bishops and the Emperor's brother Ferdinand, the summons to the founding session in Speyer on November 11, 1524 was ready to be dispatched when the Emperor in Spain vetoed this initiative with his one, momentous vote. Charles V carried on pursuing his Hapsburg design for reform in head and members consistently nonetheless, until he failed to get his agenda accepted by the Council of Trent. Rejecting the Emperor's goal of seeking limitations on the papal plenitude of power, the Council met his wishes in turning to the reform of a resident episcopate, which was (it may be said) arguably its major achievement. The ensuing story of the Catholic Reformation cannot be told without mention of the Counter Reformation. Under the leadership of Philip II and along the path from "Madrid to Purgatory," the Tridentine Reformation was complemented by a series of escalating military initiatives which would see its successes in France matched by losses in the Low Countries.

Mindful of the above-mentioned three forms of systemic reform of late-medieval Christendom with papal, conciliar, and national platforms (pivotal coordinates on any realistic map of Reformation Europe), we can take up the question of what conditions allowed for that least likely of all outcomes, namely a non-systemic Reformation. The principal hurdle for such a reformation is the legitimization of a non-papal Catholicism, for which two options presented themselves: the national-conciliar and the antihierarchical-lay solutions. Luther would have been able to retain the loyalty of many more of his early supporters if he had presented himself as a strict conciliarist or if he had been prepared to ride the strong wave of anticlericalism. However, Luther's most provocative innovation, the priesthood of all believers, and its concomitant doctrine of justification by faith alone, did not destroy but demanded an ordained priesthood—whether pope, bishop or priest—to sustain the faithful in their battle with the devil through preaching the Word, celebrating the Eucharist, and hearing (private) confession.

The explanation for the survival of Luther's Reformation has to be found in two other factors. As Manfred Schulze has shown, the so-called "reformation of the princes" is not the dismal end-product of the Protestant Reformation, as Erwin Iserloh suggested, but rather the late-medieval incubator which allowed the fledgling Reformation movement to reach maturity. In the century before the Reformation, the papacy, preoccupied with the extension of the papal states and the threat of radical conciliarism, had increasingly granted territorial princes, particularly in the Empire, privileges of ecclesiastical oversight and reform. The Saxon province of the Augustinian Observants had already become a major instrument of such a princely reformation well before it provided Luther with his first communication network. The risky protection Frederick the Wise granted Luther after the promulgation of the Edict of Worms owes far less to the private piety of this thoroughly late-medieval ruler than to his long-established electoral reform policy. There is in my mind no doubt that without this princely protection, Luther's voice and the ensuing Reformation movement would have been nipped in the bud.

The second factor is related not to a situation which Luther encountered but one which he shaped. Returning posthaste from the Wartburg to Wittenberg in March 1522, Luther confronted for the first time the communal Reformation which had accelerated the tempo of reform and, under the leadership of Karlstadt, legitimized iconoclasm. In a week-long series of sermons, he preached the gospel of patience, warning against riot and revolt *(Treue Vermahnung)*. Whereas this time Luther was able to control the situation, three years later things would be different. The spiritual allies of Karlstadt would mobilize the peasants, serving as chaplains and articulating their platform—a platform which was condemned by Luther in no uncertain terms. During a series of clashes, at Mühlhausen and, above all, in the aftermath of ruthless retaliation, some seventy thousand peasants were killed, almost as many as were slaughtered during the St. Bartholomew's Massacre in 1572.

In an incisive epitaph for the Peasants' Revolt, Peter Blickle was able to invoke a number of eminent historians for the thesis that 1525 "saw a turning point in the Reformation." Not always with a sense of disappointment, the Reformation is said to have lost "much of its vitality." Occasionally a modern perspective dominates, interested in linking the ruthless repression of the peasants with a "typical" German lack of *Zivilcourage,* matched by an overdose of civil obedience *(Obrigkeitsgehorsam)*. Without questioning these intriguing efforts to use the past to criticize the present, there should be little doubt that if Luther had sided in 1522 with the Wittenberg radicals or, three years later, with the leaders of the Peasant Revolt, the Lutheran Reformation would not merely have lost "much of its vitality," but would have been dislodged in Electoral Saxony, and elsewhere in the Empire aborted altogether. A mustering of eyewitness reports makes it clear that even initial supporters of the Peasant cause were convinced that valid protest had exploded into anarchy and chaos. The foremost opinion makers were the power-brokers in the cities, and Erasmus of

Rotterdam articulates their fears. If Erasmus can make Luther responsible for social unrest and revolt *(tumultus)*, it is not hard to imagine what his reaction would have been had Luther actually wavered.

For a non-systemic reformation, perception and, more generally, a favorable public opinion are crucial conditions for achieving change. The learned Marxist Max Steinmetz characterized the uprising of 1525 as a premature revolution. If Luther had followed in Karlstadt's footsteps, the German Reformation would have been premature as well. Yet there is something far more fundamentally flawed in the thesis of the "loss-of-vitality" in 1525. It is the outgrowth of the perspectival distortion that goes with longstanding myopia, the lopsided preoccupation with Germany: in December 1525, just months after the peak of the German Peasants' Revolution the first Huguenot protest songs were circulated in Paris; Luther's message had found a dynamic new carrier: the Reformation of the Refugees was born.

III. The Cutting Edge: The Reformation of the Refugees

Prenez en patience,
Vous serviteurs de Dieu,
Jettans vostre espérance
En nostre doux Sauveur.
C'est le seul médiateur,
Ayant toute puissance;
C'est le seul médiateur,
Rendons luy tout honneur.
(*Chanson Nouvelle*, c. December 1525)

Turning from Luther to Calvin, the same question can be asked: how do we explain the fact that the Reformation did not fail? Indeed here we are faced with an even more formidable challenge since Luther's window of opportunity was no longer available to Calvin. In contrast with Luther's chance to exploit the interim, gaining precious time with appeals to universities, the Emperor, and to a future council, Calvin had to leave Paris and seek refuge in Switzerland when university and court had already moved against the evangelical dissenters; and even before he was fully established in Geneva, he had to take up his pen to write the "Antidote" against the decrees of the Council of Trent. Above all, Calvin had to contend with the widespread disenchantment with the failings of German Lutheranism. In his 1543 manifesto on the need for reformation, *De necessitate reformandae Ecclesiae*, he listed four such points of critique specifically targeting Germany: first, theological discord; second, lack of measurable progress in the quality of Christian life; third, the slackening hold on popular religion by the abolition of fasting, pilgrimages, and spiritual exercises; and finally, the expropriation of church property by greedy princes intent on filling their own pockets. Calvin does not hesitate to declare the success of a true reformation as nothing less than a miracle, only to be compared with the resurrection of the dead. "Yet, ours is not the task to assess the chances of success," but to pray and sweat. "Ours is the task to preach the gospel, let the chips fall wherever they may, and face the consequences."

When Luther confronted his own activist wing in March 1522, he had expressed the same view but with a significant variant: "I have attacked the papacy by preaching the word of God. This word has done the job while I slept and drank Wittenberg beer *mit meynem Philippo und Amßdorff.*" Though Calvin would never have invoked beer-drinking—his was more a taste for wine—he did share Luther's view that the success of the Reformation could not be the fruit of human ingenuity. At the same time, Calvin failed to find the evidence of a great awakening on German soil: not just Luther with his Philip and Amsdorf, but the whole of Lutheranism had fallen asleep. Twenty years of emissaries beseeching German Protestant princes to support the persecuted Huguenots, begging for soldiers and money, had been to no avail. German Protestantism, content with the Peace of Augsburg and preoccupied with preserving the balance of power within the Empire, was ill prepared to be the bold ally Calvin knew he needed in the battle for Europe's soil and soul.

In order to understand the dynamics of Calvin's Reformation, we need a larger map than the one showing the original German axis from Wittenberg to Schmalkald and Innsbruck. We will want to draw the Genevan trail to Lyon, London and Emden as well as the Spanish trail from Madrid to Paris and Antwerp. The geopolitical scope of Calvin's Reformation can best be understood by tracing its course from Geneva via Paris and Antwerp to the newly emerging provinces, Zeeland and Holland. Looking in vain for support from a tired Lutheranism which was satisfied with the settlements it had acquired, French Calvinism proved to be no match for the Spanish flow of funding and troops. It was sufficiently resilient, however, to forestall a second Armada and to allow the Netherlands to emerge victoriously from its eighty-years war.

What we have sketched here is not a necessary process but the tumultuous accumulation of small skirmishes and local battles. All the more urgent is the question, what elements in Calvin's platform allowed the Reformation of the Refugees to survive as "Churches under the Cross" against the heavy odds of a rejuvenated and aggressive Catholicism; or phrased from a different perspective: what allowed the European Reformation to survive its German beginnings? In this final section, I want to concentrate on three obstacles in Calvin's message that seem most clearly to militate against a wider reception: total human depravity, the divisive doctrine of predestination, and a moral rigor which, as I argued above, when exploding in violence and iconoclasm would have been the death warrant for the non-systemic reformation in the Empire.

(1) I turn first to Calvin's radical understanding of sin and introduce it with a quotation:

> when one constitutes a society and gives laws for it, it must be taken for granted that all men are evil, and that they always will give vent to the evil will that is rooted in their minds whenever opportunity arises.

The widespread conviction that Calvin's anthropology is profoundly pessimistic seems to be clearly documented here. As a matter of fact, the passage quoted is taken from Machiavelli's *Discorsi,* written some ten years before his death in 1527. This unusual and unacademic device to mislead the audience serves the purpose of exposing a deep-seated presupposition: what seemed to be a somber view of the power of evil, typical of the pessimist Calvin proves to be the fundamental point of departure for the notorious realist, Machiavelli. Actually, there is good reason to invert the roles. From the perspective of modern political theory, Machiavelli is the pessimist, who has less confidence in the ruled than in the ruler. Calvin, on the other hand, combines a biblical realism about the force of evil with a strikingly optimistic view of the possibility for private and public improvement and sanctification. His view of the world as the "theater of God's glory" is the optimistic call for action on the basis of his radical assessment of human institutions, equally dysfunctional in the emerging absolute state, in the Church, and in popular religion. It has not been sufficiently realized that as part of Calvin's platform, depravity spells a call to arms, not despair of human endeavor.

(2) The second most formidable obstacle to be considered is the doctrine of predestination. Philip Benedict acutely captures its repulsive potential: "Moral rigor shades over easily into self-righteousness, and the elect are rarely loved when they let the remainder of the community know that it is damned." While the rest of his eminent book on Rouen during the Wars of Religion is firmly based on statistics, this particular statement is based on common sense, including a common misunderstanding of Calvin's doctrine of predestination. There is no evidence in Calvin's own writings or in the reactions of his readers that the doctrine of predestination was either intended or, in fact, functioned in this divisive way.

Our modern difficulty in grasping the dynamics of predestination is due to the fact that historians of theology have made it part of a speculative system, preferably documented by Calvin's handbook for theology, the *Institutes.* Yet it is an historian of theology, Willem van't Spijker, to whom we owe the insight that this doctrine, as puzzling in the sixteenth century as it is today, was born out of experience; and we may add, in Calvin's case, the experience of the refugees. Even the differences between Bucer and Calvin are related to their different social experiences. Bucer, the City Reformer, cannot avoid the question of why some in Strasbourg accept the gospel and others do not. As St Augustine, on the basis of the identical experience in Hippo, Bucer concludes that through God's predestination the eyes of some are opened while others are closed. Calvin accepts Bucer's Augustinian interpretation but adds another element that arises out of the transition from the City Reformation to the Reformation of the Refugees.

The doctrine of predestination is the crucial antidote against the fear that the faithful will not be able to persevere under the pressure of persecution. Election is the gospel's encouragement for the faithful and not a message of doom for the opponents. In particular, it responds to the anguish that Calvin already felt in the early wave of persecution, which pervaded Paris on the eve of his escape to Switzerland: he feared that torture would make him betray the names of the other members of his underground cell. Rather than the grounds for arrogance, predestination holds out the hope for all true Christians that they will persevere to the end even under duress. In defense of the scriptural insights fostered by this experience of persecution, a systematic theology was developed which would lose its direction and harden its doctrinal crust when the refugees later became settlers and citizens, now interpreting election as a civil right.

(3) Finally, we must turn to that sensitive issue of revolt and iconoclasm which nearly aborted Luther's reformation. No doubt, Calvin would have been sympathetic to Karlstadt's activism in 1522. Yet two crucial differences have to be highlighted. In the first place, Calvin's "war against the idols" is easily misunderstood. Carlos Eire, who so precisely inventoried the piety of Philip II in the face of death and purgatory, was misled by earlier Calvin scholarship to assume that Calvin militated against images on the platonic assumption of God's absolute transcendence. Actually, Calvin did not attack the idols because of God's transcendence beyond the world of time and space but because of God's omnipresence in every detail of reality and in every act of history. In an audacious intellectual history of iconoclasm, Alain Besançon has argued that Calvin did not change the image of God but of the world. When he chooses for this view the term *le monde dédivinisé,* his term is acceptable, provided it is interpreted in the sense that God is "de-localized." Calvin criticized popular religion for making images into idols because of the perceived implicit lack of confidence in God's presence in all matters of daily life.

The second difference brings us back to the vulnerability of the non-systemic reformation. The outbreak of iconoclasm in France and the Netherlands heavily compromised the Huguenot movement. It was essential, therefore, for Calvin to do everything in his power to restrain his followers from *tumultus,* riots and the use of force in occupying churches and breaking images. When the cause of the Reformation and the very survival of the Huguenot movement seemed jeopardized, he went as far as breaking with his own left wing, even distancing himself from his old comrade-in-arms, Guillaume Farel.

While the systemic reformation was our point of departure, iconoclasm marks the proper point of conclusion. For it is exactly this phenomenon that displays the dynamics of a theological program and how such a program can be informed and transformed by social and political factors. The emergence of iconoclasm marks the point where the original message is translated, transferred, and absorbed in a suspense-filled web of processes, of *longue* and *brève durée.* But without a firm grasp of the original message itself, neither the beginning of the Reformation in Germany nor its Calvinistic completion can be properly understood.

Calvin and the Good Life:
Augustine's Logic of *uti/frui* in *Institutes* 3:10[1]

Kyung-Y. Burchill-Limb

What we will discuss in this seminar concerns but a very small part of the *Institutes,* specifically Book 3, chapter 10, where the question is raised as to "How to use the present life and its means of aid." Here Calvin touches most closely on the theme of the good life, providing such a positive evaluation of the enjoyment of earthly goods that he has even been hailed as the prophet of "life, liberty and the pursuit of happiness." It is in the light of the late H. A. Oberman's remark that Calvin's development of the *uti/frui* dialectic went far beyond what can be seen as Augustine's "dualistic" elaboration of *uti/frui,*[2] that I hope to be able to offer some clarification of the issues involved through an examination of the logic of *uti* and of *frui,* which constituted the frame of reference for all discussions on the subject since the patristic period. Even though he neither explicitly cites nor mentions the bishop of Hippo's work in this context, it is yet clear that Calvin's thinking took place against the background provided by this inherited vocabulary and logic. Here I am less concerned with the question of influence as such, a problem that in any case is more likely to engender debate than understanding, than with trying to see how a constant and evident problem of Christian experience came to be modified in terms of Calvin's thought. Only when this has been grasped can we turn to consider the underlying problem of Calvin's modernity without ceding to anachronism. This should then provide a useful point of conclusion.

[1]Much of the preparation of the paper was done thanks to the award of a H. Henry Meeter Summer Faculty Research Fellowship at Calvin College in 1998. The author also wishes to express her gratitude to the late H. A. Oberman for a number of helpful comments at the time of the conference.

[2]Cf. H. A. Oberman, "The Pursuit of Happiness: Calvin between Humanism and Reformation," in J. O'Mally, T. Izbicki and G. Christianson, eds., *Humanity and Divinity in Renaissance and Reformation: Essays in Honor of Charles Trinkhaus,* Studies in the History and Christian Thought, vol. 51 (Leiden: Brill, 1990), 251-83.

I. Augustine's logic[3] of *uti* and of *frui*

Let me begin then with a summary account of the meaning of the words. The formula *uti/frui,* which really refers to the distinction[4] between the utility of means and the fruition of ends, is one of long-standing importance within the context of historical theology and crops up in one form or another in many of the crucial debates of the Middle Ages.[5] Though this logic can be traced back to Cicero's *honestum/utile* distinction and to Plotinus's distinction between πρὸς την χρείαν and πρὸς το τέλος,[6] and for this reason can hardly be described as Augustine's invention, yet its point of development in Christian discourse is clearly to be found with the bishop of Hippo. Already in his *De pulchro et apto,* a lost work retraceable through Book IV of the *Confessions,* this logic of distinction between functional, dependant and relative *aptum* (the seemly) and perfect, autarchic and absolute *pulchrum* (the beautiful) is evident in describing the relation of the parts to the whole and is thus closely related to Augustine's theory of knowledge.[7] Here the sense is given as follows: "et pulchrum, quod per se ipsum, aptum autem, quod ad aliquid adconmodatum deceret, definiebam et distinguebam." (4:15:24).

These two concepts had been brought together in the Roman legal concept of *usus fructus,* which determined the right to use or enjoy the benefits of an estate belonging to another. In a Christian context this was reflected in the notion of stewardship, which Augustine discusses in his *De diuersis quaestionibus LXXXIII* q. 30. Derived from contemporary practice of agrarian production, *uti* here refers to the condition of those who do not actually own but merely exploit an estate. Implicit in this language is an ethical responsibility to cultivate the land—or by extension any other benefice so held in trust—so that it could bring forth its potential of fruit. It hardly needs to be stressed that this sense of use was radically different from the utilitarian ethics of today, but the notion of stewardship came to be seen as axiomatic to any discussion of the problems associated with material wealth in the pre-modern world.

It is, of course, in this context as well that *frui* can be best defined. Although it simply refers to the enjoyment of the created order and its bounty, it was in no way to be confused with a hedonistic delight in the senses. The term rather

---

[3]For the purposes of this present paper, I am not referring to any formalized system of logic as would be apparent in one of the recognized schools of philosophy, but rather to a general approach to reasoning, something which would seem to do greater justice to the eclectic nature and scope of Augustine's mind.

[4]Cf. *De diu. quaest. LXXXIII* q. 30: "secundum hanc differentiam."

[5]Cf. V. J. Bourke, *Joy in Augustine's Ethics,* The Saint Augustine Lecture 1978 (Villanova: Villanova University Press, 1978), 67-81.

[6]Cf. Enn. 1:4:16; U. Duchrow, *Christenheit und Weltverantwortung. Traditionsgeschichte und systematische Struktur der Zweireichelehre* (Stuttgart: E. Klett, 1970), 202.

[7]Cf. De ord. 2:11:30: "Ratio est mentis motio, ea quae discuntur distinguendi et connectendi potens."

suggested a sense of peace and stability derived from the contemplation of a process brought to its natural fulfillment. Here Augustine's understanding of *frui* is closely related to expressions such as *habere deum, beatus esse/facere nos beatos, esse cum deo* and *perfrui deo,* and the delight motive is clearly to be distinguished from that derived from passing pleasures. One thing that we should keep in mind is the fact that the terms related to sensual pleasure like *uoluptas, suauitas, dulcedo, iucunditas* are employed by Augustine to describe his mystic sense of the love of God. A clear example of this usage can be found in the definition of *frui* as *capere uoluptatem* in the text from *De diuersis quaestionibus LXXXIII* q. 30. Another point to be noted is that *frui* is closely related to the concept of order, which in turn suggests the sustaining image of *tenere.* Since the one who "holds" the order of the proportioned whole is God, so man's enjoyment of this order necessarily implies his adhesion to God, though the word *inhaerere* as used in the text is perhaps even stronger. Thus briefly we might define the sense of *frui* in Augustine as the stable happiness derived from the condition of remaining (cf. *manentia*) in God.

Compared to this stability expressed through the term *in Deo,* the word *uti* is associated with the preposition *ad,* thus suggesting a sense of orientation as well as that of instrumental utility and adjustment. From a subjective standpoint, *uti* thus implies a process of evaluative judgment and is clearly related to both the rational and volitional dimensions of man. Without the exercise of such judgment in determining what to use, how to use and to what end, we do not use but misuse[8] the created order. Thus something is said to be useful only in so far as it contributes towards a predetermined end. Or to be more precise, whereas all of creation may be described as good in itself, it is yet the prerogative of rational beings to render things useful by ascribing to them a specific function and objective. That is why the value of our acts must depend on their ultimate reference, since all things will be organized with that in mind.[9] If a person's real objective is the accumulation of riches or power then one way or another his whole life will revolve around this end. It is only when one's ultimate concern is with the love of God that his or her life will be orientated with reference to that end. This logic of *uti* and *frui* thus came to constitute an important element of the Augustinian tradition, where it served as a principle relating the penultimate goals of this present life with the fulfillment of Christian existence in the world to come. Implicit within this view is a relative denigration of the things of this life as a form of diversion, if not actually an impediment to the objective of spiritual journey to God. While this should not be confused with the ascetic values of many of his contemporaries, there appears yet to be a certain dualistic residue in Augustine's thought and this was to remain an ingrained feature of the Christian tradition with its implicit opposition between temporal and spiritual goods.

---

[8]Cf. *De doctrina christiana* 1:4:4.

[9]Cf. *De diu. quaest. LXXXIII* q. 30: "utile autem quod ad aliud aliquid referendum est."

II. Calvin's teaching in *Institutes* 3:10

It is against this background that we may now turn to look at Calvin's understanding of the good life as outlined in *Institutes* 3:10, a chapter the importance of which has come into greater prominence following S. Schreiner's original and thought-provoking study on the Reformer's understanding of the created order. My own purpose, however, is simply to comment on the text in the light of the foregoing analysis of the distinction between *uti* and *frui.*

A. The positive dimension of sensual pleasure

What strikes us from the outset is Calvin's characterization of earthly goods as "means of aid" *(adiumenta)* and "support" *(adminiculum),* thus inciting his readers to view the material world in a positive light. At the start of the second section, this point is made even more explicit when it is noted: "Let this be our principle: that the use of God's gifts is not wrongly directed when it is referred to that end *[quum in eum finem refertur]* to which the Author himself created and destined them for us, since he created them for our good, not for our ruin." Here the basic belief in the goodness of earthly goods is common to both Calvin and Augustine, though the latter is much more restrained and immediately cautions against being led astray through the perversity of the human heart. Calvin on the other hand goes straight to the question of the "right use" of those things necessary to life, as well as to the legitimate pleasure that may so be derived. The difference is even more striking when we look at the choice of words used to describe sensual pleasure: terms such as *oblectamentum* and *hilaritas* are associated with the pleasures of the table; trees and fruit are noted for their *aspectus gratia* and *jucunditas ordoris;* while the sight and scent of flowers are suggested by the words *pulchritudo* and *suavitas.* At one point Calvin even goes as far as to employ the word *frui* to designate our enjoyment of the created order.[10] Furthermore, Calvin renders legitimate this pleasure of the senses in the world around, defending it as inherently praiseworthy *(commendabiles)* rather than as a grudging concession to necessity (cf. *necessarium usum*).

Immediately after this remark, at the beginning of the third section Calvin turns his scorn against the "inhuman philosophy" that sought not only to deprive humankind of the "licit fruit of divine beneficence," but also aspired to the degradation of man's natural sensitivity. Although not explicitly stated in the text, it is here clear that for Calvin a sense of delight in the material world is but a "legitimate response" to the divine message of beneficence as manifested in the creatures. The qualification is that all must be done with respect to order, a point which recalls the underwriting principle of Augustine's teaching. Here too, sensual pleasure must be seen as part of a global scheme of things and as such it must be kept within coherent bounds. The "ordering" of life is thus neither to restrain nor condemn pleasure, but to ensure that it does

---

[10] "Et ipsae naturales rerum dotes satis demonstrant quorsum et quatenus frui liceat."

not destroy itself through an excessive indulgence in the sensual pleasures, or in other words in debauchery.

B. The logic of *uti/frui* between this world and the next

All this would seem to confirm William Bouwsma's analysis, namely that the Genevan Reformer more or less consciously sought to dissociate himself from Augustine's all too rigid distinction between *uti* and *frui*. Still this point should not be exaggerated. For all that Calvin's defense of the legitimate use of sensual pleasure and his more flexible understanding of *frui* might be seen as a departure from the Augustinian tradition, it yet takes place against the background of a common set of assumptions. The theological purpose of the *uti/frui* distinction had less to do with the problem of sensual satisfaction than with providing a constant reminder of the importance of distinguishing and ordering between the temporal passage and the eternal destination. Seen in this respect, it seems to me that the kernel of Augustine's argument can be found in the fourth section of *Institutes* 3:10, where Calvin advocates "contempt" of the present life and "meditation" on heavenly immortality as a "rule" for the faithful. Here two principles are outlined on the proper conduct of this present life. The first, which had already been stated as a caveat at the beginning of the chapter, consists of recalling the Lord's teaching that "the present life is for his people as a pilgrimage through which they are hastening toward the heavenly kingdom." In this theme of life as a "journey"—be it in the sense of a passage *(cursus)* or a journey *(peregrinatio)*, we can easily trace Augustine's fundamental concern to provide an eschatological dimension to *frui* as rooted in his doctrine of creation.

Secondly, while it is true that Calvin emphasizes the positive value of sense perception in our appreciation of the created order, this point is immediately placed in perspective when we are reminded of Paul's injunction to the Corinthians to use this world "with not very much affection" (1 Corinthians 7:30), living within the world as if we were not part of it. Here *perinde affecti sint* seems to me psychologically incompatible with his defense of the legitimate *frui* of temporal goods, since enjoyment and affection normally go together in the process of sensual fulfillment. The real difference at this point, or so I would argue, is that whereas the bishop of Hippo is more suspicious of fallen man's capacity to enjoy the temporal good in an orderly way and for this reason chooses to adopt a rhetoric of constant admonition, the French Reformer is rather more preoccupied in proving a practical instruction of *modum tenere:* "But no less diligently ... we must resist the lust of the flesh, which, unless it is kept in order, overflows without measure" (3:10:2).

C. The ordering of the present life: *modum tenere*

As already mentioned, Augustine's *uti/frui* distinction is based on a theory of knowledge inherited from antiquity, according to which the ordering and disposition was of fundamental importance. Now this in itself presupposed some form of teleological principle according to which the subject matter could be arranged. This too is suggested in the third section of *Institutes* 3:10, where it is noted that the defining criteria of a well-ordered state are the recognition of God and thanksgiving for "his kindness towards us." In the relation of the faithful to God, man's duties are set forth as the fulfillment of "piety" and "vocation." Since the enjoyment of food, wine and clothes, as well as the other pleasures of life, is considered as a form of permission *(licentia)* from which one may legitimately profit, so the values of liberty and responsible judgment must go hand in hand. This is particularly important where Calvin speaks of the need for moderation with respect to abundance and poverty. The necessary "discernment" to be observed in these matters seems to me to ascribe a more exalted status to individual conscience. Faced with the evidence that some find difficulty in dealing with their wealth, while many have to struggle to overcome want, Calvin places all before their common responsibility to maintain their true liberty in looking beyond the cares and attachments of the material world "to the thought of heavenly life and zeal to cultivate the soul." This measured disposition in the management of material goods and resources was for Calvin a hallmark of piety. Its objective was to allow each to fructify the wealth with which they were entrusted (cf. *uti*), while at the same time directing their concern towards God (cf. *frui*).

It is thus that Calvin places his teaching on the regulation of material life clearly within the context of his understanding of individual vocation. Since each and every one is called to a specific mission in accordance with God's governing design, to follow in the line of this vocation means the ordering of each individual life according to its means and ends. In so doing, Calvin introduces not only the individual sense of *modus* through being faithful to one's vocation, but also the universal value of stewardship, here understood with reference to *villicatio,* the care or management of the estates of an absentee landlord. Despite the apparent diversity of God's assignment, each calling has its referential end and measure in God with which our life should be in harmony. In the absence of such a concordance with God's purpose, the appearance of an ordered life is but vain, as was noted in section six: "Perhaps, sometimes, he could contrive something laudable in appearance; but whatever it may be in the eyes of men *[in conspectu hominum],* it will be rejected before God's throne. Besides, there will be no proportion among the several parts of his life *[in ipsis vitae partibus nulla erit symmetria]*. Accordingly, your life will then be best ordered when it is directed to this goal *[proinde tum optime composita erit tua vita quum ad hunc scopum dirigetur]*."

Here we see Calvin coming back to his initial theme as declared at the opening of the chapter, namely the ordering of our life (cf. *res in componenda vitae ratione*). In other words the whole discussion concerning the right way of using and enjoying the material world is related to his dominant concern to articulate our need to assume the responsibility of an individual calling before God. The chapter should thus not be read solely as an ethical discourse on what to do with things, but rather as an invitation to that form of self-knowledge without which we cannot profit from the goods of this present life but only misuse them. This then becomes the major impediment to man's true fruition in the order of God.

III. Calvin's modernity

By way of conclusion, I would simply like to state my own position on a number of the disputed issues and this largely in the hope of inciting further discussion.

1. My first point is related to Heiko Oberman's expression, "Augustine's dualistic dialectic of *uti/frui,* " the rationale of which was explained at the beginning of this paper. There is certainly no difficulty in discerning elements of a rhetorical dichotomy in Augustine's *uti/frui* logic. Nevertheless, I wonder if we should not distinguish, in our turn, between "rhetorical language" and "logical reasoning." Moreover, since the intellectual tradition of late antiquity laid great stress on the necessity of conceptual distinction as part of the art of memory, it is hardly surprising that this should appear as characteristic of his thought. But if we follow the theological intent of his work, it becomes clear that the sense of this distinction is likewise to be found in the transformation of *uti* in terms of its final fruition in God. Rather than talking of a "dualistic dialectic," we might be better advised to treat the *uti/frui* logic as an essential part of Augustine's thought as a whole. It is important to avoid any confusion between a rhetoric of dichotomy and a dualistic dialectic.
2. If moreover it may be granted that Augustine's reasoning of *uti/frui* provided the essential backcloth to the elaboration of Calvin's ideas in *Institutes* 3:10, I should yet like to emphasize the difference in rhetorical effect as between the two thinkers. For both Calvin and Augustine earthly goods can be ascribed a positive value only when seen in the light of their creator's good providence. The differences of nuance stem from the fact that Augustine was preoccupied with the potential misuse of the created order in what was still a world founded on an essentially pagan value system, whereas in the *Institutes* Calvin is more concerned to stress the overriding beneficence of God's work. Here in passing I raise the aside as to whether the same perspective would be found in an analysis of some of the sermon literature, which was evidently produced with a different intention.
3. Finally, I should like to invite your reflection on the relation between *pura conscientia* and the doctrine of vocation, since it seems to me that it is here that we may find the key to the whole question of Calvin's modernity. The idea of *modum tenere* with its invitation to the ordering of the Christian life was to presuppose the personal commitment of individual vocation and here Calvin goes well beyond anything to be found in Augustine. In this passage of Calvin we are not simply presented with a theory concerning the proper disposition of material goods, but rather with a challenge as to how in conscience, before God, we may best use that which has been entrusted.

The Young Calvin and Later Calvin:
Changes in His Theology

Yang Ho Lee

I. Changes in Calvin's Theology

Calvin's thought changed from its earlier to its later expression. This change is discernible even in the beginning sentence of *Institutes of the Christian Religion.*[1]

1536

Nearly the whole of sacred doctrine consists in these two parts: the knowledge of God and of ourselves.

1539

Nearly all the wisdom we possess, that is to say, true and sound wisdom, contains two parts: the knowledge of God and of ourselves.

Here we can find a notable change from "sacred doctrine" to "wisdom." T. H. L. Parker explained this change from "narrow" sacred doctrine to "comprehensive" wisdom:

> The change, which he introduced in 1539, is significant. ... But more to our present point, although *sapientia* had a long ecclesiastical use, going back to the Old Testament *chochmā*, it possessed also a classical pedigree in the *sophia* of the Greek philosophers. In the sixteenth century, that stormy stretch of water where the two seas met, *sapientia* bore both a Christian and a secular connotation, and was therefore a word of comprehensive scope. Both the Church and the world were interested in wisdom, and each believed this pearl of great price to be in its own possession. Now, the first edition of the *Institutio* was tied to Calvin's *apologia* to the King of France on behalf of the persecuted French Protestants, and hence served the purpose of presenting Protestant teaching as manifestly not heretical but within the tradition of the Patristic Church. In accordance with this aim, *sacra doctrina* means "Christian doctrine", the theology of the Church and not of a sect. In the second edition, however, we may suggest that Calvin is dissatisfied with his claim

[1]"Summa fere sacrae doctrinae duabus his partibus constat: Cognitione Dei ac nostri" (CO 1:27). "Tota fere sapientiae nostrae summa, quae vera demum ac solida sapientia censeri debeat, duabus partibus constat: cognitione Dei, et nostri" (CO 1: 279).

> as being too narrow. If almost the whole of *sacra doctrina* consists in the knowledge of God and of ourselves, the question at once thrusts itself forward: Is there then a *profana doctrina,* a secular philosophy, which can demand a place alongside *sacra doctrina*? Is *sacra doctrina* only one branch of *doctrina,* and have other branches an equal validity? More generally, is Christianity just one sect in a universal pantheon?[2]

Parker continued:

> Calvin therefore changes the term to the comprehensive *sapientia,* and so cuts the ground from under the feet of the many neo-philosophies of his day. ... It is true that Calvin makes use of non-Christian philosophies; but he has no intention of attempting a synthesis. What in fact follows *sapientia nostra* throughout the four books of the *Institutio* is a statement of Christian doctrine, of *sacra doctrina.* Moreover, by beginning the work with this sentence, he speaks directly not only to the Protestants, not only to the rest of the orthodox Christian world, but also to the philosophers, the humanists and even the atheists, and declares to them the comprehensiveness of the Biblical teaching on God, man, and the universe—such a comprehensiveness that, although "nature" and "heathen philosophers" may confirm it, they can add nothing to it.[3]

William J. Bouwsma, however, explained matters differently. He described this as a change from "a traditional conception of theology as God's truth rather than ours" to "the best sort of knowledge we limited creatures can manage." He wrote:

> He understood, at least sometimes, that theology, as a human enterprise, does not state truths in an absolute sense, from God's standpoint. Its truths are as limited as the human beings who develop them. It may be that he did not himself immediately or fully recognize this. The first sentence in the first edition of the *Institutes* reads: "Almost the whole of sacred doctrine *[sacra doctrina]* consists of two parts: knowledge of God and of ourselves," a formula he had taken from Cicero. This rather absolute wording suggested that he held, in 1536, a traditional conception of theology as God's truth rather than ours. But the second edition, three years later, made an interesting change, as though something had troubled him about the earlier wording. Now, for "sacred doctrine," he substituted "our wisdom *[sapienta* [sic] *nostra]*," that is, the best sort of knowledge we limited creatures can manage.[4]

As we will consider in the following, Calvin estimated astronomy or philosophy more positively in his later days. In this respect, the thought of the later

---

[2]T. H. L. Parker, *Calvin's Doctrine of the Knowledge of God* (Edinburgh: Oliver and Boyd, 1969), 15-16.

[3]Ibid., 16-17.

[4]William J. Bouwsma, *John Calvin: A Sixteenth Century Portrait* (New York: Oxford University Press, 1988), 160.

Calvin became more comprehensive. It seems that Calvin wanted to change his *Institutes* from narrow sacred doctrine to comprehensive wisdom.

Calvin, as was just stated, spoke highly of astronomy or philosophy in his later days. In his *Commentary on the Book of Genesis,* published in 1554, he wrote: "For astronomy is not only pleasant, but also very useful to be known: it cannot be denied that this art unfolds the admirable wisdom of God."[5] Also Calvin admired philosophers in the 1559 edition of the *Institutes,* saying "I, indeed, agree that the things they teach are true, not only enjoyable, but also profitable to learn, and skillfully assembled by them. And I do not forbid those who are desirous of learning to study them."[6] In the same edition of the *Institutes,* he said, "Hence Plato's opinion is more correct, because he considers the image of God in the soul."[7] Furthermore, in regards to the doctrine of providence, Calvin, in the 1539 edition of the *Institutes,* rejected the doctrine of universal providence. However, in the 1559 edition of the *Institutes,* he wrote, "I do not wholly repudiate what is said concerning universal providence."

> 1539
>
> Therefore, *as we rightly rejected a little above the opinion of those who imagine a universal providence of God* which does not stoop to the especial care of any particular creature, yet first of all it is important that we recognize this special care toward us.[8]
>
> 1559
>
> Yet *I do not wholly repudiate what is said concerning universal providence,* provided they in turn grant me that the universe is ruled by God, not only because he watches over the order of nature set by himself, but because he exercises especial care over each of his works.[9]

---

[5]"Nam astrologia non modo iucunda est cognitu, sed apprime quoque utilis: negari non potest quin admirabilem Dei sapientiam explicet ars illa" (*Commentary on the Book of Genesis* 1:16 [hereafter cited as *Comm. Gen.* followed by chapter and verse], CO 23:22).

[6]"Vera quidem esse, nec iucunda modo cognitu, sed etiam utilia esse fateor, dextreque ab illis collecta quae docent: nec vero ab eorum studio prohibeo qui discendi cupidi sunt" (*Inst.* 1.15.6, OS 3:183:19-23).

[7]"Inde autem Platoni rectior sententia, quod imaginem Dei in anima considerat" (*Inst.* 1.15.6, OS 3:182.21-22). Also cf.: "Plato, whom he seems hardly to have known before, now becomes one of the writers to whom he most often refers, although he generally avoids doing so by name" (François Wendel, *Calvin: The Origins and Development of His Religious Thought,* trans. Philip Mairet (Glasgow: William Collins, 1950), 115). The time—"now"—to which Wendel refers is 1539.

[8]"Quanquam itaque merito supra mihi permisi explodere eorum opinionem, qui universalem Dei providentiam comminiscuntur, quae non speciatim ad curam uniuscuiusque creaturae se demittat, in primis tamen specialem hanc curam erga nos recognoscere operae pretium est" (CO 1:895) (italics added).

[9]"Neque tamen quod de universali providentia dicitur in totum repudio: modo vicissim hoc mihi concedant, mundum a Deo regi, non tantum quia positum a se naturae ordinem tuetur, sed quia peculiarem uniuscuiusque ex suis operibus curam gerit" (*Inst.* 1:16:4, OS 3:194:9-13) (italics added).

It is perhaps not surprising that the later Calvin, who spoke highly of astronomy or philosophy, did not wholly repudiate the doctrine of universal providence.

Development can be seen in other areas as well. For example, in the first edition of the *Institutes,* Calvin spoke only of a two-fold messianic unction:

> We also believe that Christ himself was sprinkled with all the graces of the Holy Spirit. These are called "oil" (Ps. 45, 89) because without these we waste away, dry and barren. And as the Spirit has rested upon him, and has poured itself out wholly upon him, in order that we may all receive from his fullness (that is, whoever of us are partners and partakers of him through faith) (Is. 11, 61; John 1), so do we believe in short that by this anointing he was appointed *king* by the Father to subject all power in heaven and on earth (Ps. 2), that in him we might be kings, having sway over the devil, sin, death, and hell (1 Pet. 2). Then we believe that he was appointed *priest,* by his self-sacrifice to placate the Father and reconcile him to us, that in him we might be priests, with him as our Intercessor and Mediator, offering our prayers, our thanks, ourselves, and our all to the Father (Rev. 1; Ps. 110; Heb. 5, 13).[10]

In the 1539 edition of the Institutes, however, Calvin began to refer to the prophetic office of Christ:

> The name "Christ" is added, which, though not inappropriately attributed to others, is none the less his by a peculiar right. For the Lord anoints all on whom he sheds the graces of his Spirit. And there is no one faithful, nor has there been any, whom he did not fill with his unction. Therefore it comes about that all the faithful were anointed. The prophets have their own unction also, and the kings have it, and the priests, not in the manner of outward ceremony only but spiritually. ... Therefore the oil whereby *prophets* as well as *priests* and *kings* were consecrated was not a useless symbol but a sacrament of that true and unique anointing.[11]

[10]"Credimus et Christum ipsum esse, hoc est, omnibus sancti spiritus gratiis perfusum; quae oleum ideo dicuntur (Psal. 45. 89), quod sine his aridi et steriles tabescimus, sicque, ut spiritus super ipsum requieverit, ac sese totum in eum effuderit: ut de plenitudine eius omnes accipiamus, quicunque simus per fidem eius consortes ac participes (Ies. 11. 61. Ioan. 1); hac denique unctione constitutum esse a parte regem, qui omnem sibi potestatem in coelo et in terra subiiceret (Psal. 2), ut in ipso reges essemus, imperium habentes supra diabolum, peccatum, mortem et inferos (1 Petr. 2). Deinde sacerdotem, qui suo sacrificio patrem nobis placaret ac reconciliaret, ut in ipso sacerdotes essemus: ipso intercessore ac mediatore, patri preces, gratiarum actiones, nosmetipsos, et nostra omnia offerentes (Apoc. 1. Psal. 110. Hebr. 5. 13)" (CO 1:68-69) (italics added).

[11]"Christi elogium annectitur, quod tametsi aliis non absurde attribuitur, illi tamen peculiari quodam iure competit. Ungit enim omnes Dominus quibus spiritus sui gratias instillat. Atqui nemo est fidelium, nec unquam fuit, quem non eiusmodi unctione irrigaverit. Omnes igitur fideles unctos esse conficitur. Habent suam quoque unctionem prophetae; habent et suam tum reges, tum sacerdotes; non illam modo caeremonialem et externam sed spiritualem. ... Quare oleum illud quo tam prophetae quam sacerdotes et reges inaugurabantur, non inane erat symboloum, sed verae illius et unicae unctionis sacramentum" (CO 1:513-14) (italics added).

And in the 1559 edition of the Institutes, Calvin wrote:

> Now it is to be noted that the title "Christ" pertains to these three offices: for we know that under the law prophets as well as priests and kings were anointed with holy oil. Hence the illustrious name of "Messiah" was also bestowed upon the promised Mediator. As I have elsewhere shown, I recognize that Christ was called Messiah especially with respect to, and by virtue of, his kingship. Yet his anointing as *prophet* and as *priest* have their place and must not be overlooked by us.[12]

Concerning this change, John Frederick Jansen declared, "We need to ask ourselves whether the formula represents a peripheral or an essential theological change. ... I would contend that the change is peripheral rather than essential. ... The essential structure of his doctrine of Christ's work remains two-fold. If such be the case, then the *munus triplex* is not the truest expression of his theology."[13] Jansen rightly held that "the change is peripheral rather essential." However, when he said, "The essential structure of his doctrine of Christ's work remains two-fold," he was, in our judgment, mistaken. For, it seems that for Calvin the two-fold messianic offices of Christ were central and the prophetic office was peripheral. More shall be said about this in Part II of this paper.

If we turn to Calvin's doctrine of faith, we can also see development and change. The thesis of R. T. Kendall, who argued that for Calvin faith was intellectual,[14] provoked a heated controversy among Calvin scholars. Calvin, however, in the 1536 edition of the *Institutes,* like Luther, said that first of all faith was hope and trust:

> The other [form of faith] is the faith whereby we not only believe that God and Christ are, but also believe in God and Christ, truly acknowledging him as our God and Christ as our Savior. Now this is not only to adjudge true all that has been written or is said of God and Christ; but to put all *hope and trust* in one God and Christ, and to be so strengthened by this thought, that we have no doubt about God's good will toward us.[15]

---

[12]"Porro notandum est ad haec tria munera Christi pertinere elogium; scimus enim sub Lege sacro oleo tam Prophetas quam sacerdotes ac reges fuisse unctos. Unde et celebre Messiae nomen promisso Mediatori fuit impositum. Etsi autem fateor peculiari regni intuitu et ratione dictum fuisse Messiam (ut etiam alibi ostendi) prophetica tamen et sacerdotalis unctio gradum suum obtinent, neque sunt a nobis negligendae" (Inst. 2:15:2, OS 3:473:6-12) (italics added).

[13]John Frederick Jansen, *Calvin's Doctrine of the Work of Christ* (London: James Clarke, 1956), 51.

[14]R. T. Kendall, *Calvin and English Calvinism to 1649* (Oxford: Oxford University Press, 1981), 19.

[15]"Altera est: qua non modo Deum et Christum esse credimus, sed etiam in Deum credimus, et Christum, vere ipsum pro Deo nostro ac Christum pro salvatore agnoscentes. Hoc vero est, non modo verum reputare id omne, quod de Deo ac Christo vel scriptum est, vel dicitur, sed spem omnem ac fiduciam in uno Deo ac Christo reponere, hacque cogitatione sic offirmatos esse, ut de bona Dei erga nos voluntate nihil dubitemus" (CO 1:56) (italics added).

Yet in the 1539 edition of the *Institutes,* Calvin emphasized the intellectual nature of faith, criticizing the implicit faith of the Scholastics:[16]

> Is this what believing means—to understand nothing, provided only that you submit your feeling obediently to the church? *Faith rests not on ignorance, but on knowledge.* ... For when the apostle says, "With the heart a man believes unto righteousness, with the mouth makes confession unto salvation" (Rom. 10:10), he indicates that it is not enough for a man implicitly to believe what he does not understand or even investigate. But he requires explicit recognition of the divine goodness upon which our righteousness rests.[17]

In the meantime, Calvin, in the same edition of the *Institutes,* made an effort to keep the balance between the volitional side and the intellectual side of faith:

> Now we shall possess a right definition of faith if we call it a firm and certain knowledge of God's benevolence toward us, which, founded upon the truth of the freely given promise in Christ, is through the Holy Spirit both revealed to our *minds* and sealed upon our *hearts.* [18]

However, one can also find in the same edition of the *Institutes,* Calvin emphasizing the volitional side of faith rather than the intellectual side:

> That very assent itself—as has already been explained—is *more of the heart than of the brain, and more of the disposition than of the understanding.*[19]

Change can also be seen in Calvin's doctrine of the church. In the first edition of the *Institutes* he insisted on the invisible aspect of the church:

> This is what we mean when we say, "we believe the church." For by faith are believed things *that cannot be seen with the naked eye.* By this it is made plain that

---

[16]Cf. Wendel, *Calvin,* 240-41. Wendel said, "But from 1539 onwards, Calvin was no longer content with this definition which identified faith with confidence and hope" (241). Also cf. "For example in the 1536 *Institutio* Calvin, like Luther, insisted that above all faith was trust and hope. In 1539 he made more of the intellectual nature of faith. Not that one can accuse him of intellectualism, but, in insisting that 'understanding is linked together with faith,' he simply meant to reject all confusion with the implicit faith of the schoolmen" (Jean-Daniel Benoît, "The History and Development of the *Institutio:* How Calvin Worked" in G. E. Duffield (ed.), *John Calvin* (Appleford: Sutton Courtenay Press, 1961), 104).

[17]"Hoccine credere est, nihil intelligere, modo sensum tuum obedienter ecclesiae submittas? Non in ignoratione, sed in cognitione sita est fides; ... Nam quum dicit apostolus (Rom. 10, 10), corde credi ad iustitiam, ore confessionem fieri ad salutem, non satis esse indicat, si quis implicite credat quod non intelligat, nec etiam inquirat; sed explicitam requirit divinae bonitatis agnitionem, in qua consistit nostra iustitia" (CO 1:473) (italics added).

[18]"Nunc iusta fidei definitio nobis constabit, si dicamus esse divinae erga nos benevolentiae firmam certamque cognitionem, quae gratuitae in Christo promissionis veritate fundata per spiritum sanctum et revelatur mentibus nostris et cordibus obsignatur" (CO 1:456) (italics added).

[19]"Siquidem assensionem ipsam cordis esse magis quam cerebri, et affectus magis quam intelligentiae, iam expositum est" (CO 1:472) (italics added).

> *it is not a physical thing* which ought to be subjected to our sense perception, or *enclosed within a definite space, or fixed in some spot.*[20]

Meanwhile, Calvin mentioned both the invisible church and visible church in the 1543 edition of the Institutes:

> For we have said that Holy Scripture speaks of the church in two ways. Sometimes by the term "church" it means that which is actually in God's presence, into which no persons are received but those who are children of God by grace of adoption and true members of Christ by sanctification of the Holy Spirit. Then, indeed, the church includes not only the saints presently living on earth, but *all the elect* from the beginning of the world. Often, however, the name "church" designates the *whole multitude of men* spread over the earth who profess to worship one God and Christ. ... In this church are mingled many hypocrites who have nothing of Christ but the name and outward appearance.[21]

And in the 1559 edition of the *Institutes,* Calvin used the phrase, "not only ... but also" to describe the church.[22]

> 1559
> The article in the Creed in which we profess to "believe the church" refers not only to the visible church (our present topic) but also to all God's elect, in whose number are also included the dead.

Additionally, Calvin did not distinguish between the outer call and the inner call of the minister in the first edition of the *Institutes.* He, however, distinguished them from 1543 onwards, as can be seen from the following:

> 1536
> This is the place to explain the meaning of the call. It consists of two things, namely, that we should understand who are the ones to institute bishops or presbyters, and by what rite or ceremony to initiate them. Evidence for lawful institution cannot be sought from the institution of the apostles, who

---

[20]"Quin potius nihil horum nisi fide, intelligitur, quod ipsum significamus, cum dicimus: nos ipsam credere. Creduntur enim quae praesenti oculo spectari nequeunt. Quo planum fit, non rem esse carnalem, quae sensibus nostris subiici, aut certo spatio circumscribi, aut in sede aliqua figi debeat" (CO 1:77) (italics added).

[21]"Bifariam enim de ecclesia sacrae literae loquuntur. Interdum enim, quum ecclesiam nominant, eam intelligunt quae revera est coram Deo, in quam nulli recipiuntur, nisi qui et adoptionis gratia filii Dei sunt, et spiritus sanctificatione, vera Christi membra. Ac tunc quidem non tantum sanctos qui in terra habitant comprehendit, sed electos omnes, qui ab origine mundi fuerunt. Saepe autem ecclesiae nomine universam hominum multitudinem in orbe diffusam designat, quae unum se Deum et Christum colere profitetur. ... In hac autem plurimi sunt permixti hypocritae, qui nihil Christi habent praeter titulum et speciem" (CO 1:542) (italics added).

[22]"In Symbolo, ubi profitemur nos credere Ecclesiam, id non solum ad visibilem, de qua nunc agimus, refertur, sed ad omnes quoque electos Dei, in quorum numero comprehenduntur etiam qui morte defuncti sunt" (*Inst.* 4:1:2, OS 5:2:5-8).

awaited no human call, but by the command of the Lord alone girded themselves for their task. Nor is it clear enough what order the apostles themselves held, except that Paul, whom we cited a moment ago in that passage, stated that he left Titus in Crete to appoint bishops in every city (Titus 1).[23]

1543

I am speaking of the *solemn call* which has to do with the public order of the church. I pass over that *secret call,* of which each minister is conscious before God, and which does not have the church as witness.[24]

1559

I am speaking of the *outward and solemn call* which has to do with the public order of the church. I pass over that *secret call,* of which each minister is conscious before God, and which does not have the church as witness.[25]

Calvin's doctrine of the sacraments reveals similar qualities. So Calvin, like Luther, emphasized God's act in the 1536 edition of the *Institutes.* In the 1543 edition of the *Institutes,* however, he, like Zwingli, mentioned man's attestation.[26]

1536

First, we must consider what a sacrament is. It is an outward sign by which the Lord represents and attests to us his good will toward us to sustain the weakness of our faith.

1543

First, we must consider what a sacrament is. It seems to me that a simple and proper definition would be to say that it is an outward symbol by which the

[23]"Porro quae sit ratio vocationis, nunc docendi locus est. Ea in duobus versatur: nempe ut habeamus et a quibus instituendi sint episcopi seu presbyteri, et quo ritu quave caeremonia initiandi. Legitimae institutionis documentum ex apostolorum institutione peti non potest, qui humana vocatione non expectata, sed solo Domini mandato instructi, operi se accinxerunt. Nec quem ipsi apostoli ordinem tenuerint satis constat: nisi quod Paulus, eo quem nuper citavimus loco tradit, se reliquisse Titum in Creta ut episcopos per civitates constitueret (Tit. 1), et alibi Timothem admonet, ne cui temere manum imponat (1 Tim. 5)" (CO 1:186).

[24]"De solenni vocatione loquor, quae ad publicum ecclesiae ordinem spectat; arcanam vero illam, cuius sibi quisque minister coram Deo conscius est, ecclesiam testem non habet, omitto" (CO 1:568) (italics added).

[25]"De externa et solenni vocatione loquor, quae ad publicum ecclesiae ordinem spectat; arcanam vero illam, cuius sibi quisque minister coram Deo conscius est, ecclesiam testem non habet, omitto" (Inst. 4:3:11, OS 5:52:21-24) (italics added).

[26]"Principio animadvertere convenit, quid sit sacramentum. Est autem signum externum, quo bonam suam erga nos voluntatem Dominus nobis repraesentat ac testificatur, ad sustinendam fidei nostrae imbecillitatem" (CO 1:102). "Principio animadvertere convenit, quid sit sacramentum. Videtur autem mihi haec simplex et propria fore definitio, si dixerimus externum esse symbolum, quo benevolentiae erga nos suae promissiones conscientiis nostris Dominus obsignat, ad sustinendam fidei nostrae imbecillitatem: et nos vicissim pietatem erga eum nostram apud homines testamur" (CO 1:937-38); Cf. John W. Riggs, "Emerging Ecclesiology in Calvin's Baptismal Thought, 1536-1543" in *Church History* 64 (1995), 29-43.

Lord seals on our consciences the promises of his good will toward us in order to sustain the weakness of our faith; and we in turn attest our piety toward him before men.

Concerning the three forms of government, that is to say, monarchy, aristocracy and democracy, Calvin, in the first edition of the *Institutes,* said, "it is not easy to distinguish which one of them excels in usefulness." Yet, in the 1543 edition of the *Institutes* he said, "aristocracy, or a system compounded of aristocracy and democracy, far excels all others."[27]

1536
And if you compare the forms of government among themselves apart from the circumstances, it is not easy to distinguish which one of them excels in usefulness, for they contend on such equal terms. The fall from kingdom to tyranny is easy; but it is not much more difficult to fall from the rule of the best men to the faction of a few; yet it is easiest of all to fall from popular rule to sedition.

1543
And if you compare the forms of government among themselves apart from the circumstances, it is not easy to distinguish which one of them excels in usefulness, for they contend on such equal terms. The fall from kingdom to tyranny is easy; but it is not much more difficult to fall from the rule of the best men to the faction of a few; yet it is easiest of all to fall from popular rule to sedition. For if the three forms of government which the philosophers discuss be considered in themselves, I will not deny that aristocracy, or a system compounded of aristocracy and democracy, far excels all others.

In addition, in 1555 Calvin declared in a sermon on Deuteronomy 17: 14-18: "if we discuss human government, we can say that it is far better to live in a free state than under a prince."[28]

Thus, as has been seen above, Calvin's thought changed from its earliest expression to its later, more mature formulation. Generally speaking, the change was from either/or to both/and. Here the both/and is not a both/and

[27]"si ipsos etiam status citra circumstantias inter se compares, non facile sit discernere, quis utilitate praeponderet adeo aequis conditionibus contendunt. Proclivis est a regno in tyrannidem lapsus; sed non multo difficilior, ab optimatum potestate in paucorum factionem; multo vero facillimus a populari dominatione in seditionem" (CO 1:232-33). "Et si ipsos etiam status, citra circumstantias, inter se compares, non facile sit discernere, quis utilitate praeponderet, adeo aequis conditionibus contendunt. Proclivis est a regno in tyrannidem lapsus; sed non multo difficilior, ab optimatum potestate in paucorum factionem. Multo vero facillimus a populari dominatione in seditionem. Equidem si in se considerentur tres illae, quas ponunt philosophi, regiminis formae, minime negaverim vel aristocratiam, vel temperatum ex ipsa et politia statum aliis omnibus longe excellere" (CO 1:1105).

[28]"si on disputoit des gouvernemens humains, qu'on pourroit dire, que d'estre en un estat libre, c'est une condition beaucoup meilleure, que d'estre sous un prince" (*Sermons on Deuteronomy,* 17:14-18, CO 27:458).

of equals but a both/and which indicates that one concept or idea is central and another peripheral. Calvin, in the first edition of the *Institutes,* articulated narrow sacred doctrine. However, from 1539 onwards, he wanted to set forth a wisdom that was more comprehensive in its scope. So, for example, in his later days, Calvin spoke highly of astronomy and philosophy. Additionally, as we have seen, the young Calvin rejected the doctrine of the universal providence while the later Calvin did not wholly repudiate it. Likewise, the young Calvin spoke only of two messianic offices whereas the later Calvin mentioned three messianic offices. The young Calvin emphasized trust and hope in the Christian faith, but the later Calvin mentioned both the volitional side and the intellectual side of faith. The young Calvin did not distinguish between the visible and the invisible church while the later Calvin distinguished between them. The young Calvin spoke only of the outer call of ministers, but the later Calvin mentioned both the outer and inner call. The young Calvin followed Luther's doctrine of the sacrament while the later Calvin accepted both Luther's and Zwingli's ideas. The young Calvin preferred aristocracy whereas the later Calvin favored a mixture of aristocracy and democracy. In short, the thought of the later Calvin was more comprehensive. The later Calvin's system was a great synthesis; that is to say, a great synthesis of theology and philosophy, of Roman Catholicism and Protestant radicalism, of Lutheran and Zwinglian ideas. For this reason, he deserves the great name of the father of modern ecumenical theology.

II. The Structure of Theology in the Later Calvin

Calvin scholars have been puzzled by the problems involved in identifying the structure of Calvin's theology. Some Calvin scholars have attempted to find the principle that governs his thought in the construction of his theology. Others have tried to find the structure of Calvin's theology by analyzing the final edition of his *Institutes.*

To Ernst Troeltsch, the central doctrine of Calvin's theology is the idea of God's predestination. "The first distinctive feature of Calvinism, and the most important one, is the idea of predestination, the famous central doctrine of Calvinism."[29] In the idea of predestination, Calvin is "trying to express the character of God as absolute sovereign will."[30] For Calvin "the chief point is not the self-centered personal salvation of the creature, and the universality of the Divine Will of Love, but it is the Glory of God."[31] In short, to Troeltsch Calvin was a theocentric thinker who emphasized the predestination, sovereign will, and glory of God.

---

[29]Ernst Troeltsch, *The Social Teaching of the Christian Churches,* trans. Olive Wyon (2 vols.; London: George Allen & Unwin, 1931), 2:581.

[30]Ibid., 582.

[31]Ibid., 583.

On the other hand, Wilhelm Niesel regards Calvin as a christocentric thinker. "In every aspect of doctrine Calvin is concerned only about one thing: namely, the God revealed in flesh."[32] He goes on to say, "Jesus Christ controls not only the content but also the form of Calvinistic thought."[33]

Differently again, Benjamin B. Warfield regards Calvin as "the Theologian of the Holy Spirit."[34] "But in the same sense in which we may say that the doctrine of sin and grace dates from Augustine, the doctrine of satisfaction from Anselm, the doctrine of justification by faith from Luther, we must say that the doctrine of the work of the Holy Spirit is a gift from Calvin to the Church."[35] He also says, "In his hands, for the first time in the history of the Church, the doctrine of the Holy Spirit comes to its rights. ... But, above everything else, it is the sense of the sovereign working of salvation by the almighty power of the Holy Spirit which characterizes all Calvin's thought of God. And above everything else he deserves, therefore, the great name of the theologian of the Holy Spirit."[36]

So one might ask whether Calvin is a theocentric thinker, or a christocentric thinker, or a pneumatocentric thinker. If one investigates the writings of Calvin, one learns that the above-mentioned interpretations are all possible. As Calvin himself says, "When, therefore, we treat of the merit of Christ, we do not place the beginning in him, but we go back to God's ordination, which is the primary cause."[37] "Christ, apart from God's good pleasure, could not merit anything."[38] Certainly, these expressions show that Christ is subordinated to the sovereign will of God. On the other hand, Calvin says in the *Commentary on the Gospel of John,* "from the beginning of the world all the patriarchs drew whatever gifts they had from Christ."[39] And in the *Institutes* he says, "through him alone we escape the imputation of our sins to us."[40] But, at the same time, the work of the Holy Spirit is much emphasized in the theological system of Calvin. It is the

---

[32]Wilhelm Niesel, *The Theology of Calvin,* trans. Harold Knight (Philadelphia: Westminster Press, 1956), 246.

[33]Ibid., 247.

[34]Benjamin B. Warfield, *Calvin and Augustine,* ed. Samuel G. Craig (Philadelphia: Presbyterian and Reformed, 1971), 484.

[35]Ibid., 485.

[36]Ibid., 487.

[37]"Quum ergo de Christi merito agitur, non statuitur in eo principium: sed conscendimus ad Dei ordinationem, quae prima causa est" (*Inst.* 2:17:1, OS 3:509:15-17).

[38]"Nam Christus nonnisi ex Dei beneplacito quicquam mereri potuit" (*Inst.* 2:17:1, OS 3:509:25-26).

[39]"omnes ab initio mundi patres a Christo hausisse quidquid habuerint donorum" (*Comm. Jn.* 1:16, CO 47:17).

[40]"ut revera per ipsum solum consequimur ne imputentur nobis peccata" (*Inst.* 2:16:3, OS 3:485:6-7).

Holy Spirit who gave inspiration to the writers of the Scriptures, and gives inner testimony to the readers of the Scriptures, and gives us graces through the sacraments. By the secret efficacy of the Spirit, "We come to enjoy Christ and all his blessings."[41]

If we consider these passages, we have to say that God, Christ, and the Holy Spirit are all emphasized in the theology of Calvin. In other words, the central theme of Calvin's theology is the triune God. So, for example, God, Christ, and the Holy Spirit are all mentioned in the following short definition of faith:

> Now we shall have a right definition of faith if we say that it is a firm and certain knowledge of the divine benevolence toward us, founded upon the truth of the free promise in Christ, both revealed to our minds and sealed upon our hearts through the Holy Spirit.[42]

We can find many such trinitarian schemes in the writings of Calvin. Calvin thinks that this trinitarian scheme roughly agrees with the four causes of Aristotle. In our salvation, the efficient cause is God the Father, the material cause Christ, the formal or instrumental cause faith, and the final cause the glory of God.[43] Also in the *Commentary on the Acts* he says, "Therefore when we treat of the remission of sins, we must look for no other originator of it than the Heavenly Father; we must imagine no other material cause than the blood of Christ. But when it comes to the formal cause, the Holy Spirit indeed plays the leading role, but an inferior instrument is added, the preaching of the Gospel and baptism itself."[44] Generally speaking, Calvin thinks that God is the efficient cause, Christ the material cause, and the work of the Holy Spirit the formal cause. In the case of the final cause, however, Calvin does not mention it in his commentary on Acts 22:16. Therefore, it seems that though Calvin thought that his trinitarian scheme roughly agreed with the four causes of Aristotle, he did not try to make the four causes the fundamental basis of his doctrine. They merely furnished him with a subsidiary argument.

In 1917 Louis Goumaz attempted such an interpretation in his *La Doctrine du salut d'après les commentaires de Jean Calvin sur le Nouveau Testament*. According to him, God the Father is the efficient cause of the salvation, Christ the material cause of the salvation, the action of the Holy Spirit the formal cause of the sal-

---

[41]"ac de arcana Spiritus efficacia inquirere, qua fit ut Christo bonisque eius omnibus fruamur" (*Inst.* 3:1:1, OS 4:1:22-24).

[42]*Inst.* 3:2:7, OS 4:16:31-35.

[43]*Inst.* 3:14:17, OS 4:235.

[44]"Ergo quum de remissione peccatorum agitur, non alius quaerendus est eius autor quam coelestis pater: non alia materialis causa fingenda est quam Christi sanguis. Ubi vero ad formalem causam venitur, primas quidem tenet spiritus sanctus: sed accedit inferius organum, evangelii praedicatio et baptismus ipse" (Comm. Act. 22:16, CO 48:496).

vation, and the glory of God the final cause of the salvation.[45] As we mentioned, however, Calvin did not try to base his doctrine on the four causes of Aristotle, as Goumaz attempts to do in his book. In spite of this defect, it is unfortunate that Calvin scholars have not sufficiently noted the work of Goumaz.

In this connection, we can observe some deficiencies in earlier studies of Calvin. Troeltsch misunderstood the efficient cause as if it were the whole of Calvin's theology. Niesel exaggerated the material cause as if it were the central theme of Calvin. Warfield overestimated the formal cause and therefore called Calvin "the theologian of the Holy Spirit." They emphasized only one aspect of Calvin's thought. Calvin, however, emphasized all three.

Meanwhile, Benjamin Charles Milner, Jr. insists that the unifying principle in Calvin's theology is the absolute correlation of the Spirit and the Word.[46] He argues that by the "theological" and the "christological" interpretations of Calvin "the work of the Holy Spirit is neither fully nor accurately gauged."[47] He is right when he emphasizes both the Spirit and the Word. However, his failure is that he does not fully consider predestination and the sovereign will of God the Father in Calvin's thought.

Recently, Charles Partee suggested in an essay entitled "Calvin's Central Dogma Again" that a central dogma in Calvin might be union with Christ. He explained that "The purpose of this essay is to suggest that a newer quest for a central dogma in Calvin might well consider the doctrine of 'Union with Christ,' which offers a useful way of summarizing the contents of the *Institutes*."[48] However, though union with Christ might be one of the important doctrines in Calvin, this opinion also cannot escape the critique which was leveled again Niesel.

As mentioned earlier, some Calvin scholars have tried to find the structure of Calvin's theology by analyzing his *Institutes*. The editors of the Geneva edition of Calvin's works interpret the *Institutes* as follows:

> The author has a two-fold aim—*scopus duplex*—in this *Institutio Christiana:* the former the knowledge of God, by which we arrive at blessed immortality; the latter the knowledge of ourselves, determined to that former. For this purpose he makes use of the form of the Apostles' Creed, as being the most familiar to all Christians. For just as the Creed is in four parts (i.e. the first on God the Father, the second on the Son, the third on the Holy Spirit, and the fourth on the Church), so also our author has divided his *Institutio* into four books so as to accomplish both parts of the scope that we mentioned.[49]

---

[45]Louis Goumaz, *La Doctrine du salut d'après les commentaries de Jean Calvin sur le Nouveau Testament* (Lausanne: Libraire Payot, 1917), 129ff.

[46]Benjamin Charles Milner, Jr., *Calvin's Doctrine of the Church* (Leiden: E. J. Brill, 1970), 4.

[47]Ibid., 191-92.

[48]Charles Partee, "Calvin's Central Dogma Again" in *The Sixteenth Century Journal*, 18 (1987), 191.

[49]*Iohannis Calvini Opera Omnia Theologica in Septem Tomos Digesta* (Geneva: Iohannes Vignon, Petrus & Iacobus Chouet, 1617), sig. **4a, quoted in Parker, *Calvin's Doctrine,* 8.

This interpretation has been generally accepted. In 1868, however, J. Köstlin insisted that the *Institutes* could be divided into two parts,[50] and in the present century, E. A. Dowey developed further the opinion of Köstlin.[51] According to Köstlin and Dowey, the 1559 edition of the *Institutes* is arranged in the following way in accordance with the *duplex cognitio Domini:*

1. The doctrines of God the Father, Son, and Spirit, and his creation and world government in general, apart from sin and the redemptive revelation and redemptive activity that sin makes necessary—and similarly of mankind, apart from sin and the necessity for salvation. (Book I).
2. The historical revelation and activity of God for the salvation of the sinner, as follows:
   a. The establishing of salvation through the incarnate Son, for which preparation had already been made under the Old Covenant. (Book II).
   b. The application through the Holy Spirit of the salvation given in Christ, as follows:
      i. The process of salvation which is realized inwardly by the Spirit in individuals, extending until the perfection of these persons in the resurrection. (Book III).
      ii. The outer means which God uses in this activity of the Spirit. (Book IV).[52]

François Wendel also says that the *Institutes* consists of two main parts:[53]

> The first is constituted by Book I, and is concerned with the doctrine of God (Trinity, Creator, Providence), the scriptural revelation and man (independently of sin and of the need for salvation). The second part extends over the other three books, and deals with the historic revelation and the plan of salvation. This in its turn is subdivided into two parts: firstly, preparation for the work of salvation, under the old covenant, and its accomplishment in the incarnation of the Son of God (Book II); and secondly, the attribution and application of salvation by the Holy Spirit, (a) by the intimate operation of the Holy Spirit within the believer, even to its completion in the future life (Book III); and (b) by the external means that the Holy Spirit employs to complete this operation and bring it to its right end (Book IV).[54]

---

[50]J. Köstlin, "Calvins Institutio nach Form und Inhalt, in ihrer geschichtlichen Entwicklung," *Theologische Studien und Kritiken* (1868), 6-62, 410-86.

[51]Edward A. Dowey, Jr., *The Knowledge of God in Calvin's Theology* (New York: Columbia University Press, 1952).

[52]Ibid., 42.

[53]Wendel, *Calvin,* 121.

[54]Ibid.

The analysis of A. Dakin is also not very different from the analysis of Dowey and Wendel.[55]

However, since T. H. L. Parker thinks that the *Institutes* consists of four parts in accordance with the four parts of the Apostles' Creed, he criticizes the division of Dowey. "Such a reordering of the material must be regarded as illegitimate textual criticism because in assessing the nature of the subject, it does not take the order itself into account ... but imposes upon the order what is in fact a presupposition."[56] Recently, Parker reiterated this viewpoint in his *Calvin: An Introduction to His Thought.* Parker wrote, "We may therefore complete our labeling of the recensions by calling this the 'credal' *Institutio.*"[57] However, as Richard C. Gamble points out, "Calvin scholarship has shown increasing unanimity that the *[duplex cognitio Dei]* must be reckoned with as either a controlling principle of his theology or the controlling principle."[58]

In short, although the final edition of the *Institutes* consists of four books, it can be divided into two parts: the knowledge of God the Creator and knowledge of God the Redeemer. This point is mentioned several times in the final edition of the *Institutes,* and the *locus classicus* of it is the following:

> Since, therefore, the Lord first appears, as much in the fashioning of the world as in the general doctrine of Scripture, simply as the Creator, and afterwards as the Redeemer in the face of Christ: hence arises a twofold knowledge of him: of which the former is now to be considered, and the other will follow in its order.[59]

Milner, however, objects to the opinion that the final edition of the Institutes was written according to the *duplex cognitio Domini.* Milner says in the above-mentioned book,

> Now I would like to suggest that it is not the *duplex cognitio Domini* which underlies the final organization of the *Institutes,* but Calvin's conception of order as that is structured in the correlation of the Spirit and the Word. Thus, Book I describes the original order of creation, *i.e.,* the doctrines of God and man apart from sin; Book II.i-v the disruption of that order in the fall; and books II.vi-IV the restoration of order, i.e., the Word (Book II) brought to us by the Spirit (Book III) through the external means (Book IV).[60]

---

[55]A. Dakin, *Calvinism* (London: Duckworth, 1940), 247-48.

[56]Parker, *Calvin's Doctrine,* 7.

[57]T. H. L. Parker, *Calvin: An Introduction to His Thought* (Louisville: Westminster/John Knox Press, 1995), 8.

[58]Richard C. Gamble, "Current Trends in Calvin Research, 1982-90" in Wilhelm H. Neuser (ed.), *Calvinus Sacrae Scripturae Professor* (Grand Rapids: Eerdmans, 1994), 106.

[59]"Quia ergo Dominus primum simpliciter creator tam in mundi opificio, quam in generali Scripturae doctrina, deinde in Christi facie redemptor apparet: hinc duplex emergit eius cognitio: quarum nunc prior tractanda est, altera deinde suo ordine sequetur" (*Inst.* 1:2:1, OS 3:34:21-25).

[60]Milner, *Calvin's Doctrine,* 193.

In this interpretation, the church as an institution for the restoration of order stands in the center: "this understanding . . . confirms . . . the centrality of Calvin's doctrine of the church for his theology as a whole; since the church is the restoration of order in the world, not only Book IV, but Book II.vi-IV must be understood as its exposition, with Book I (the conception of order), and Book II.i-v (the disruption of order), serving as its presupposition."[61] However, in this thesis, God who is creating even now is overlooked, and only God who is redeeming is emphasized. In the thought of Calvin, since creation includes preservation, creation is not simply a past event. Calvin himself says, "Moreover, to make God a momentary Creator, who once for all finished his work, would be cold and barren; and we must differ from profane men especially in that we see the presence of divine power shining not less in the perpetual state of the world than in its first creation."[62] In short, for Calvin God not only redeems us through the church, but also continues to create in the world. Therefore, the linear scheme of Milner's interpretation, the creation of order, followed by the disruption of order, followed in turn by the restoration of order, does not correspond to Calvin's scheme.

On the other hand, E. David Willis suggests the possibility of another interpretation, though he does not reject the *duplex cognitio* scheme:

> There is "De Cognitione Dei Creatoris" and "De Cognitione Dei Redemptoris," but no "De Cognitione Spiritus Sancti." Even if it be decided that the *duplex cognitio* scheme and not the three articles of the Creed provides the primary instrument for structuring the final edition of the *Institutes,* still the subject of books III and IV is generally the work of the Holy Spirit, as the subject of Book I is generally God the Creator and of Book II generally the Redeemer.[63]

Willis rightly recognizes that Calvin's *duplex cognitio Dei* is not *creatoris et Christi* but *creatoris et redemptoris.*[64] This is so "because for Calvin Christ is not only the redemptive Word of God but also the creative Word of God."[65] Since Christ also participates in creation, that is to say, since Christ is also creator, Willis rightly says that the two facets of our knowledge of God are not *creatoris et Christi* but *creatoris et redemptoris.* Unfortunately, however, Willis does not see that the knowledge of God the Father is included in *"De Cognitione Dei Redemptoris,"* just as the knowledge of Christ is included in *"De Cognitione Dei Creatoris,"* because he does

[61]Ibid., 193-94.

[62]"Porro Deum facere momentaneum creatorem, qui semel duntaxat opus suum absolverit, frigidum esset ac ieiunum. Atque in hoc praecipue nos a profanis hominibus differre convenit, ut non minus in perpetuo mundi statu quam prima eius origine praesentia divinae virtutis nobis illuceat" (*Inst.* 1:16:1, OS 3:187:10-14).

[63]E. David Willis, *Calvin's Catholic Christology* (Leiden: E. J. Brill, 1966), 123.

[64]Ibid., 121.

[65]Ibid.

not realize that Book 2 of the *Institutes is "De Cognitione Dei Redemptoris,"* not *"De Cognitione Christi."* Moreover, even though Willis rightly says that "for Calvin Christ is not only the redemptive Word of God but also the creative Word of God, just as the Spirit is not only regenerative but also creative,"[66] he needs *"De Cognitione Spiritus Sancti,"* because he does not comprehend that the knowledge of God, the Father, the Son, and the Holy Spirit is included in both *"De Cognitione Dei Creatoris"* and *"De Cognitione Dei Redemptoris."*

In short, for Calvin God, the Father, the Son, and the Holy Spirit, that is, the triune God, is included in *"De Cognitione Dei Creatoris."* As well, God, the Father, the Son, and the Holy Spirit, that is, the triune God, is included in *"De Cognitione Dei Redemptoris."* In other words, Book I of the *Institutes* deals with the triune God as Creator, and Books II-IV deal with the triune God as Redeemer. That is to say, the subject of the *Institutes* is the work of creation and redemption of the triune God. And we may say that the subject of Calvin's theology is the work of creation and redemption of the triune God, because the *Institutes* is the most comprehensive and systematic work of Calvin.

Meanwhile, Partee divided the *Institutes* into two parts on the basis of his viewpoint that Calvin's central dogma is union with Christ.

A. God for us
  I. As Creator (Book I)
    a. His creation
    b. His providence
  II. As Redeemer (Book II)
    a. The revelation
    b. The natures and person
    c. The offices
B. God in us
  I. As Individuals (Book III)
    a. Faith
      1. Regeneration
      2. Justification
    b. Election
  II. As a Community (Book IV)
    a. The ministry
    b. The sacraments
    c. The state[67]

However, the division of Partee cannot be maintained because, as he himself says, "It cannot be demonstrated, and should not be asserted, that Calvin consciously organized the four books in an objective (God for us) / subjective (God in us) fashion.

---

[66]Ibid.

[67]Partee, "Calvin's Central Dogma," 195.

If the subject of Calvin's theology is the work of creation and redemption of the triune God, what, then, is the relation between the creation of the triune God and the redemption of the triune God? In this connection, we must deal with the thesis of Hermann Bauke. According to Bauke, the distinguishing features of Calvin's theology are "the formal-dialectical rationalism"[68] and "the *complexio oppositorum*"[69] on the basis of his "biblicism."[70] And so Bauke regards Calvin as "a dialectician rather than a systematizer, or at best a dialectic systematizer."[71] "The single fundamental elements of dogmatic stand side by side and are bound together dialectically, not deductively deduced from one or two fundamental principles."[72]

While Bauke argues that Calvin was not a systematic theologian who deductively deduced his theology from one or two fundamental principles, Niesel attempts to find the one fundamental principle and he insists that this fundamental principle is Christ, as we have noted. Dowey argues that the relation of the knowledge of God the Creator to the knowledge of God the Redeemer is a dialectic one.[73] On the other hand, Karl Barth says, "It is true that, according to Calvin, the knowledge of God in Christ includes a real knowledge of the true God in creation. Includes! This means that it does not, as Brunner seems to think, bring forth a second, relatively independent kind of knowledge, so that the circle would become an ellipsis after all."[74] On the contrary, according to Emile Doumergue, the method and system of Calvin is a contradiction,[75] and "the thought of Calvin is an ellipse with two foci."[76] Also, whereas Raymond K. Anderson says, "we have found relatively little support in the present study for the common caricature of his work as an eclectic or dialectic combination of diverse principles,"[77] Alexandre Ganoczy speaks of "the dialectical structure of the thought of Calvin."[78]

---

[68]Hermann Bauke, *Die Probleme der Theologie Calvins* (Leipzig: Verlag der J. C. Hinrichs'schen Buchhandlung, 1922), 13.

[69]Ibid., 14.

[70]Ibid., 19.

[71]Ibid., 16.

[72]Ibid., 32.

[73]Dowey, *Knowledge,* 238.

[74]Karl Barth, "No! Answer to Emil Brunner" in *Natural Theology,* trans. Peter Fraenkel (London: The Centenary Press, 1946), 108-109.

[75]Emile Doumergue, *Le Caractère de Calvin* (Neuilly: La Cause, 1931), 76.

[76]Emile Doumergue, *Jean Calvin: Les hommes et les choses de son temps* (7 vols: Lausanne: Georges Bridel & Cie, 1899-1927), 4: 279.

[77]Raymond K. Anderson, *Love and Order: The Life-Structuring Dynamics of Grace and Virtue in Calvin's Ethical Thought* (Chambersburg: Wilson College, 1973), 395.

[78]Alexandre Ganoczy, *Calvin: Théologien de l'Église et du ministère* (Paris: du Cerf, 1964), 59.

Is the character of Calvin's thought elliptical (according to Doumergue) or not (according to Barth)? Is it dialectic (according to Dowey), or deductive (according to Niesel)? In this connection, we do well to consider the so-called *extra Calvinisticum. Extra Calvinisticum* is the doctrine that the Eternal Son of God, even after the Incarnation, was united to the human nature to form one Person but was not restricted to the flesh.[79] The doctrine received its name when Lutheran theologians, upon hearing the Calvinists insist that the Son's existence also beyond the flesh of Jesus Christ *(etiam extra carnem)* was being threatened by the Lutheran version of the *communicatio idiomatum,* labelled the Reformed contention "that Calvinistic 'beyond'" *(illud extra Calvinisticum).*[80] Calvin says, "Marvelously, the Son of God descended from heaven in such a way that he did not leave heaven: marvelously, he willed to be born in the Virgin's womb, to live on the earth, and to hang upon the cross, and yet always filled the world as from the beginning."[81] Even though Niesel says, "It might be objected that it is false to regard the *extra Calvinisticum* as the most essential feature of Calvinistic Christology,"[82] the *extra Calvinisticum* is very important in Calvin's theology, as Heiko A. Oberman points out.[83]

The thought form of Calvin in the so-called *extra Calvinisticum* is neither an ellipse with two foci nor a circle with one center, but two concentric circles in which two different objects are related as core and shell. What, then, is the structure of Calvin's theology? The subject of Calvin's theology is the work of creation and redemption of the triune God, and the relation between the creation of the triune God and the redemption of the triune God is a relation of concentric circles, that is, a relation of core and shell. In other words, the creation of the triune God is peripheral, and the redemption of the triune God is central.

In the meantime, according to B. G. Armstrong the structure of Calvin's thought is a hypothetical structure. "[T]he whole general tenor and structure of Calvin's theology is built around a hypothetical or conditional base."[84] Armstrong argues "that Calvin lived intimately in the two worlds of Renaissance and Reformation, and that he never was able to resolve the conflict of fundamentally different ideologies, and that his theology was accommodated to con-

---

[79]Cf. Willis, *Calvin's Catholic Christology,* 1.

[80]Cf. Ibid.

[81]"Mirabiliter enim e caelo descendit Filius Dei, ut caelum tamen non relinqueret: mirabiliter in utero Virginis gestari, in terris versari, et in cruce pendere voluit, ut semper mundum impleret, sicut ab initio" (*Inst.* 2:13:4, OS 3:458:9-13).

[82]Niesel, *Theology,* 119.

[83]Heiko A. Oberman, "The 'Extra' Dimension in the Theology of Calvin" in *Journal of Ecclesiastical History* 21 (1970), 43-64.

[84]B. G. Armstrong, "The Nature and Structure of Calvin's Thought According to the *Institutes:* Another Look" in *John Calvin's Institutes: His Opus Magnum* (Potchefstroom: Potchefstroom University for Christian Higher Education, 1986), 64-65.

flicting ideologies in such a way that there will always be two poles, two aspects, two dialectical and conflicting elements in each theological topic which he discusses."[85] Also he said, "The hypothetical and actual, the ideal and the real, structure which characterizes Calvin's theology is nowhere more clearly seen than in the discussion of the doctrine of Justification by Faith and its relationship to the doctrine of Sanctification."[86] Armstrong's argument that Calvin lived in the two worlds of Renaissance and Reformation, and accommodated to conflicting ideologies in such a way that there will always be two poles in each theological topic which he discusses seems to be partially right. However, Armstrong failed to grasp the fact that Calvin did not put the same value on Renaissance and Reformation but put a great (central) value on Reformation and a little (peripheral) value on Renaissance.

According to William J. Bouwsma, two Calvins coexist uncomfortably within the same historical personage. "One of these Calvins was a philosopher, a rationalist and a schoolman in the high Scholastic tradition represented by Thomas Aquinas, a man of fixed principles, and a conservative."[87] The other Calvin was a rhetorician and humanist, a skeptical fideist in the manner of the followers of William of Ockham, flexible to the point of opportunism, and a revolutionary in spite of himself."[88] Bouwsma's argument that there are two Calvins within the historical Calvin seems to be right. However, the two Calvins are not "philosophical Calvin" and "humanistic Calvin" but Calvin the Reformer and Calvin the humanist. Bouwsma overestimated Calvin's humanism. In fact, Calvin the Reformer is in the center, and Calvin the humanist is on the periphery.

As stated above, the subject of Calvin's theology is the creation and redemption of the triune God, and these two works of God are in a relation of shell and core, or a relation of the peripheral and the central. Now let us consider the doctrines of the later Calvin from this standpoint.

First of all, according to Calvin God is the Creator and Redeemer. As stated above, Calvin's statement of the twofold knowledge of the Lord can be found in many places of the *Institutes*. And the titles of Book I and Book II of the *Institutes* show clearly the twofold knowledge of the Lord. The fact that the knowledge of the Redeemer is central and the knowledge of the Creator is peripheral in Calvin's theology comes out in his concern and the space which he devoted to each in the *Institutes*. Dowey rightly says, "Calvin's thought has a soteriological center which dominates all his theology."[89] Also as stated above,

---

[85]Ibid., 56.

[86]Ibid., 74.

[87]Bouwsma, *John Calvin*, 230.

[88]Ibid., 231.

[89]Edward A. Dowey, Jr., "The Structure of Calvin's Theological Thought as Influenced by the Two-fold Knowledge of God" in Wilhelm H. Neuser (ed.), *Calvinus Ecclesiae Genevensis Custos* (Frankfurt am Main: Peter Lang, 1984), 137.

there is a distinction between "Christ in the flesh" and "Christ who is also beyond the flesh" in Calvin's theology. In this distinction, "Christ in the flesh" is central and "Christ who is also beyond the flesh" is peripheral. Because Calvin's theology has a soteriological center, the crucifixion and resurrection of Jesus Christ must be central. Also according to Calvin there are two kinds of grace of the Holy Spirit, that is to say, special grace and general or common grace. Calvin says about "the general grace of God"[90] the following:

> If we regard the Spirit of God as the sole fountain of truth, we shall neither reject the truth itself, nor despise it wherever it shall appear, unless we wish to dishonor the Spirit of God. . . . Shall we deny that the truth shone upon the ancient jurists who established civic order and discipline with such great equity? Shall we say that the philosophers were blind in their fine observation and artful description of nature? ... No, we cannot read the writings of the ancients on these subjects without great admiration. ... But shall we count anything praiseworthy or noble without recognizing at the same time that it comes from God?[91]

If one considers these passages, Calvin seems to be a humanist as Erasmus. However, if one considers the *Institutes* as a whole, one can find that Calvin rejected the viewpoint of Erasmus about humankind and his free will.

One can find in many of Calvin's doctrines a form of thought which distinguishes the central from the peripheral. Now we are going to consider some of them. First of all, consider the problem of natural revelation. The problem of natural theology in Calvin is one of the controversial issues in Calvin scholarship. According to Calvin, from nature we know the hands and feet of God, though through Christ we know not only God's heart, but also God's hands and feet. Calvin says:

> There, in short, the invisible kingdom of Christ occupies all things and his spiritual grace is diffused through all. Yet this does not prevent us from applying our senses to the consideration of heaven and earth, that we may thence seek confirmation in the true knowledge of God. For Christ is that image in which God presents to our view, not only his heart, but also his hands and his feet. I give the name of his heart to that secret love with which

---

[90]"generalem Dei gratiam" (*Inst.* 2:2:17, OS 3:259:33).

[91]"Si unicum veritatis fontem, Dei Spiritum esse reputamus, veritatem ipsam neque respuemus, neque contemnemus, ubicunde apparebit: nisi velimus in Spiritum Dei contumeliosi esse; ... Veritatem affulsisse antiquis iureconsultis negabimus, qui tanta aequitate civilem ordinem et disciplinam prodiderunt? Philosophos caecutisse dicemus cum in exquisita ista naturae contemplatione, tum artificiosa descriptione? ... Imo ne sine ingenti quidem admiratione, veterum scripta legere de his rebus poterimus: ... Porro laudabilene aliquid aut praeclarum censebimus, quod non recognoscamus a Deo provenire?" (*Inst.* 2:2:15, OS 3:258:14-30).

he embraces us in Christ: by his hands and feet I understand those works of his which are displayed before our eyes.[92]

According to these sentences, the knowledge of God from nature is peripheral, and the knowledge of God from Christ is central.

Secondly, we might consider the problem of *indicia.* Warfield says, "we find the surest indication that he thought of the *indicia* as co-working with the testimony of the Spirit to this result."[93] Of course, Calvin thought of the *indicia* as co-working with the testimony of the Spirit, but the *indicia* are peripheral, and the testimony of the Spirit is central. Calvin says, "Unless this certainty, higher and stronger than any human judgment, be present, it will be vain to fortify the authority of Scripture by arguments, to establish it by common agreement of the Church, or to confirm it with other helps."[94] Also Calvin says, "Scripture will ultimately suffice for a saving knowledge of God only when its certainty is founded upon the inward persuasion of the Holy Spirit. Indeed, these human testimonies which exist to confirm it will not be vain if, as secondary aids to our feebleness, they follow that chief and highest testimony."[95] In short, the inward persuasion of the Holy Spirit is central; *indicia,* human testimonies, are peripheral.

Thirdly, let us consider the problem of the inspiration and inerrancy of the Scripture. Warfield says, "In point of fact, Calvin not only asserts the freedom of Scripture as given by God from all error, but never in his detailed dealing with Scripture allows that such errors exist in it."[96] However, Calvin found some errors in the Scriptures. Calvin says, in the commentary on Matthew 27:9, "How the name of Jeremiah crept in I cannot confess to know nor do I make much of it: obviously Jeremiah's name is put in error for Zechariah (13:7)."[97] In short, according to Calvin one can find some errors of a trivial nature in the Scriptures, but one cannot find any error in the doctrine, that is to say, the cen-

[92]"Denique illic invisibile Christi regnum omnia occupat, et spiritualis eius gratia per omnia diffusa est. Verum hoc non obstat quominus sensus nostros ad coeli terraeque considerationem applicantes, inde etiam petamus quae nos in vera Dei notitia confirment. Christus enim imago est, in qua non modo pectus suum nobis Deus conspicuum reddit, sed manus quoque et pedes. Pectus appello arcanum illum amorem quo nos in Christo complexus est: per manus autem et pedes, quae oculis nostris exposita sunt opera intelligo" (CO 23:9-12).

[93]Warfield, *Calvin,* 89.

[94]"Haec nisi certitudo adsit quolibet humano iudicio et superior et validior, frustra Scripturae authoritas vel argumentis munietur, vel Ecclesiae consensu stabilietur, vel aliis praesidiis confirmabitur" (Inst. 1:7:1, OS 3:71:39-72:2).

[95]"Quare tum vere demum ad salvificam Dei cognitionem Scriptura satisfaciet, ubi interiori Spiritus sancti persuasione fundata fuerit eius certitudo. Quae vero ad eam confirmandam humana extant testimonia, sic inania non erunt, si praecipuum illud et summum, velut secundaria nostrae imbecillitatis adminicula, subsequantur" (*Inst.* 1:7:13, OS 3:81:22-28).

[96]Warfield, *Calvin,* 65.

[97]"Quomodo Ieremiae nomen obrepserit, me nescire fateor, nec anxie laboro: certe Ieremiae nomen errore positum esse pro Zacharia (13, 7)" (Comm. Matt. 27:9, CO 45:749).

tral message of Scripture. Calvin says, "For we must always distinguish, when we speak of the prophets and the apostles, between their doctrine, which was pure, free from every imperfection, and their own persons, as they commonly say, or themselves. ... yet his doctrine was absolutely free from every defect."[98]

Fourthly, Calvin distinguishes between central and peripheral doctrines. Calvin says:

> For not all the articles of true doctrine are of the same sort. Some are so necessary to know that they should be certain and unquestioned by all men as the proper principles of religion. . . . Among the churches there are other articles of doctrine disputed which still do not break the unity of faith. . . . Does this not sufficiently indicate that a difference of opinion over those non-essential matters should in no wise be the basis of schism among Christians?[99]

In short, in the Christian doctrines, there are essential doctrines and non-essential doctrines.

Fifthly, let us consider his doctrine of the church. Calvin distinguishes between invisible church and visible church. The invisible church which consists of the elect is a small invisible church in the visible church *[ecclesiola in ecclesia]*. In the visible church "are mingled many hypocrites who have nothing of Christ but the name and outward appearance."[100]

Sixthly, as stated above, the later Calvin distinguishes outer call and inner call. Calvin says, "I am speaking of the outward and solemn call which has to do with the public order of the church. I pass over that secret call, of which each minister is conscious before God, and which does not have the church as witness."[101] Also Calvin says, "But two things are required in anyone who would be heard in the church and occupy the position of a teacher; he must be called by God to that office, and be faithful in carrying out its duties."[102] The inner call is central, and the outer call is peripheral.

---

[98]"Nam semper distinguere oportet, quum agitur de prophetis et apostolis, inter ipsam doctrinam, quae pura fuit ab omni sorde, et inter ipsorum personas, ut vulgo loquuntur, hoc est inter ipsos. ... interea doctrina prorsus caruit omni naevo" (Comm. Jer. 15:18, CO 38:231).

[99]"Non enim unius sunt formae omnia verae doctrinae capita. Sunt quaedam ita necessaria cognitu, ut fixa esse et indubitata omnibus oporteat, ceu propria religionis placita; ... Sunt alia, quae inter Ecclesias controversa, fidei tamen unitatem non dirimant. ... Annon satis indicat, dissensionem de rebus istis non ita necessariis, dissidii materiam esse non debere inter Christianos?" (*Inst.* 4:1:12, OS 5:16:6-21).

[100]"In hac autem plurimi sunt permixti hypocritae, qui nihil Christi habent praeter titulum et speciem" (*Inst.* 4:1:7, OS 5:12:19-21).

[101]*Inst.* 4:3:11, OS 5:52:21-24.

[102]"Duo autem requiruntur, ut quis in ecclesia audiatur docendique locum habeat. Nam vocatum esse a Deo oportet ad id munus, et in eo exsequendo bona fide versari" (*Comm. 1 Cor.* 1:1, CO 49:303).

Seventhly we may consider the doctrine of the sacraments. According to Calvin, the sacrament is "an outward sign by which the Lord seals on our consciences the promises of his good will toward us."[103] And "I say that Christ is the matter or (if you prefer) the substance of all the sacraments; for in him they have all their firmness, and they do not promise anything apart from him."[104] What, then, is the relation between the outward sign and the substance of the sacraments? Calvin says, "Hence that distinction (if it be duly understood), often noted by the same Augustine, between a sacrament and the matter of the sacrament. For the distinction signifies not only that the figure and the truth are contained in the sacrament, but that they are not so linked that they cannot be separated; and that even in the union itself the matter must always be distinguished from the sign, that we may not transfer to the one what belongs to the other."[105] Therefore, Calvin criticizes the "false doctrine" of the Roman Catholics, "by which the cause of justification and the power of the Holy Spirit are enclosed in elements, just as in vessels or vehicles."[106] On the other hand, Calvin criticized Protestant radicals, "Fanatical men (like Schwenckfeld) pervert this testimony ridiculously by wanting to take away from sacraments all their power and effect."107 In the sacraments, the outward sign is peripheral, and the substance is central.

Lastly, let us consider Calvin's political thought. According to Marc-Edouard Chenevière, "Calvin ... was a determined adversary of modern democracy, that is to say, of the political doctrine which makes the people the only possible and legitimate holder of power and sovereignty."[108] On the other hand, according to Hudson, "The thought of Calvin provided the potential basis for the elaboration of democratic ideas. Not only did he provide a basis for resistance to the exercise of arbitrary power, but his thought did not preclude the formulation of a definitively democratic philosophy of government."[109] As stated above,

---

[103]"externum esse symbolum, quo benevolentiae erga nos suae promissiones conscientiis nostris Dominus obsignat" (Inst. 4:14:1, OS 5:259:3-5).

[104]"Christum Sacramentorum omnium materiam, vel (si mavis) substantiam esse dico: quando in ipso totam habent suam soliditatem, nec quicquam extra ipsum promittunt" (*Inst.* 4:14:16, OS 5:273:15-17).

[105]"Hinc illa, si rite intelligatur, inter Sacramentum et rem sacramenti ab eodem Augustino saepius notata distinctio; neque enim significat duntaxat, figuram et veritatem illic contineri, sed non ita cohaerere quin separari queant: ac in ipsa etiam coniunctione oportere semper discerni rem a signo, ne ad alterum transferamus quod alterius est" (*Inst.* 4:14:15, OS 5:272:15-20).

[106]"Interim illud tollitur figmentum quo iustificationis causa virtusque Spiritus sancti elementis ceu vasculis ac plaustris includitur" (*Inst.* 4:14:17, OS 5:275:23-25).

[107]"Caeterum hoc testimonium perperam detorquent fanatici homines (ut Schvincfeldius) dum sacramentis omnem vim et effectum detrahere volunt" (*Comm. 1 Pet. 3:21,* CO 55:268).

[108]Marc-Edouard Chenevière, *La Pensée politique de Calvin* (Genève: Slatkine Reprints, 1970), 10, n. 4.

[109]Winthrop S. Hudson, "Democratic Freedom and Religious Faith in the Reformed Tradition," *Church History* 15 (1946), 179.

Calvin says, "I will not deny that aristocracy, or a system composed of aristocracy and democracy, far excels all others."[110] Also Calvin says, "the Lord confirmed it by his authority when he ordained among the Israelites an aristocracy bordering on democracy, since he willed to keep them in the best condition."[111] As McNeill says, "his notion of 'aristocracy tempered by democracy' approaches our conception of representative democracy."[112] In other words, Calvin advocates a form of political government which consists of government by the best men amongst the people. The people are the outer circle, and the best men the inner circle.

---

[110] *Inst.* 4:20:8, OS 5:478:23-24.

[111] "tum sua quoque authoritate Dominus confirmavit quum aristocratiam politiae vicinam apud Israelitas instituit, quum optima conditione eos habere vellet" (*Inst.* 4:20:8, OS 5:479: 3-6).

[112] John T. McNeill, "The Democratic Element in Calvin's Thought" in *Church History* 18 (1949), 169.

Mettre ordre en l'Eglise de Dieu: The Election of Officers in Calvin's Sermons on the Acts of the Apostles

Wilhelmus H. Th. Moehn

In his letter to Cardinal Sadolet, Calvin described the Reformation as "restoring the better form of the Church."[1] One of the most important sources for Calvin's image of the *vetusta ecclesiae facies* is the book of Acts. From those sermons he held on this book, 44 sermons have survived in manuscript; seven sermons were already published in the sixteenth century.[2]

The subject matter of the first part of the Acts offers the preacher a regular opportunity to draw a line from the early church to the actions of contemporary church life. Calvin, amongst other things, pays attention to the care for the poor, the duty of officers, the functioning of the "Consistoire" and the marks of the church (Acts 2:42).

In this article, we will confine ourselves to one sermon in which Calvin pays attention to the way in which officers should be elected. How does he translate the details as described in the book of Acts into his sixteenth-century Geneva?

I. Elections According to Acts 6

Acts 6:1-3 offers an opportunity to consider not only the diaconal responsibility of the congregation, but also the way in which officers are elected in a Christian congregation. For the purpose of our research we are mainly interested in the way the members of the congregation participate in this process and the way their role should be assessed. In relation to the attention which is paid

---

[1]J. Calvin, *Responsio ad Sadoleti Epistolam* (OS 1:466): "... non modo longe meliorem nobis cum antiquitate consensionem esse quam vobis, sed nihil aliud conari quam ut instauretur aliquando vetusta illa ecclesiae facies." See for Calvin's valuation of the early church, D. Fischer, "L'histoire de L'Église dans la pensée de Calvin," *Archiv für Reformationsgeschichte* 77 (1986), 103-107.

[2]The 44 sermons have been edited by W. Balke and W. H. Th. Moehn: J. Calvin, *Sermons on the Acts of the Apostles,* SC 8 (Neukirchen-Vluyn: Neukirchener Verlag des Erziehungsvereins, 1994). The seven sermons which have been edited in the *Calvini Opera* are now being prepared for the COR edition. The "Premier sermon de la Pentecoste" (CO 48:623-36) does not belong in the *lectio continua* series on Acts; see SC 8:xvi, n. 49.

to the care for the poor and to the polemics with regards to the Roman Catholic view of the diaconate, relatively little attention is paid to the actual *election* of the deacons. Calvin gives his attention to this theme only in two short fragments in *Sermon* 23. He attempts to draw a line from the first Christian community to the practice of the election in his own age. It is remarkable that in both these fragments he criticises the way the members of the congregation participate in the elections. The apostles gathered the entire congregation *[toute l'Eglise],* as usual with Christians. At the end of the sermon, Calvin expressly claims that not just a few, but all people should look for suitable persons.[3]

> It would please God also at this moment, if this rule was still applied, that there would be an election for the entire people for all public offices, so that no person would be admitted unless he was approved. This is the custom with worldly offices and spiritual tasks. They treat the matter lightly, so that it seems that they are merely asking to elect him in private. But when a servant of God's word is to be elected, everyone should be burning with zeal in order to be able to elect the most suitable person for this office; there should be a public election and everyone should be invited. Mais quoy? Herewith we demonstrate that we only possess half a Christianity and that we hardly care for the way in which God's church is governed.[4]

The procedure involving the election of the "seven" is not exclusively used for the election of the deacons, but also for the election of the "ministres" and the government officials. Calvin uses general rules from the actual election of seven suitable persons in Jerusalem, which should apply in his age as well.

The quotation demonstrates that the situation in Geneva is not entirely according to Calvin's wishes. On the other hand, the sermon does not provide a clear image of the abuses he refers to. Also when he talks about the elections for the second time, he does not give an explanation: "Whenever there are elections—no matter which one—it is as if we ask for God's wrath when we mock him. Whenever elections of officers and deacons are concerned, we

[3]SC 8:203:25-26: "Or il n'est pas seulement dict qu'il faille qu'il y en ait quelzques ungs qui ayent le regard à cela, c'est à sçavoir d'eslire gentz propres à cest estat, mais il est commandé à toute l'Eglise d'en avoir soing." Cf. *Comm. Acts* 6:3 (COR II/12/1:166:14-15; CO 48:120): "Quod ad praesentem locum spectat, primum electio permittitur Ecclesiae."

[4]SC 8:197:15-22: "Et pleust à Dieu que fust encores aujourd'huy observé, qu'en toutes les commissions et charges publicques, il y avoit election de tout le peuple, afin que nul n'y fust admis, sinon qu'il fust bien approuvé. On faict cela aux offices de ce monde et aulx charges spirituelles. On s'en acquictera legierement, qu'il semble qu'on ne demande qu'à le couler soubz le bras, que s'il est question d'eslire ung ministre de la parolle de Dieu, il fauldroit bien qu'ung chacun eust ung zele ardent de pouvoir choisir ung homme tel qu'il conviendroit bien à cest estat, qu'il y eust election publicque et qu'ung chacun fust convocqué. Mais quoy? En cela monstrons nous que nous avons seulement une chrestienté à demy, et qu'il ne nous chault guieres comment l'Eglise de Dieu soit gouvernée."

should realise that these are not unimportant."[5] In what way are the elections a mockery? Which people give reason for the accusation of "une chrestienté à demy"? The members of the congregation themselves, the magistrates or perhaps even the preachers? In order to be able to answer these questions, we should first consider the way officers were elected in Geneva, as well as the theological motivation in the background.

II. The Task of Ministers and Congregation

There are several ways in which officers might be elected within a congregation. "Someone now asks whether the minister ought to be chosen by the whole church *[a tota Ecclesia]*, or only by his colleagues and the elders charged with the censure of morals, or whether he ought to be appointed by the authority of a single person."[6] Those who appeal to the method of Timothy in Ephesus or Titus in Crete, thinking that they could decide everything according to their wish, are mistaken. "For they were over the rest only to give good and salutary advice to the people, not that they alone, in disregard of all the rest, might do what they pleased!"[7] Also in the case of the Greeks and Romans the people were actively involved in the elections. Appealing to Cyprian,[8] Calvin deems it justified that the priest is elected in the presence of the people *[plebe praesente]* while all eyes are on him, and that the priest is considered dignified and suitable in public judgement and testimony *[publico iudicio ac testimonio]*. "In the same way Matthias is appointed to the company of the apostles; in the same way the seven deacons are created—with the people looking on and approving."[9] On the basis of the Scriptures Calvin concludes that there is a double responsibility of both the congregation and the already confirmed officers: "We there-

[5]SC 8:203:27-29: "Quand donc on faira des elections, je ne sçay quelles, c'est autant comme si nous amassions l'ire de Dieu sur nous, en nous mocquant de luy. Quand il est question d'eslire des ministres et des diacres, il fault que nous congnoissons que ce n'est pas petite chose."

[6]*Inst.* 4:3:15 (OS 5:55:10-12). Translations from the *Institutes* are from the McNeill-Battles edition.

[7]Ibid. (OS 5:55:18-20): "Praefuerunt enim tantum ut bonis et salutaribus consiliis populo praeirent: non ut soli, exclusis aliis omnibus, agerent quod placeret." Cf. *Comm. Tit.* 1:5 (CO 52:409): "Sed videtur nimium Tito permittere, dum iubet eum praeficere omnibus ecclesiis ministros. Haec enim fere regia esset potestas: deinde hoc modo et singulis ecclesiis ius eligendi, et pastorum collegio iudicium tollitur: id vero esset totam sacram ecclesiae administrationem profanare. Verum responsio facilis est, non permitti arbitrio Titi ut unus possit omnia, et quos voluerit episcopos ecclesiis imponat: sed tantum iubet ut electionibus praesit tanquam moderator, sicuti necesse est."

[8]On Calvin's use of Cyprian see A. Zillenbiller, *Die Einheit der katholischen Kirche. Calvins Cyprianrezeption in seinen ekklesiologischen Schriften*, Veröffentlichungen des Instituts für Europäische Geschichte Mainz. Abteilung für abendländische Religionsgeschichte 151 (Mainz: Philipp von Zabern, 1993), 106-111.

[9]*Inst.* 4:3:15 (OS 5:56:9-10).

fore hold that this call of a minister is lawful according to the Word of God, when those who seemed fit are created by the consent and approval of the people *[ex populi consensu et approbatione]*; moreover, that other pastors ought to preside over the election in order that the multitude may not go wrong either through fickleness, through evil intentions, or through disorder."

Calvin does not only seek an association with the Scriptures, he also looks at the practice of the early church. "Moreover, the holy fathers took care that this freedom of the people should in no way be diminished. Consequently, when the universal synod which was gathered at Constantinople ordained Nectarius, it refused to do so without the approval of *all clergy and people*."[10] Calvin also mentions the Council in Laodicea, where it was ordained that the election should not be left entirely to the people. According to Calvin, however, this was decided in order to avoid that such an election would cause confusion and strife. The intention was to withstand the foolish desires of the people. That is the reason why the people were given the task to ratify a certain appointment after it was made.

An election could be realised in two ways:

(a) First the clergy alone made their choice; they then presented the person they had chosen to the magistrates or senate and leading citizens. The latter, after deliberation, ratified the election if it seemed just; if not, they chose another whom they preferred. Then they brought the matter before the people, who although not bound by the previous decisions, nevertheless could not raise a tumult.

(b) Or if they began with the people, this was done only to find out whom they especially desired. After the people's desires were heard, the clergy then made their choice. Thus, neither were the clergy allowed to appoint whom they wished, nor was it necessary for them to follow the foolish desires of the people.[11]

Until this moment, the government stayed out of sight, but during the Council of Laodicea, which took place in the fourth century, the government or the council came between the clergy and the members of the congregation —a place which the government would maintain in Geneva as well, as we shall soon see.

Calvin envisaged a good cooperation between officers and members of the congregation. Referring to 2 Corinthians 8:18, he said: "In this procedure lead-

---

[10]*Inst.* 4:4:11 (OS 5:68:27-31, emphasis added): "... id facere noluerit sine totius cleri et populi approbatione." See for the appeal to the early church also J. Bohatec, *Calvins Lehre von Staat und Kirche mit besonderer Berücksichtigung des Organismusgedankens,* Untersuchungen zur deutschen Staats- und Rechtsgeschichte 147 (Breslau: M. & M. Marcus, 1937; reprint Aalen: Scientia Verlag, 1968), 482-91 and R. J. Mooi, *Het kerk- en dogmahistorisch element in de werken van Johannes Calvijn* (Wageningen: H. Veenman & Zonen, 1965), 74-75.

[11]*Inst.* 4:4:12 (OS 5:69:15-24).

ers of authority and counsel took precedence and regulated the election while the common people cast their votes."[12] However, the heart of the matter is with the officers. In connection with this issue, it is remarkable that he frequently mentions his concern about whether the multitude is able to judge.[13] Calvin recognises the dangers of tyranny and autocracy, but he is mainly concerned about the threat of the anonymous crowd: "And this is the middle way between tyranny and disorderly licence, for it means that nothing indeed may be done except by the consent and approval of the people; but on the other hand that the pastors may rule with their authority like a bridle to hold in check the impulses of the people, to prevent their enthusiasm running away with them."[14] The short survey of the theological and church-historical foundation of the practice of the election in Geneva justifies the conclusion that the call originated from the entire congregation, even though the preachers played a decisive role in the election.[15]

III. The Ecclesiastical Ordonnances

In the procedure for the election of preachers, *Les Ordonnances ecclésiastiques* (1541) explicitly refer to the Scriptures and the practice of the early church. First of all, the preachers choose a person who according to them should be confirmed in the office. Subsequently, this person is introduced to the Council.

---

[12] *Comm. 2 Cor. 8:18* (Calvin, *The Second Epistle of Paul the Apostle to the Corinthians and the Epistles to Timothy, Titus and Philemon,* eds. D. W. & T. F. Torrance (Grand Rapids: Eerdmans, 1964), 116.; COR II/15:146:15-17; CO 50:103-104): "In qua praeibant authoritate et consilio primores totamque actionem gubernabant. Plebs autem sciscebat."

[13] Cf. *Inst.* 4:3:15 (OS 5:56:17-18), Inst. 4:4:12 (OS 5:69:29-33) and SC 8:195:35-36: "Ce proverbe là est aussi veritable, comme il est ancien, 'que multitude engendre confusion'." Calvin expresses his opinion of the "multitude" in his commentary on Seneca's *De clementia,* ed. F. L. Battles, A. M. Hugo, Renaissance Text Series 3 (Leiden: E. J. Brill, 1969), 4:31-33: "Multitudinem seditiosam, discordem &c.) sunt haec epitheta perpetua multitudinis, seditiosa, discors, impotens: nec sine ratione imposita." Cf. *De clementia* 4:38-5:11. Preaching on Acts 4:32 "Qu'il y avoit ung coeur et une ame en la multitude des croyans," Calvin said: "Sainct Luc parle expressement de la multitude, ... car c'est une chose plus admirable, quand nous voyons une grande assemblée de gentz, qui toutesfoys s'accordent, que s'il y avoit deux ou troys hommes ou une douzaine qui eussent amytié ensemble. Il se peult faire qu'ilz se pourront accorder. Mais quand il y a multitude, sinon que le sainct Esprit gouverne, il fault qu'il y ait confusion et que les hommes se monstrent telz qu'ilz sont de nature. ... Et ainsi c'est ung miracle evident quand il y a une grande multitude qui vit en paix," SC 8:114:6-15.

[14] *Comm. Acts 6:3* (Calvin, *The Acts of the Apostles,* eds. D. W. & T. F. Torrance (Grand Rapids: Eerdmans, 1977), 1:161; COR II/12/1:166:19-23; CO 48:120-21): "Atque hoc inter tyrannidem et confusam licentiam medium est, ut nihil quidem agitur nisi ex consensu et approbatione plebis; pastores tamen moderentur, ut eorum authoritas instar fraeni sit ad cohibendos plebis impetus, ne ultra modum exultent." See also *Comm. Acts* 14:23 (COR II/12/2:22; CO 48:333).

[15] Cf. B. Ch. Milner, *Calvin's Doctrine of the Church,* Studies in the History of Christian Thought 5 (Leiden: E. J. Brill, 1970), 140: "The call comes from the church as a body, even though the 'college of pastors' will have played a decisive role in the election."

The Council receives and accepts him, if in fact they approve of him. They recommend him, in order to propose him during the service *[en la predication]* to the community of saints, so that he might be received by common consent. If he is legitimately proven to be unworthy, the procedure has to be repeated to appoint someone else.[16] The *Ordonnances ecclésiastiques* provide the Council with the opportunity to bring legal objections against a candidate. If there are valid reasons, the vote of the members of the Council is of such consequence that a new candidate will have to be appointed.

IV. Participation of Laymen

What light is shed by *Sermon* 23 on the question of the importance which Calvin attaches to the vote of the congregation? We already heard how Calvin voiced his criticism of the Genevan situation: "they treat the matter lightly, so that it seems like they merely ask to appoint him in private"; "here should be a public election and everybody should be admitted" and "we demonstrate herewith that we only possess half a Christianity and we hardly care for the way in which God's church is governed." Especially the second admonition about a public election justifies the conjecture that Calvin is not really criticising the members of the congregation, but "le Conseil," which is not giving sufficient attention to the third phase of the procedure—the agreement of the congregation. An editorial note in the adapted *Ordonnances ecclésiastiques* from 1561 confirms this idea: "Addition of that which has been discussed and decreed in the Council of the two hundred on 9 February 1560, in order to explain how this article on the presentation should be understood and to repair the mistaken customs regarding this issue."[17] The specification demonstrates that preachers who had been approved by the Council had been introduced to the

[16] *Ord. eccl., Registres de la Compagnie des Pasteurs de Genève au temps de Calvin* (henceforth RCP), vol. 1, 1546-53, ed. R. M. Kingdon, J.-F. Bergier, Travaux d'Humanisme et Renaissance 55 (Genève: Droz, 1964), 2 (OS 2:329:23-31). A. Ganoczy, *Ecclesia ministrans. Dienende Kirche und kirchlicher Dienst bei Calvin,* Ökumenische Forschungen 1. Ekklesiologische Abteilung 3 (Freiburg: Herder, 1968), 262 does not involve the sentence "S'il estoit trouvé indigne et demonstré tel par probations legitimes, il fauldroit lors proceder à nouvelle election pour en prendre un aultre" in his analysis. The edition of the *Ord. eccl.* in the *Opera Selecta* easily gives cause for a deletion of this final sentence. Because of an extended addition in 1561, this sentence has ended up on p. 330, l. 32-34. See, however, the better arranged edition in RCP 1:2 and E. Rivoire, V. van Berchem, ed., *Les sources du droit du canton de Genève,* Les sources du droit Suisse, xxiie partie, 4 vols. (Arau: Sauerländer, 1927-1935), 2:378:19-21. H. Höpfl, *The Christian Polity of John Calvin,* Cambridge Studies in the History and Theory of Politics (Cambridge: Cambridge University Press, 1982), 92 does pay attention to this sentence, but he minimalises its significance: "The possibility of a candidate being found unworthy, and hence of the need for a new election, was indeed mentioned, but no arrangements were provided for such an eventuality." In our view, the sentence "il fauldroit lors proceder à nouvelle election" refers back to the beginning of the article on the election of preachers, and is at this place sufficiently mentioned with regards to the procedure which had to be followed.

[17] *Ord. eccl.,* OS 2:330:1-4.

congregation, but it had not been asked for an approbation. As a result, the audience and the entire body of the church were deprived of their freedom and awareness.[18] If members of the congregation are opposed to an appointed preacher, they will have the opportunity forthwith to bring their objections forward on the day before his presentation. This procedure attempted to avoid confusion at the moment the congregation is asked for its approval. Also, from the *Registres de la Compagnie des Pasteurs* it does not appear that members of the congregation were asked for their approval. On 13 September 1549 Jehan Fabri was chosen by the preachers instead of Jean Ferron, who had been deposed because of sexual abuse. There is only an "oath in front of the members of the council in the accustomed manner."[19] Within the rule of church life, Calvin is wary of a gagged congregation. Although it would take until 1561 for an alteration in the *Ordonnances ecclésiastiques,* Calvin already in his sermon of 10 August 1550 reminded the government of its task to take seriously the opinion of the audience regarding the candidate. It cannot be that a preacher is forced upon a congregation against its will.

In the decade between the sermon on Acts 6 and the underscoring of the text of the *Ordonnances ecclésiastiques,* Calvin's attention to the position of members of the congregation can be demonstrated at several times. On Friday 24 April 1556, Lois Enoch is elected as preacher. On Sunday 10 May, he is presented to the congregation together with Jean Macart; the audience are mentioned explicitly:

> ... M. Jean Macart, ministre de Ressin et de Dardainiés, estant appellé pour prescher en la ville, fut presenté, ensemble ledit M. Lois Enoch, au peuple, assavoir en la predicacion du matin 8 heures à Sainct Pierre, et à .3. heures après midi à St. Gervais.[20]

[18] *Ord. eccl.,* OS 2:330:5-12: "Item, sur ce que lesdits spectables Ministres nous ont remonstré, que l'ordonnance faicte sur leur presentation n'avoit point esté gardee, d'autant que ceux qui estoyent esleuz et acceptez par la Seigneurie ont esté presentez simplement au temple, sans demander si on les approuvoit: et que par cela le peuple et tout le corps de l'Eglise ont esté fraudez de leur liberté, enquoy aussi il nous est apparu qu'on s'estoit destourné de ce qui avoit esté bien estably du commencement." See for this alteration also J. Plomp, *De kerkelijke tucht bij Calvijn* (Kampen: J. H. Kok, 1969), 191.

[19] RCP 1:62-63: "Le lundi 28e jour d'octobre les freres de la ville furent pardevant Messieurs pour presenter lad. Fabri et fere rapport de ce qu'ilz avoient entendu de luy tant de sa vie que de sa doctrine. ... Led. Fabri fut receu pour ministre de ceste eglise de Geneve, et feit le serment devant nosd. Seigneurs à la maniere acoustumee." See for the procedure of the deposition of Ferron RCP 1:58-61. Also in the election of Nicolas Colladon the congregation is not mentioned: "Le 12e jour de may 1553 fut esleu au lieu de maistre Philippes de Ecclesia maistre Nicolas Coladon. Et après avoir proposé et presché selon la coustume, après avoir esté examiné, fut presenté à Messieurs le jeudi 18e dud. mois, qui luy assignerent lieu à Vandouvre et Couloigny" (RCP 1:160).

[20] RCP 2:67.

Three years later—Calvin is preaching on the Synoptic Gospels—he informs the congregation twice at the end of a sermon about the election of preachers. They are given an opportunity to mention their objections, if they have any. After Calvin held a sermon on Mark 1:23-27, he announced preceding the final prayer:

> Or il reste de vous advertir que pour annoncer la parole de Dieu en ceste ville, il y a Maistre Iean Remond Merlin qui a esté eleu et accepté de Messieurs: et d'autant qu'il sera presenté Dimanche prochain, au plaisir de Dieu, si quelqu'un sçait à redire sur luy, ou en sa vie ou en sa doctrine, qu'il le vienne dire où il appartiendra.[21]

Merlin had already been elected preacher of Poissy on 17 March 1559.[22] At the appointment "en ceste ville," a short period later, the *Compagnie des pasteurs* deemed it necessary to grant the audience a period of time in which they could react. Some weeks later, a preacher had to be elected once again. Once again, the audience were invited to react, whenever they thought it necessary to do so. At this point, it also becomes clear to the body of the congregation what motivation is at the background of this appeal:

> Or il y a encores un petit mot, c'est que Messieurs ont accepté que nostre frere N. soit appelé en ceste ville, lequel a desia servi au ministere par ci devant à Iussi. Mais *afin que la liberté soit gardée à toute l'Eglise,* d'autant qu'il doit estre presenté Dimanche prochain, si quelqu'un sçavoit à redire sur luy, qu'il l'aille annoncer à Messieurs entre ci et Dimanche.[23]

The combination of the details from the sermons and the *Registres de la Compagnie des Pasteurs* clearly show that on the one hand Calvin desired to guarantee the freedom of the audience and to respect it as much as possible while,

---

[21]Serm. 59, Mark 1:23-27, par. (CO 46:748). Cf. the next sermon on Mark 1:29-39, par. (CO 46:758): "Or maintenant (comme il vous a esté predit) d'autant que nostre Seigneur en a retiré quelques uns de ceste Eglise, les uns par mort, les autres par absence, il faloit que nous fussions pourveus afin que l'ordre de l'Eglise s'entretiene. Et suyvant l'advertissement qui vous en a esté fait, le frere qui est yci present a esté eleu et accepté de Messieurs. Que reste-il? Il faut que maintenant, puis qu'il y a un Ministre à instituer, nous pensions à ce que dit nostre Seigneur Jesus Christ..."

[22]See RCP 2:86.

[23]Serm. 63, Matt. 5:5-7, par. (CO 46:798, emphasis added). See also Serm. 64, Matt. 5:8-10, par. (CO 46:808-809): "Au reste, pource que le temps ne porteroit pas que ceci fust deduit plus au long: maintenant, d'autant que le frere qui est yci present, ayant desia auparavant servi en un endroit au ministere de ceste Eglise, a esté accepté de Messieurs, et ordonné pour y servir d'oresenavant en ceste ville: que toutesfois et quantes qu'il y a un ministre à recevoir, nous cognoissions à quelle fin c'est..." Cf. RCP 2:64: "Vendredy 28e dudit mois de juing [1555]... M. Pierre Airebaudouse fut esleu pour estre envoié à Jussy, au lieu de M. Nicolas des Galars," and RCP 2:93: (date: Septembre 1560) "Le (blanc) notre frere maistre Pierre de Airebaudouze, ministre à Jussi fut appellé de là en ceste ville pour le mesme office, et maistre Jehan Pinaut, qui enseignoit les enfans de l'hospital, fut esleu et envoyé à Jussi pour y administrer la Parole de Dieu."

on the other hand, the announcements in subsequent sermons evidently demonstrate a silent acceptation by the members of the congregation.[24]

V. Conclusion

The sermon on Acts 6:1-3 shows that for a preacher the involvement of the entire congregation in the elections is an important affair. It would be a good thing if the entire congregation would be involved in the approval. In research, however, the question about the assessment of this approval is not an undisputed issue. A. Ganoczy prefers a minimal interpretation: the congregation is only allowed to give its consent.[25] F. Wendel also agrees that the actual election is an affair of preachers and magistrates. For the members of the congregation the election is reduced to "une simple approbation" of the choice of the preachers and magistrates.[26] In his view, this is in accordance with Calvin's aristocratic tendencies. However, W. Niesel thinks that the election belongs to the congregation.[27] In practice this concerns a cooperation between preachers and the entire congregation. Niesel arrived at this positive judgement because he eliminates the role of the magistrate entirely and exclusively analyses the *Institutes* and the commentaries, without involving the *Ordonnances ecclésiastiques.*

A well-balanced appreciation of Calvin's point of view cannot be achieved by placing a framework of the twentieth-century model of democratic elections over Calvin's statements. His care for the independence of the members of the congregation should be seen in the light of the position of the church in the sixteenth century. On the one hand, the right to vote that members of the congregation possessed is limited to the giving of consent to an election which in effect took place by the members of the *Compagnie des pasteurs* and the members of the Council. On the other hand, the *Ordonnances* of 1561 guaranteed the freedom of the entire congregation because of its approval. We also observed that a rejec-

[24]See Calvin's letter to Olevianus, 25 November 1560 (CO 18:235, nr. 3272): "Primum eliguntur ministri a nostro collegio: ac datur illis scripturae locus, in cuius interpretatione specimen suae dexteritatis edant. Deinde examen habetur de praecipuis doctrinae capitibus: tandem coram nobis perinde ut apud populum concionantur. Adsunt etiam duo ex senatu. Si probatur eorum eruditio, eos senatui cum testimonio offerimus: in cuius arbitrio est non admittere, si minus idoneos esse iudicet. Quod si recipiuntur (ut semper hactenus contigit) tum nomina promulgamus coram populo, ut si quod vitium latuerit, liberum sit singulis ante octo dies indicare. *Qui tacitis omnium suffragiis probantur,* eos commendamus Deo et ecclesiae" (emphasis added).

[25]Ganoczy, *Ecclesia ministrans,* 263, 266: "Das Volk wird nur um die Zustimmung gebeten... die Rolle des Volkes beschränkte er auf die bloße Zustimmung" (emphasis added).

[26]F. Wendel, Calvin. *Sources et évolution de sa pensée religieuse* (Paris: Presses Universitaires de France, 1950), 231. Cf. H. J. Grimm, *The Reformation Era 1500-1650* (New York: Macmillan, 2nd edition, 1973), 278 and Höpfl, *The Christian Polity,* 92: "The congregation's part in all this was that of a cypher."

[27]W. Niesel, *Die Theologie Calvins,* Einführung in die evangelische Theologie 6 (München: Chr. Kaiser, 2nd edition, 1957), 204: "Die Wahl steht grundsätzlich der Kirche, d.h. der Gemeinde, zu."

tion by the congregation—if justified—has to be allowed. However, because the church is a *corpus permixtum,* it has to be taken into account that also hypocrites and dissemblers are involved in the election of officers. For this reason, Calvin thinks it is unwarranted to place the election entirely in the hands of the congregation. Instead, he argues in favour of a leading role of the officers, and he means herewith to follow the example of the Scriptures and the early church, if an election is not against the will of the congregation. Calvin clearly demonstrates his sense of reality regarding this issue.[28] The way in which he declares his wishes and ideals regarding (church) elections leads to the conclusion that he was looking for a maximum participation of the members of the congregation in the elections within the contemporary context of the church. The election by the people, "afin que nul n'y fust admis, sinon qu'il fust bien approuvé,"[29] includes a condition which should not be neglected or underestimated.

---

[28]Cf. Bohatec, *Calvins Lehre,* 494.

[29]SC 8:197:16-17; see above note 4.

Calvin lecteur de la Bible en chaire

Max Engammare

Il s'est agit dans ce séminaire de commencer par déterminer l'exemplaire de la Bible en hébreu avec laquelle Calvin montait en chaire à Saint-Pierre de Genève ou à la Madeleine pour prêcher tous les jours, une semaine sur deux, à partir d'un texte de l'Ancien Testament. Dans un second temps, nous avons recherché quelques usages et principes du Calvin prédicateur face à sa traduction établie chaque jour sans note.

La Bible ou mieux les Bibles qu'utilisait Calvin

Au début de chacune de ses prédications, Calvin commence par traduire le texte du jour. Pour une prédication fondée sur un texte vétéro-testamentaire, il utilise une Bible en hébreu, T.H.L. Parker, le premier, l'a mis en évidence pour les sermons sur Esaïe.[1] Je le confirme sans hésiter pour les sermons sur la Genèse, grâce à la critique textuelle et à l'examen des traductions, mais également avec une remarque comme celle que l'on trouve dans le 23e sermon sur la Genèse, à propos de Genèse 4:8.

> Or il est vray que les Juifz mettent icy comme un espace en blanc, à cause qu'il leur semble que l'oraison n'est point accomplie. Mais Moise a parlé comme en suspend et a voulu signifier en somme que Cain a fait ses plaintes, comme si son frere l'avoit grevé et qu'il luy eust fait grande injure, d'autant qu'il estoit plus agreable à Dieu.[2]

Cette remarque n'a de sens que devant une Bible en hébreu. En effet, la deuxième *Biblia rabbinica* de Daniel Bomberg saute une ligne;[3] les *Quinque libri*

---

[1]Cf. T. H. L. Parker, *Calvin's Preaching* (Edinburgh: T & T Clark, 1992), 80ss et appendix 3 (172ss); *Sermons sur le livre d'Esaïe, chapitres 30-41,* Supplementa Calviniana 3, éd. T. H. L. Parker et F. M. Higman (Neukirchen-Vluyn: Neukirchener Verlag, 1995), XX-XXV.

[2]23e sermon sur la Genèse. Je me réfère à mon édition, *Sermons de Jean Calvin sur la Genèse, chapitres 1 à 20,4,* Supplementa Calviniana 11/1 et 11/2 (Neukirchen-Vluyn: Neukirchener Verlag, 2000), 264.

[3](Venise, 1524-1525), f° [Ivi]a.

Legis de Robert Estienne laissent un blanc d'une demi-ligne.[4] En revanche la seconde *Biblia hebraica de Münster*,[5] donne simplement la réclame "beth," première lettre du premier mot de la ligne suivante: "biheyôtham" ("quand ils étaient, furent"), sans espace inséré. La première édition de Münster possédait bien, quant à elle, un blanc d'un quart de ligne.[6] Le commentaire de Calvin ne dit mot de cet espace, pas davantage que Münster, Fagius,[7] Musculus, Borrhaeus, sans parler de Luther ou Zwingli, chez les contemporains; Rashi et Ibn Ezra ne relèvent pas davantage cet intervalle. Seul Pellikan, à ma connaissance, mentionne ce blanc.[8] Cette remarque sur l'espace, indice indéniable du fait que Calvin prêchait à partir du texte hébreu, se voit confirmée par l'étude des traductions, nous y reviendrons.

Il est quasi certain que Calvin lisait l'hébreu dans la *Biblia hebraica* de Münster. En effet, dans la traduction à l'entame du cinquième sermon, les derniers mots du verset 24 et les premiers du verset 25 de Genèse 1 manquent. Ces mots correspondent, au dernier mot près, à une ligne de l'édition de Münster 1534 (f° 1b, ligne hébraïque 25) ou 1546 (p. 2, ligne hébraïque 21), mais non aux Bibles de Bomberg, ni à celles d'Estienne 1539-1544 (in-quarto) ou 1543-1544 (in-16°):

wayehî-qèn waya'as 'élohîm 'ét-ḥayyath hâ'âréṣ lemînâh.[9]

Le dernier mot "lemînâh" ("selon son [ou leur] espèce") commençant déjà la ligne précédente, on comprend facilement que le doigt de Calvin ait glissé. Dans mon étude sur la prédication de Calvin sur Genèse 3,[10] je n'avais mentionné que la Bible de 1546, comme Tony Lane l'a fait remarquer.[11] La com-

---

4(Paris, 1544), f° biia.

5(Bâle: M. Isengrinus & H. Petrus, 1546), 10.

6*Hebraica biblia* (Bâle: M. Isengrinus & H. Petrus, 1534), f° 3b.

7Fagius ne mentionne pas l'espace blanc, mais rapporte la leçon du Targum de Jérusalem qui a pallié l'absence du dialogue en l'inventant. Cf. Paul Fagius, *Exegesis sive expositio dictionum hebraicarum literalis et simplex, in quatuor capita Geneseos, pro studiosis linguae hebraicae* (Isnae, 1542), 131s.

8"Habent hic Hebraeorum codices intercapedinem, quasi aliquid inde ablatum sit ex versu." Cf. Konrad Pellikan, *Commentaria Bibliorum et illa brevia quidem ac catholica,* t. 1 (Zurich: Christophorus Froschauer, 1532), f° 8a.

9"Et fut ainsi fait. Dieu donc fit l'animau de la terre selon son espece."

10"Le paradis à Genève. Comment Calvin prêchait-il la Chute aux Genevois?" *Etudes théologiques et religieuses* 69 (1994), 332s (329-47).

11Anthony N. S. Lane, "The sources of Calvin's citations in his Genesis commentary," in A. N. S. Lane, ed., *Interpreting the Bible. Historical and Theological Studies in Honour of David F. Wright* (Leicester: Apollos, 1997), 63, n. 62 (47-97).

position de cette ligne étant identique dans les deux éditions (j'avais distribué une photocopie des deux passages), on ne peut juger sur cet unique élément, ni d'ailleurs sur le fait que seule l'édition de 1534-35 est mentionnée dans le catalogue de la Bibliothèque de l'Académie en 1572, pour avancer que Calvin possédait la première édition.[12] Pourtant l'espace blanc en Genèse 4:8, matérialisé en 1534-35 et non en 1546, constitue un indice bien plus important pour avancer que Calvin utilisait la première édition de Münster, ayant pu l'acheter quand il suivit les cours de l'hébraïsant à Bâle en 1535-1536.

On doit pourtant se rappeler que Calvin possédait également une Bible rabbinique, celle qui avait appartenu à Olivétan. Le 5 septembre 1539, Christophe Fabri (Libertet), l'ami d'Olivétan, écrivait à Calvin pour lui parler de la Bibliothèque de son parent, puisqu'il en avait hérité une partie. Quelques semaines plus tard, Calvin répondait, remerciait et souhaitait que les livres soient vendus (ce qui est du reste étonnant d'un point de vue intellectuel, mais se comprend d'un point de vue financier: Calvin étant peu fortuné), à l'exception de la Bible hébraïque reliée en deux volumes, le Psautier ayant été séparé des autres livres. Calvin justifiait d'ailleurs son choix:

> Je souhaite cependant avoir deux volumes, si cela ne te dérange pas: la Bible vénitienne et le Psautier. Je sais en effet que les psaumes manquent au volume principal. La raison de mon souhait est qu'Olivétan a numéroté scrupuleusement tous les versets.[13]

Si Calvin possédait cette Bible de Bomberg, facile à utiliser pour un néophyte, puisque complètement numérotée à la main, il ne semble pas, à cause du saut de ligne relevé, que Calvin l'ait utilisé en chaire (d'autant plus qu'il s'agissait d'un instrument juif et non chrétien, au contraire de l'édition de Münster).

Alt- sondern kein Neutestamentler, je n'ai pas poussé très loin les recherches pour le Nouveau Testament, mais si Willem Balke et Wilhelmus Moehn, les derniers à avoir édité des sermons de Calvin sur le Nouveau Testament, n'ont pas affirmé fortement que Calvin prêchait à partir du grec, leurs remarques nous invitent à aller jusque là, puisque la traduction que Calvin donne des premiers chapitres sur les Actes diffère des Bibles neuchâteloise de 1535 et genevoises de 1546 et 1551.[14]

---

[12]Cf. Alexandre Ganoczy, *La Bibliothèque de l'Académie de Calvin,* Études de Philologie et d'Histoire 13 (Genève: Droz, 1969), 160; mais également 4s (car ce ne sont pas tous les livres de Calvin qui furent choisis par Bèze en 1564, que certains furent déjà vendus en 1569, et que d'autres fonds furent rapidement incorporés aux livres de Calvin).

[13]"Duos tantum habere optem, nisi tibi molestum erit: Biblia veneta et psalterium. Scio enim psalterium a majori volumine abesse. Causa haec est meae cupiditatis, quod Olivetanus diligenter omnes versus suis numeris notavit" (A.-L. Herminjard, *Correspondance des réformateurs dans les pays de langue française,* 9 vols (Genève-Paris: H. Georg, 1866-1897), 6:30s (lettre n° 818)). La lettre du 5 septembre 1539 correspond au n° 816 (ibid., 13-27).

[14]*Sermons on the Acts of the Apostles,* Supplementa Calviniana 8, éd. Willem Balke et Wilhelmus H. Th. Moehn (Neukirchen-Vluyn: Neukirchener Verlag, 1994), XX.

Il faudrait maintenant identifier l'édition grecque que Calvin utilisait. Il y a fort à parier que ce fut une édition d'Erasme, puisqu'il critiqua constamment les leçons et options du grand humaniste. On pourrait même supputer qu'il s'agissait de la quatrième édition de 1527, ou une édition antérieure, puisque la cinquième édition, parut en 1535, un an avant la mort d'Erasme; or, à cette date, Calvin s'était déjà intéressé au Nouveau Testament. En 1539, il ne demande d'ailleurs pas à Fabri de conserver pour lui l'édition du Nouveau Testament avec les annotations érasmiennes que possédait Olivétan.

Peut-on cependant estimer que Calvin montait en chaire avec une édition dont il ne partageait pas toutes les options? La discussion est ouverte.

L'usage des langues originales

Pourtant cette prédication à partir de l'hébreu n'est pas toujours sans surprise. Régulièrement la traduction de la péricope du jour laisse à désirer: oubli de mots, traductions fantaisistes, résumés, et autres approximations.[15] Les écarts de traduction n'apparaissent pas toujours devant des *hapax legomena,* mais sont également causés par des expressions difficiles. Plus intéressant, quand la traduction d'un jour a été approximative (celle des sermons 8 et 11 par exemple), le jour ou la semaine qui suivent, les traductions sont parfaites, que l'hébreu comporte des difficultés ou non (ainsi aux sermons 9 et 12). Il est indéniable que Calvin connaissait relativement bien l'hébreu biblique, la majorité des traductions données au début d'un sermon en font foi. Pourtant Calvin avait besoin de se préparer, de lire son texte du jour, d'utiliser un instrument de Münster si nécessaire pour offrir depuis la chaire une traduction parfaite.

J'ai montré ailleurs qu'il arrivait même à Calvin de se souvenir de la Vulgate, plutôt que de traduire l'hébreu, le "faciamus ei" étant l'un des exemples les plus probants.[16] Au sermon 11, sur Genèse 2:18-21, Calvin a traduit 'é'éséh-lô, non pas "je lui ferai," mais "faisons luy," égal au "faciamus ei," leçon de la traduction latine commune.[17]

Pire, j'ai même le soupçon qu'il est arrivé à Calvin de lorgner sur la traduction latine de Münster. C'est ce que je vous propose de regarder ensemble, pour que vous confirmiez ou infirmiez mon soupçon.

Au début du 75e sermon sur la Genèse du 22 mars 1560, Calvin donne la traduction de Genèse 16:1-4:

---

[15] On trouvera au début de chaque sermon l'analyse détaillée de la traduction biblique. Cf. également les démonstrations données dans mes articles "Le Paradis à Genève," 332-34, et "Joannes Calvinus trium linguarum peritus? La question de l'hébreu," *Bibliothèque d'Humanisme et Renaissance* 58 (1996), 35-60.

[16] Cf. "Le paradis à Genève."

[17] Cf. *Sermons de Jean Calvin sur la Genèse,* 125.

Or Sarai, la femme d'Abram, ne luy avoit point enfanté. Elle avoit une chambriere egyptienne nommée Agar. Sarai donc dit à Abram: Voicy maintenant le Seigneur m'a fermé la matrice, que je n'enfante point. Entre donc à ma chambriere, si je pourray estre edifiée d'elle. Abram obeit à la voix de Sarai. Et Sarai, femme d'Abram, print Agar, sa chambriere, au bout de dix ans qu'il avoit habité en la terre de Chanaan, et la donna à Abram, son mary, pour femme. Et estant entré à Agar, elle conceut. Et voyant qu'elle estoit enceinte, elle mesprisa sa maistresse.

Les différences entre l'hébreu et la traduction française de Calvin sont ici bien grandes:

Au v. 1, *lo' yâledâh* est simplement rendu "avoit point enfanté;" dans le commentaire: "avoit enfanté nul enfant (pepererat)." Surtout au v. 2, Calvin a rendu *'aṣâranî millédéth* par "m'a fermé la matrice," ce qui coïncide à la traduction latine du commentaire ("conclusit me ne parerem"), non au français: "m'a empeschée d'enfanter." Au v. 3, Calvin conserve la syntaxe de l'hébreu dans le sermon, comme dans le commentaire latin, alors qu'il redistribue autrement les informations dans la version française du commentaire.[18] Pour ce sermon, on pourrait même soupçonner Calvin d'avoir simplement traduit non l'hébreu, mais le latin de Münster (avec un doute pour le verset 2), tant le français de Calvin ressemble au latin de l'hébraïsant, dont je donne la version: "Itaque Sarai uxor Abram non genuit illi; habuit autem ancillam Aegyptiam, nomine Hagar. Dixitque Sarai ad Abram: en prohibuit me Dominus ne parerem; ingredere quaeso ad ancillam meam, si forte aedificer ex ea. Et obediebat Abram voci Sarai. Tulitque Sarai uxor Abram Hagar Aegyptiam ancillam suam a fine decem annorum, quo habitavit Abram in terra Chnaan, et dedit eam Abram marito suo in uxorem. Qui cum ingressus esset ad Hagar, concepit illa; videns quod se gravidam, vilipensa est domina eius in oculis suis."[19]

Ici encore la discussion est ouverte.

Le principe de la *lectio continua*

Dans sa prédication, comme dans ses leçons ou les congrégations, Calvin a adopté, à la suite des Zurichois et des Strasbourgeois,[20] le principe de la *lectio continua,* commençant l'explication d'un livre biblique au premier verset du

---

[18]Cf. *Commentaire de M. Jean Calvin sur le premier livre de Moyse, dit Genese* (Genève: Jean Girard, 1554), 182; *In Primum Mosis librum, qui Genesis vulgo dicitur, Commentarius* (Genève: Robert Estienne, 1554) [ci-après *Commentaire et Commentarius*] (CO 23:221s).

[19]Cf. Münster , *Biblia hebraica* [1534], f° 13v° (édition de 1546, 33).

[20]Cf. Gottfried Locher, *Die Zwinglische Reformation im Rahmen der europäischen Kirchengeschichte* (Göttingen et Zürich: Vandenhoeck & Ruprecht, 1979), 161s; François Wendel, *L'Eglise de Strasbourg, sa constitution et son organisation 1532-1535,* Études d'histoire et de philosophie religieuses publiées par la Faculté de théologie protestante de l'Université de Strasbourg 38 (Paris: Presses Universitaires de France, 1942), 210s.

premier chapitre et ne l'abandonnant qu'au dernier verset de l'ultime chapitre. Ce principe est bien connu, on sait qu'il rompt avec la pratique homilétique catholique romaine, ainsi qu'avec la pratique luthérienne, et on pourrait se satisfaire de ce constat. Ce principe génère pourtant un double effet pervers, que nous pouvons discuter, après une brève présentation.

Calvin prêche tous les dimanches et, une semaine sur deux, tous les jours sur des textes bibliques. Chaque nouveau sermon, selon un principe immuable, commence par un bref rappel de ce qui a été vu la veille ou la semaine précédente. Ce rappel, didactique, n'est pas fait pour l'absent, mais sert d'aide-mémoire à l'auditeur qui a oublié de quoi le prédicateur a parlé la veille. Les registres du Consistoire, dans les années 1540, mais encore en 1559 et 1560, sont d'ailleurs remplis de cas de personnes incapables de dire sur quel texte on a prêché la veille ou quelques jours auparavant (le sommes-nous toujours davantage?). L'absent, celui qui a manqué une prédication ou, pire, plusieurs, se trouve irrémédiablement lésé, exclut de fait de la structure homilétique. C'est le premier effet pervers du principe de la *lectio continua:* vous ne pouvez manquer un seul sermon, car un chaînon manque de façon irrémédiable.

Calvin, bien plus que ne le firent les exégètes médiévaux, porte une attention aux moindres détails du texte biblique, voulant rendre raison de tout le texte et de ses circonstances d'élocution. Les commentateurs anciens, il est vrai, avaient à leur disposition des outils allégoriques et typologiques qui ne nécessitaient pas une attention aussi excessive, outils qu'utilise peu Calvin. Dès le premier sermon, et l'histoire de la Création, Calvin cherche à comprendre comment cette transmission est parvenue jusqu'à nous:

> Voilà pourquoy oultre ce que Dieu s'est manifesté en ses oeuvres, il nous a voulu aussy donner l'histoire de la creation du monde, telle qu'elle est icy contenue. Or *il est vray que Moyse n'estoit pas de ce temps là,* mays nous sçavons que le peuple d'Israel sçavoit dont il estoit sorty. Car de main en main, tousjours les sainctz peres ont enseigné leurs successeurs de ce qui leur estoit necessaire à salut. Voilà Abraham qui a tesmoignage, comme nous verrons cy apres, qu'il instruira sa famille en toute bonne doctrine. Depuys la mort d'Abraham, vray est que les Juifs n'ont pas esté tousjours si diligens qu'ilz debvoyent, excepté Isaac et Jacob avec les sainctz patriarches. Mays quoy qu'il en soyt, si est ce qu'ilz ont tousjours retenu quelques principes, et n'ont point esté pleinement esgarés.[21]

Ailleurs, c'est la question de la beauté de Sarai, alors qu'elle était âgé de près d'un siècle (sermon 57, f° 395a). C'est encore la raison du choix du sexe masculin pour recevoir la marque de l'alliance (sermon 80, f° 526a-b). En Genèse 15:13, ce sont les quatre cents ans qui ne correspondent pas au temps de la captivité en Egypte (sermon 72, f° 462b). En Genèse 16:15, pour qu'Abraham

[21]Cf. sermon 1, (p. 2) (c'est moi, une nouvelle fois, qui souligne).

sache comment nommer Ismaël, il a fallu que la servante Hagar lui raconte son aventure (sermon 77, f° 505a), alors qu'il est étonnant qu'Abraham, homme riche et important, surveille les passants depuis l'entrée de sa tente (sermon 80, f° 556b). Un dernier exemple, mais on en rencontre bien d'autres dans les sermons sur la Genèse ou sur Esaïe, c'est celui de l'aveuglement des Sodomites, certes, mais alors qu'il faisait nuit (sermon 91, f° 613b). Calvin répond bien évidemment par la foi à ces questions de détails, qu'il est parfois le premier à soulever, mais il a bel et bien posé les questions auxquelles la critique historique apportera des réponses davantage sceptiques. Une précision toutefois: Calvin travaille rarement les incohérences du texte biblique: aussi se tait-il au sujet des deux récits de la mort de Judas. Cet attachement à la lettre du texte, qui permettra d'ailleurs, plus tard, les revendications de l'inerrance biblique, et ce désir de s'arrêter aux moindres détails de l'Ecriture constituent le second effet pervers de la *lectio continua* parcourant la totalité d'un texte biblique.

Les erreurs de citations de l'Ecriture

J'ai écrit un article pour chercher à sérier, puis à expliquer, les citations erronées de l'Ecriture dans les sermons de Calvin sur la Genèse[22] et j'en ai repris les grandes lignes dans un article en anglais qui a paru dans *Church History*.[23] Il apparaît que, du haut de la chaire, le Réformateur use de l'Ecriture avec une grande liberté, pour étayer sa théologie et l'accentuer. Aussi Calvin n'est pas toujours au service de l'Ecriture; c'est l'Ecriture parfois qui est convoquée pour la défense et l'illustration de ses propos. Les variations peuvent n'être que de détail (le coût d'un passereau, l'amalgame au lieu de la séparation des opérations du Père et du Fils, la circoncision des enfants en rapport avec Christ ou les mentions de deux, trois femmes, lors de la création d'Eve); d'autres écarts témoignent d'un usage de l'hyperbole. Calvin généralise ou accentue des passages bibliques: les bêtes se changent en hommes; un retrait partiel de l'esprit de Dieu devient un retrait radical; l'image de la gloire de Dieu est transformée en image de Dieu; une exhortation évolue en condamnation; l'affection charnelle couvre soudain tous les sentiments humains, etc. Ces modifications sont d'ailleurs les plus nombreuses. Il arrive encore à Calvin de forger un verset à partir de quelques passages, d'insérer des images qu'il estime et ses idées dans une citation, et même de créer une nouvelle occurrence biblique qu'aucun texte scripturaire ne porte: ainsi les ténèbres chez ceux qui annoncent l'Evangile ou les humains qui ne sont que pourriture. J'associe ces écarts avec la fonction prophétique, juste commentateur de l'Ecriture, que Calvin revendiquait.

---

[22]Cf. "Calvin connaissait-il la Bible? Les citations de l'Ecriture dans ses sermons sur la Genèse," *Bulletin de la Société d'Histoire du Protestantisme Français* 141 (1995), 163-84.

[23]"Calvin. A Prophet without a Prophecy," *Church History* 67 (1998), 643-61.

On trouve les mêmes types de confusion quand Calvin utilise Eusèbe, et c'est ce qu'a parfaitement montré Irena Backus,[24] mais également avec le droit romain ou avec la science païenne, et je n'avance que deux exemples.

Dans le 43e sermon sur Genèse 9:3-7, du 9 janvier 1560, Calvin cite la Loi, il ne s'agit pourtant pas de la Loi biblique, mais de la loi romaine. Sainte confusion, puisqu'elle permet à Calvin d'utiliser un syllogisme qu'il pratique volontiers: si dans un cas concernant quelque chose ou quelqu'un de moins important qu'un fidèle, Dieu agit de telle manière, tant plus nous bénira-t-il ou nous chatiera-t-il quand il s'agira de nous ("que sera-ce de nous?").

> Il est bien mesmes ordonné en la Loy[25] que, quand une beste furieuse, ou de nature maligne, aura devoré un homme, qu'elle soit mise pour exemple en un gibet, et que cela engendre quelque fraieur. Non pas que la beste de soy soit coulpable, mais le tout est pour l'instruction des hommes, afin que nous recongnoissions, *[1a] si Dieu ne supporte point les bestes, et qu'il ne leur pardonne pas une cruauté qu'elles auront commise, [1b] combien qu'elles ne savent qu'elles font, [2a] que sera ce, quand par certaine malice, [2b] sachans bien que nous* devons espargner la vie de nos prochains, neantmoins nous aurons oublié tout ce qui a esté imprimé en nos coeurs, quand Dieu nous fait sentir combien nous sommes redevables à nos prochains?[26]

Pour inviter ses auditeurs à pratiquer l'amour fraternel, Calvin a confondu droit romain et Loi biblique.

On peut bien évidemment minimiser ces erreurs de citations, mais il me semble plus juste de discerner là une fréquentation utilitaire des sources au service d'une idée que défend Calvin, tout en précisant que jamais ces confusions ou ses créations n'amènent Calvin à forger un nouveau dogme. L'on peut évoquer le principe augustinien de l'amour: quelle que soit la voie pour y parvenir, les chemins de traverse ne sont pas interdits.[27]

---

[24]"Calvin's Judgment of Eusebius of Caesarea: An Analysis," *Sixteenth Century Journal* 22 (1991), 419-37.

[25]En Dt. 21:1-9, c'est une génisse qui est sacrifiée, en cas de meurtre anonyme. En Dt 21:22s, c'est un homme qui est pendu au bois. Le texte allégué par Calvin ne se trouve pas dans la Bible. Dans son commentaire Calvin explique Gn 9:5, dans un sens proche de celui développé dans ce sermon: "Quant à ce qu'il <Dieu> dit qu'il punira les bestes qui auront violé la vie de l'homme, cela est dit pour l'exemple." *Commentaire,* 118s; *Commentarius,* col. 146. Je n'ai pas trouvé trace d'un tel commandement ni dans le droit canonique romain, ni dans le Talmud, en particulier dans le traité Tohorot de la Michna. Cf. Jacob Neusner, éd., *A History of the Mishnaic Law of Purities,* part. 11 et 12, Studies in Judaism in Late Antiquity 6, part. 11 et 12 (Leiden: E. J. Brill, 1976). En revanche le droit romain ordonnait de tuer l'animal homicide, puis de l'exposer en public. Cf. *Corpus juris civilis,* volumen primum, *Digesta* lib. 48, cap. 19, lex 28:15s. Je remercie Christoph Strohm pour cette dernière référence.

[26]Cf. *Sermons de Jean Calvin sur la Genèse,* 478s.

[27]Cf. *De Doctrina christiana* 1:36:40s.

Ce que Calvin fait avec la Bible ou le droit romain, il le fait également avec le savoir antique. Il lui arrive en effet de modifier ou d'appréhender une citation antique de manière partiale, telle la mention de Brutus, choisie chez Dion Cassius, non chez Plutarque, dans un des sermons sur la Genèse.[28] Et il s'agit du quatrième extrait dans les feuilles de préparation que vous avez reçues.

L'apport de la science païenne à la lecture de la Bible

J'ai déjà montré comment Calvin utilisait le savoir antique dans la localisation du Paradis. Expliquant Genèse 2, 10-14, Calvin adopte la localisation mésopotamienne. Il fonde néanmoins sa démonstration sur les connaissances géographiques antiques: Pline, Pomponius Méla, Arrien citant Néarque, Quinte-Curce, et surtout Strabon sont tour à tour convoqués, légion de témoins que Calvin est loin de toujours appeler dans ses autres travaux bibliques ou polémiques. Le recours au savoir géographique des Anciens est confiant et total. Les Anciens en l'occurrence, toujours *auctoritates,* offrent à Calvin des appuis indispensables à son argumentation. Quand le Réformateur ajoute au texte biblique un "assemblement ou confluent qu'[il a] marqué en la figure" et qu'il affirme que cette confluence du Tigre et de l'Euphrate a été naturelle, non creusée par les hommes, c'est fort des propos de Strabon.[29]

J'aimerais maintenant commenter le quatrième extrait (cf. annexe), en particulier le passage souligné (sermon 73, f° 467a-b):

> L'un d'entre eux qui a esté renommé en prouësse et en telle magnanimité que c'estoit merveilles, quand ce vient à la mort, et qu'il est contraint par desespoir de se tuer soymesme: "Et qu'est-ce de vertu, dit-il, ce n'est que fatraz."

C'est au cours du 73e sermon sur la Genèse (15:15s: "Dieu dit à Abram: Tu t'en iras avec tes peres en paix, et seras enseveli en bonne vieillesse. Et au 4e aage tes enfans retourneront icy, car l'iniquité des Amorrheens n'est pas encores accomplie") que Calvin amène cette référence "payenne." L'évocation scripturaire de la mort d'Abraham amène Calvin à un propos général: tout le

---

[28]Cf. sermon 73, *Sermons de Jean Calvin sur la Genèse,* 819, et la note y afférente. On pense souvent à Erasme, reprenant l'anecdote citée par Jérôme (*Adnotationes in Acta Apostolorum* 17:23) in *Eloge de la folie* 64, Paul ne conservant que les deux derniers mots de l'inscription "Aux dieux de l'Asie, de l'Europe et de l'Afrique, et aux dieux inconnus et étrangers;" dont Erasme dit: "omettant les mots qui pouvaient gêner sa cause, il n'en garda que les deux derniers... A cet exemple la famille théologienne détache d'un contexte, ici et là, quelques petits mots dont elle altère le sens pour l'accommoder à ses raisonnements. Peu lui importe qu'il n'y ait aucun rapport avec ce qui précède et ce qui suit, ou même qu'il y ait contradiction. L'impudent procédé vaut tant de succès aux théologiens qu'ils en excitent maintes fois l'envie des jurisconsultes."

[29]Calvin, *Commentaire,* 52; Calvin, *Commentarius,* col. 42 (appui sur Strabon, Geographia 11:12:3). Cf. mon "Portrait de l'exégète en géographe. La carte du paradis comme instrument herméneutique chez Calvin et ses contemporains," *Annali di storia dell'esegesi* 13 (1996), 572s (565-81).

monde doit mourir, riche ou pauvre, grand ou petit, mais c'est un bien inestimable que de mourir en paix. Or les adultères, les ivrognes, les débauchés, et ceux qui se seront enrichis sur le dos d'autrui ne peuvent obtenir cette paix. A l'appui de son propos Calvin ajoute: "les payens mesmes ont bien veu cela."[30] Voilà pour le contexte, si important dans le développement de la pensée et du discours homilétique de Calvin.

Sans le nommer, Calvin évoque ici une certaine tradition de la figure de Brutus, comme il l'a déjà fait en commentant les Psaumes (1557):

> Brutus..., comme estant de la secte des Philosophes stoïciens, parloit excellemment de vertu et de la providence de Dieu, et la magnifioit: toutesfois se voyant finalement vaincu par Antoine, il vint à s'escrier, que tout ce qu'il avoit creu touchant vertu, n'estoyent que paroles en l'air et vrayes niaiseries, et que toute la peine qu'on prenoit à vivre honnestement et vertueusement n'estoit qu'autant perdu, pource que fortune domine és choses humaines.[31]

On ne lit pourtant pas ce récit chez Plutarque,[32] Plutarque que Calvin connaissait et citait régulièrement, au contraire ces propos sont relevés par Plutarque dans son *De superstitione,* sans que le nom de Brutus y soit associé.[33] C'est chez Dion Cassius qu'on trouve le mot attribué à Brutus:[34] au moment de mourir, Brutus aurait dit: "Malheureuse vertu! Tu n'étais qu'un mot; je te cultivais comme une réalité, et tu étais l'esclave de la fortune."[35] Est-il besoin de rappeler que Dion Cassius vécut un siècle après Plutarque (ca 155- ca 235).

---

[30] *Ibid.,* f° 467a.

[31] Cf. *Commentaires de Jehan Calvin sur le livre des Pseaumes,* 2 tomes (Paris: C. Meyrueis, 1859), 2:35, sur le Ps 73; CO 31:674.

[32] Cf. *Vie de Brutus* 50-52.

[33] Cf. 1:165a, *in Moralia* 14.

[34] *Histoire romaine* 47:49.

[35] On peut encore penser à Caton d'Utique, dit le Jeune. Si d'après Plutarque, Caton le Jeune, réputé pour sa magnanimité et sa rectitude, en se suicidant, ne tint pas de tels propos (cf. Plutarque, *Vie de Caton le Jeune* 65-70), Sénèque rapporte que Caton, en se suicidant, désespéra du genre humain: "nunc quoniam deploratae sunt res generis humani" (cf. *Lettres à Lucilius* liv. 3, lettre n° 24:6-8, ici 7; cf. aussi liv. 8, lettres n° 70:4 en part. 4, et 71:11-16, et son *De providentia* 2:10); rien de tel en revanche chez Augustin (*De civitate Dei* 1:17-27). Qu'il s'agisse de Platon, de Sénèque ou d'un des suicidés que nomme Erasme (Diogène, Xénocrate, Cassius, Brutus, in *Encomium moriae* 31), aucun n'a tenu, au moment de mourir, un tel propos contredisant tout son enseignement. Cf. pour Platon, le *Phédon,* en part. 115a-118a, et l'*Apologie de Socrate,* en part. 40a-42a; Xénophon, *Apologie de Socrate,* en part. 33s; Diogène Laërce, *Vies des philosophes,* en part. 2:5, "Socrates;" pour Sénèque, Tacite, *Annales* 15:61-64. Suétone ne fait que relater le suicide du philosophe (*Vie des douze Césars,* Néron 35), tout comme Jérôme, qui l'insère dans ses hommes illustres, à cause de la pseudo-correspondance avec Paul (*Liber de viris illustribus* 12). Giannozzo Manetti, qui composa au milieu du XVe siècle une *Vita Socratis et Senecae, Vita* très souvent copiée, n'a pas davantage transformé les suicides dans ce sens. Cf. l'édition critique d'Alfonso De Petris, Florence, 1979, en part. 156-66 (pour Platon) et 194-201 (pour Sénèque). Anaxagore, en se suicidant, ne tint pas, lui non

La source antique est sélectionnée en vertu du message que Calvin veut faire passer, et que je rappelais ci-dessus en définissant le contexte du passage souligné.

L'ordo dogmaticus

Apparaît ainsi le donné dogmatique qui conduit la pensée du prédicateur et son discours homilétique. Chez Luther, on le sait, c'est Christ qui est la clé de lecture de l'Ecriture; chez Calvin on pourrait dire que règne le primat de la doctrine générale de la révélation.

Les prédications sont marquées par un fort accent dogmatique, en particulier celles sur Esaïe et la Genèse que j'ai étudiées attentivement. Cette dogmatique au fil du texte est catéchétique. Elle actualise constamment le texte biblique pour le bien croire et le bien craindre des auditeurs. On peut en effet parler, au sujet des sermons de Calvin, d'une homilétique de la crainte de Dieu.[36] Le prédicateur veut que son auditoire acquière la crainte de Dieu, crainte dans le sens de révérence, crainte également dans le sens d'obéissance craintive. Ce fort accent dogmatique, propre à Calvin, se trouve certainement renforcé par la dernière version de *l'Institution de la religion chrestienne* qu'il entreprend au même moment (1558-1559), puis traduit dans la foulée (1559-1560). Pourtant cette prédication propose quelques écarts intéressants avec *l'Institution* dans sa manière de lire et d'interpréter l'Ecriture.

Comme dernier texte pour notre discussion, je vous propose l'un de ces écarts entre la prédication dogmatique et *l'Institution de la religion chrestienne:* l'expulsion du paradis (Genèse 3, 22-24) (cf. *extrait n° 3 des textes en annexe*). Le prédicateur genevois revient tout d'abord sur l'arbre de vie, dont la vertu n'est pas dans le bois, mais dans le fait que c'est un signe visible et un sacrement.[37] Calvin

---

plus, de tels propos (cf. Diogène Laërce, *Vies des philosophes 2:3*). Parmi quelques théologiens chrétiens qui ont cité l'exemple de Socrate, on ne trouve rien de tel; ainsi chez Basile de Césarée, en part. dans son *Aux jeunes gens, sur la manière de bien tirer profit des lettres helléniques* 7 et 9; ou chez Grégoire de Nazianze, dans sa lettre 32 à Philagrios, lettre dans laquelle il évoque la mort de Socrate (cf. *Lettres,* éd. Paul Gallay (Paris: les Belles Lettres, 1964), 1:42). Le propos de Calvin ne peut considérer Lucrèce, dont on rapportait le suicide, à la suite du mot de Jérôme ("propria se manu interfecit, anno aetatis XLIV," addition à la chronique d'Eusèbe). Rappelons encore, pour finir, l'histoire de Francesco Spiera, qui s'est suicidé en 1548, par désespoir, après avoir abjuré sa foi protestante devant l'inquisition vénitienne, par peur de perdre sa charge d'avocat. Calvin ne parle pas de Brutus ni de Caton dans sa préface à l'*Exemplum memorabile desesperationis in Francisco Spiera, propter abjuratam fidei confessionem* (Genève: J. Gerardus, 1550) (cf. CO 9:855-58). Cf. sur ce suicide, en dernier lieu, M. A. Overell, "The Exploitation of Francesco Spiera," *Sixteenth Century Journal* 26 (1995), 619-37. Cf. enfin le récent papier de Jeffrey R. Watt, "Calvin on Suicide," *Church History* 66 (1997), 463-76.

[36]L'on connaît la place de la crainte de Dieu dans l'*Institution,* par exemple dans les chapitres 2 et 3 du livre III; cf. *Inst.* 3:2:26.

[37]Sermon 20, *Sermons de Jean Calvin sur la Genèse,* 231s, qui renvoie au sermon 10, 112.

cite Jean 1:4, pour avancer que ce qui "estoit là signifié" c'est que "la parole de Dieu a esté la vie des hommes."[38] Calvin affirme alors: "Et ainsi en somme cest arbre de vie luy a esté un sacrement, comme aujourd'huy le baptesme et la Cene nous sont." Comme il en a coutume, Calvin a actualisé l'histoire pour son auditoire. Expulsion, sacrement, on voit se profiler l'excommunication. Calvin va-t-il oser aller jusque là? Suit un développement sur le baptême et la Cène, avant que Calvin précise à nouveau que l'arbre de vie était un sacrement,[39] et de conclure: "nous pourrons aisement cognoistre que Dieu l'excommunie de ce sacrement." Le but de cette excommunication est d'amener Adam à repentance et à salut. Calvin alors n'a plus besoin que d'actualiser à nouveau:

> En somme, ce que Moise recite est comme un excommuniement fait à Adam, comme aujourd'huy, quand on verra quelqu'un de vie scandaleuse, un homme endurci et obstiné qui ne veut recevoir nulle correction. Est-il ainsi? Il faut donc que ce miserable soit excommunié et comme retranché du corps des fideles, à fin qu'il cognoisse tant mieux son mal, et qu'il en soit navré, et que cela l'induise à avoir honte de ses fautes, et qu'il apprenne de s'humilier et demander pardon. Voilà donc comme encores aujourd'huy nostre Seigneur veut que l'excommunication soit exercée en son Eglise, à fin d'attirer les pecheurs à repentance, pource qu'ils ne sentent point leur mal, et aians scandalisé l'Eglise, ils ne font que torcher leur bouche.[40]

L'excommunication de la Cène, et l'on connaît combien ce problème de discipline fut au centre de tant de difficultés de Calvin jusqu'en 1555, trouve dans l'arbre de vie une justification inattendue. La suite du sermon développe encore longuement la question.[41] Impossible, bien évidemment, de trouver un tel développement dans l'*Institution* ou dans le commentaire.

Brève conclusion

Je crois avoir montré une utilisation très personnelle de la Bible chez Calvin quand il prêche: que ce soit une prédication à partir d'une édition en langue originale, hébreu ou grec, ou sa manière de citer la Bible, voire la convocation d'*auctoritates* antiques pour servir à son propos. Deux mots résument les rapports de Calvin avec la Bible quand il prêche et commente en chaire: liberté et contrainte.

Au risque de me répéter, mais je ne vois pas comment l'expliquer autrement, quand Calvin lit, prêche et commente la Bible, il use de la liberté du prophète de l'Ancien Testament.

---

[38]Sermon 20, ibid., 232.

[39]"Mais icy l'arbre de vie a bien signifié que la parole de Dieu estoit la source et l'origine de nostre vie" (Ibid.)

[40]Sermon 20, *Sermons de Jean Calvin sur la Genèse,* 232s.

[41]Sermon 20, *Sermons de Jean Calvin sur la Genèse,* jusqu'à la page 237, c'est-à-dire plus de huit pages, plus de la moitié de la prédication. La fin s'intéresse aux chérubins, des anges pour Calvin.

Cette liberté est néanmoins bornée par une contrainte, en raison du principe de la lectio continua, mais également de l'ordre dogmatique qui informe et conduit toute lecture de l'Ecriture.

Annexe: Quatre extraits de sermons sur la Genèse qui ont été discutés pendant le séminaire

1). Début du 57e sermon sur la Genèse du 8 février 1560 (Genèse 12:11-16), (*Sermons de Jean Calvin sur la Genèse,* 632).

Comme il aprochoit d'Egipte, et qu'il estoit prest d'y entrer, il dit à Sarai sa femme: Voicy je say que tu es femme belle de regard. Ainsi, quand les Egiptiens t'auront veue, ilz diront: "Ceste femme icy est femme de luy," et me tueront, et tu seras gardée en vie. Dy donc que tu es ma seur, afin qu'il me soit bien en faveur de toy, et que mon ame vive pour l'amour de toy. Or il advint, quand Abram fut venu en Egipte, quand les Egiptiens eurent veu la femme, ilz la trouverent fort belle. Et les princes de Pharao l'ayans veue la louerent à Pharaon. Et la femme fut ravie et menée au palais de Pharao, lequel fit du bien à Abram à cause d'elle, tellement qu'il eut beufz, asnes, serviteurs, chambrieres, asnesses et chameaux.

2). Début du 72e sermon sur la Genèse du 19 mars 1560 (Genèse 15:11-14), (*Sermons de Jean Calvin sur la Genèse,* 804).

Les oyseaulx descendirent du ciel sur les corps mortz, et Abram les chassoit. Et comme le soleil se couchoit, un sommeil tomba sur Abram. Et voyci un horreur obscur et de grande fraieur tomba sur luy. Et Dieu dit: Abram, sçaiches pour vray que ta semence sera estrangere en une terre qui ne sera point sienne, qu'on les affligera en servitude, voire on les tourmentera par l'espace de quatre cens ans. Mais je jugerai le peuple qui les aura asserviz; et de là s'en retourneront avec grandz biens.

3). 20e sermon sur la Genèse du 18 octobre 1559 (Genèse 3:22-24), (*Sermons de Jean Calvin sur la Genèse,* 232s).

Or maintenant, puis que nous savons de quoy l'arbre de vie a profité à Adam et à quel usage luy a servi la defense qui luy est faite de cest arbre de vie, nous pourrons aisement cognoistre que Dieu l'excommunie de ce sacrement qu'il luy avoit donné, à fin qu'il soit plus estonné en soy mesme et que, s'estant rendu coulpable, il aspire mieux au remede et soit incité de cercher son salut là où il le peut recouvrer, cognoissant qu'en luy, il n'y a qu'abomination. *En somme ce que Moise recite est comme un excommuniement fait à Adam* [c'est moi qui souligne] Comme aujourd'huy, quand on verra quelqu'un de vie scandaleuse, un homme endurci et obstiné qui ne veut recevoir nulle correction. Est-il ainsi? Il faut donc que ce miserable soit excommunié et comme retranché du corps des fideles, à fin qu'il cognoisse tant mieux son mal, et qu'il en soit navré, et que cela l'induise à avoir honte de ses fautes, et qu'il apprenne de s'humilier et demander pardon. Voilà donc comme encores aujourd'huy nostre Seigneur veut que l'excommunication soit exercée en son Eglise, à fin d'attirer les pecheurs à repentance, pource qu'ils ne sentent point leur mal, et aians scandalisé l'Eglise, ils ne font que torcher leur bouche. Quand donc on void qu'ils sont ainsi elourdis, il faut qu'on les pique et qu'on leur donne comme une saignée.

4). 73e sermon sur la Genèse du 20 mars 1560 (Genèse 15:15-16), (*Sermons de Jean Calvin sur la Genèse,* 818-20).

Mais comme il ne nous faut point avoir honte d'apprendre de ces paovres aveugles qui n'ont point cognu Dieu, aussi d'autre costé il nous faut regarder en quoy ilz ont failly. Ils ont bien une bonne entrée pour se mettre au bon chemin, mais puys apres ilz se sont esgarez, car ilz ont prins l'ombre pour le corps et la substance. Et qu'ainsi soit si nous cerchons bonne esperance en ce que nous aurons vescu sainctement et en toute pureté. Helas, qui est celuy de nous qui pourra testifier qu'il ait satisfaict en son debvoir en tout et par tout? Nous en sommes bien loin. Car quelque affection et desir que nous ayons de cheminer en l'obeissance de Dieu, tant y a que nous clochons tousjours et faisons beaucoup de faux pas, tellement que, si nous alleguons un poinct à Dieu, il en aura mille au rebours, tellement que nous demeurons là confuz. Ainsi donc il faut cercher un meilleur fondement pour avoir esperance, c'est que nous cheminions/ en integrité, que nous puissions protester devant Dieu et ses anges qu'il n'y a point eu de faintise en nous, que nous n'ayons voulu cheminer selon la reigle qu'il nous avoit donnée. Mais outre cela il faut que nous ayons nostre recours à sa misericorde, à fin qu'il supplée à noz deffautz, et qu'il ne nous impute point encores tant de vices, lesquelz restent en nous. Car ceux qui se sont ainsi fondez sur leurs vertus ont monstré que cela ne les pouvoit pas conduire jusques au sepulchre.

L'un d'entre eux qui a esté renommé en prouësse et en telle magnanimité que c'estoit merveilles, quand ce vient à la mort, et qu'il est contraint par desespoir de se tuer soymesme: "Et qu'est-ce de vertu, dit-il, ce n'est que fatraz" [c'est moi qui souligne]. Et pourquoy? Car ilz estoyent abbreuvez de ceste folle presomption qu'ils pouvoyent beaucoup d'euxmesmes, et ne cognoissoyent pas que s'ils cerchoyent la vertu, ils en estoyent encores bien loing, et qu'il failloit que Dieu approchast avec sa misericorde, pour suppleer à ce que defalloit à ceste vertu. Voylà comme l'arrogance les a abysmez. Et ainsi en est-il de tous ceux qui se veullent fonder sur leurs personnes. Mais de nostre part cognoissons que nostre esperance ne peut avoir nulle vertu ne fermeté, sinon en la grace de Dieu. Et ceste grace de Dieu est double. D'un costé, quand il nous reçoit à mercy; et ce pendant par son Saint Esprit il nous gouverne tellement, que nous desirons de bien faire, et le faisons en partie, encores que ce ne soit pas du tout. Or quoy qu'il en soit ceste sentence est procedée de Dieu, quand il est dit que l'esperance est la nourrice de vieillesse. Moyennant donc que nous cognoissions en quoy nous devons esperer, et de qui, et de quoy, voylà comme l'esperance sera une bonne nourrice pour nostre vieil aage et nous conduira jusques à la mort.

Calvins Gebrauch des Begriffs "religio"

Peter Opitz

Eine Untersuchung der Verwendung eines bestimmten Begriffes bei Calvin, wie sie diesem Seminar aufgegeben wurde,[1] wird bald einmal mit den Folgen dessen konfrontiert, dass Calvin weder der "Scholastik" noch der—bereits während seiner Lebzeiten anbrechenden—sogenannten "reformierten Orthodoxie" zuzurechnen ist, sondern in bibel-humanistischer Tradition steht. Eine lebendige und flexible Sprachgestalt, wie er sie schon in den biblischen Texten selbst beobachtet, stellte für ihn die Eindeutigkeit der ausgesagten Sache nicht in Frage, und wurde nur in begrenztem Maße von ihm weiter konzeptualisiert. Dennoch verstand es der Jurist Calvin dort, wo es darum ging, theologische Einsichten unzweideutig zu formulieren, auch den verwendeten Begriffen einen deutlichen Sinn zu geben. Gerade das von ihm eingehaltene Maß zwischen Lebendigkeit und Klarheit ist ein nicht zu unterschätzendes Element der Wirkung seiner Schriften. Dass jede "Definition" eines Begriffs und jede klare Beschreibung eines Sachverhalts auf noch nicht definierte, aber in ihrem Sinn als verständlich vorausgesetzte Begriffe zurückgreifen muss, versteht sich von selbst, ebenso wie die Tatsache, dass alle Begriffe erst im Kontext ihrer Verwendung und im Zusammenhang einer Aussage eindeutig werden. Calvins Verwendung des Terminus "religio" kann diese allgemeinen Feststellungen illustrieren.

I. Bedeutungsfelder von "religio"

In der *Institutio* von 1559 begegnen Ausdrücke mit der Wurzel "relig": In Buch I an 56 Stellen, in Buch II an 37 Stellen, in Buch III an 27 Stellen und in Buch IV an 102 Stellen. Eine umfassende Untersuchung diese, sondern über die *Institutio* hinaus zahlreiche weitere Texte in den Blick nehmen und präsentieren, was im Rahmen unserer Aufgabe nicht geleistet werden kann, zumal für

[1]Der folgende Text ist eine im Anschluss an den Calvinkongress von 1998 in Seoul erfolgte Ausarbeitung der dort mündlich vorgetragenen und diskutierten Thesen und Texte. Zum Hintergrund vgl. Peter Opitz, *Calvins theologische Hermeneutik* (Neukirchen-Vluyn: Neukirchener Verlag, 1994).

das Verständnis der theologischen Bedeutung und inhaltlichen Füllung dieses Begriffs damit noch wenig gewonnen wäre. Wir werden uns hier mit einer Auswahl an Stellen, an welchen Calvin den "religio"-Begriff dezidiert verwendet, begnügen müssen, die aber so getroffen wurde, dass grundlegende Aspekte seines Umgangs mit diesem zeitgenössisch häufig verwendeten Ausdruck in den Blick kommen.

A. Wichtige Quellen für Calvins "religio"-Begriff

Obwohl dem Begriff "religio" bei Calvin keine zentrale Bedeutung zukommt, begegnet er doch, wie bereits die Statistik für die *Institutio* zeigt, immer wieder. Calvin kannte den Ausdruck "religio" als einen geläufigen, keiner Analyse und keiner Präzisierung bedürftigen lateinischen Terminus, der ihm, wie allen seinen gebildeten Zeitgenossen, sowohl durch die Schriften der römischen Antike wie durch die kirchlich-theologische Tradition vertraut war.

Bereits in seinem Kommentar zu Senecas *De clementia* hatte Calvin den Satz zu erläutern: "Ergo quemadmodum religio deos colit, superstitio violat ..." Er führt dazu Ciceros Etymologie, aber auch andere Autoren an.[2] Als Gottesverehrung in einem weiten, nicht scharf umrissenen Sinn begegnet "religio" auch bei Cicero, einem für Calvin diesbezüglich wichtigen Zeugen. Der Begriff steht hier wesentlich in Verbindung mit "cultus," "caeremonia" und "metus," aber auch mit "pietas," "iustitia," "sanctitas."[3] Das sich bei Cicero spiegelnde "religio"-Verständnis der römischen Antike kann in etwa umrissen werden als die mit Ehrfurcht bzw. Scheu erfüllte sorgfältige Beachtung dessen, was den Göttern gegenüber zu tun ist. Es ist die "im Unterschied zur eher persönlichen, aber nicht innerlichen 'pietas' die mehr auf den äußeren Vollzug zielende Einstellung der Römer gegenüber den Göttern ..., die verbal 'deos colere' heißt."[4]

Auch bei wichtigen Zeugen der Alten Kirche ist "religio" die Gott geschuldete menschliche Haltung der Ehrfurcht (so sind "metus" und "timor" in diesem Zusammenhang zu übersetzen), die sich in bestimmten menschlichen Handlungen ("cultus," "caeremonia") ausdrückt.[5] Als menschliches

[2]Vgl. CO 5:155-56.

[3]Einige wenige Beispiele sollen genügen: "Religionem eam, quae in metu et caeremonia deorum est, appellant pietatem" (*Invent.* 2:22:66). "Religio est, quae superioris cuiusdam naturae, quam divinam vocant, curam caeremoniamque affert" (*Invent.* 2:53:161). "In communione autem quae posita pars est, iustitia dicitur erga deos religio, erga parentes pietas, creditis in rebus fides ..." (*Part. or.* 22:78). "... religione id est cultu deorum ..." (*De nat.* 2:9). "... non modo superstitionem tollunt, in qua inest timor inanis deorum, sed etiam religionem, quae deorum cultu pio continentur" (*De nat.* 1:117).

[4]E. Feil, *Religio I. Die Geschichte eines neuzeitlichen Grundbegriffs vom Frühchristentum bis zur Reformation* (Göttingen: Vandenhoeck & Ruprecht, 1986), 49.

[5]Z.B. Augustin: "Quale autem illud est, quod, cum religiosum a superstitioso ea distinctione discernat, ut a superstitioso dicat timeri deos, a religioso autem tantum vereri ut parentes, non ut hostes timeri ..." (civ. 6:9). "Religiosum a superstitioso optime discernitur: superstitiosus

Verhalten Gott gegenüber in allen seinen Dimensionen hatte dann Zwingli im *Commentarius* von 1525 den religio-Begriff gefasst: "Nos enim 'religionem' hic accipimus pro ea ratione, quae pietatem totam christianorum, puta: fidem, vitam, leges, ritus, sacramenta, complectitur."[6]

So ist auch für Calvin "religio" zunächst ganz allgemein das aufgrund des göttlichen Wirkens (vornehmlich in Schöpfung und Providenz)[7] auf Gott gerichtete, ihm geschuldete Verhalten des Menschen, "Gottesverehrung" im umfassenden Sinn.

B. Das Verhältnis von "religio" und "pietas"

"Religio" wird dabei im Gebrauch manchmal kaum von "pietas" unterschieden.[8] So kann Calvin in Inst. 1:12:1 die Begriffe abwechselnd gebrauchen. Andererseits scheinen die beiden Begriffe doch nicht einfach deckungsgleich zu sein. Darauf lassen bereits die beiden sicherlich mit Bedacht formulierten Stellen eingangs der Institutio von 1559 schließen. In *Inst.* 1:2:1 heißt es:

> Nam hic virtutum Dei sensus nobis idoneus est pietatis magister, ex qua religio nascitur. Pietatem voco coniunctam cum amore Dei reverentiam quam beneficiorum eius notitia conciliat.[9]

Und in *Inst.* 1:2:2 wird die "pia mens" beschrieben als eine, die

> Deum loco patris amat et reveretur, loco domini observat et colit, etiamsi nulli essent inferi, solam tamen eius offensionem horret. En quid sit pura

---

pertimescit Deum ut hostem, religiosus Deum veneratur ut parentem" (civ. 4:30). Oder Lactanz: "Quae cum ita se habeant, ut ostendimus, apparet nullam aliam spem vitae homini esse propositam, nisi ut abiectis vanitatibus, et errore miserabili, Deum cognoscat, et Deo serviat, nisi huic temporali renuntiet vitae, ac se rudimentis iustitiae ad cultum verae Religionis instituat. Hac enim conditione gignimur, ut generanti nos Deo iusta et debita obsequia praebeamus; hunc solum noverimus, hunc sequamur. Hoc vinculo pietatis obstricti Deo et religati sumus; unde ipsa Religio nomen accepit, non ut Cicero interpretatus est, a relegendo ... Quid ergo est? Nimirum religio veri cultus est, superstitio falsi. Et omnino quid colas interest, non quemadmodum colas, aut quid precere. Sed quia deorum cultores religiosos se putant, cum sint superstitiosi, nec religionem possunt a superstitione discernere, nec significantiam nominum exprimere, dicimus nomen Religionis a vinculo pietatis esse deductum, quod hominem sibi Deus religaverit, et pietate constrinxerit; quia servire nos ei ut domino, et obsequi ut patri necesse est. Melius ergo id nomen Lucretius interpretatus est, qui ait, religionum se nodos exsolvere. ... superstitiosi ergo qui multos ac falsos deos colunt. Nos autem religiosi, qui uni et vero Deo supplicamus" (*Divin. inst.* 4:28).

[6]Zwingli, *De vera et falsa religione commentarius*, Z 3:639:15-18.

[7]Vgl. *Inst.* 1:2:1; dazu Cicero, De nat. 1:3, 2:153, 3:86, usw.

[8]Vgl. dazu: S.-Y. Lee, "Calvin's Understanding of Pietas," in W. H. Neuser and B. G. Armstrong, eds., *Calvinus sincerioris religionis vindex* (Kirksville, MO: Sixteenth Century Journal Publishers, 1997), 225-39. Die "Wesensgleichheit beider Begriffe" behauptet schon J. Bohatec, *Budé und Calvin. Studien zur Gedankenwelt des französischen Frühhumanismus* (Graz: Hermann Böhlaus, 1950), 245; Belege ebd.

[9]OS 3:35:2-5. Vgl. dazu OS 3:34:10.

germanaque religio, nempe fides cum serio Dei timore coniuncta: ut timor et voluntariam reverentiam in se contineat, et secum trahat legitimum cultum qualis in Lege praescribitur.[10]

Obwohl sich die Inhalte von "pietas" und "religio" überschneiden, scheint die "pietas"—verstanden als "vera" pietas—eher die Gott gegenüber angemessene menschliche Haltung zu meinen, die aus der Erkenntnis von Gottes Werken und Wohltaten fließt, eine "liebende Ehrerbietung" aufgrund der Einsicht in die väterliche Fürsorge des göttlichen Schöpfers, die wesentlich eine affektive Zuwendung zu Gott ist.[11] Die "religio" umfasst dies ebenfalls (zumindest wenn sie "pura" und "germana" ist), besitzt aber einen weiteren Radius. Zwar gibt es ohne das individuelle Bewusstsein der Gegenwart Gottes ("conscientia") auch keine—zumindest keine "vera"—"religio."[12] Im Vergleich zur "pietas" aber erstreckt sich die "religio" zugleich auf die—gleichsam phänomenologisch erfassbaren—menschlichen Handlungen, den Gottesdienst im öffentlichen Leben, sowohl im kultischen wie im ethischen Sinn ("cultus").[13] Zu diesem Verständnis passt auch, dass Calvin die zeitgenössische praktizierte römische "religio" als geheuchelte Zeremonie und eigennützige Selbstkasteiung bezeichnet, die mit einer "impietas" im Herzen einhergehen kann, und eben darum nur scheinbar "religio" ist.[14]

Die bei Cicero zu beobachtende Nähe zwischen "religio" und "metus" als "Gottesfurcht" findet sich bei Calvin ebenfalls, allerdings in klar qualifiziertem Sinn. Zur "pura" religio gehört nach ihm konstitutiv eine Gott angemessene "Ehrfurcht," wie das oben angeführte Zitat zeigt, eine Ehrfurcht, die allerdings gerade das Gegenteil einer vor Gott fliehenden Angst ist, weil sie aus dem Glauben—als Vertrauen—fließt ("fides cum serio Dei timore coniuncta"). In

---

[10]OS 3:37:5-10.

[11]Vgl. *Katechismus 1537/38:* "Vera autem pietas non in timore sita est qui Dei iudicium libenter quidem fugiat, sed quia effugere nequeat, formidet: sed sincero magis affectu constat, qui Deum non secus ac patrem diligat, perinde ac dominum timeat ac revereatur, iustitiam eius amplexetur, offensionem morte peius horreat" (CO 5:324). Vgl. *Inst.* 3:2:27 (OS 4:37:12ff.).

[12]"Ego autem illis deesse dico, quod est in vera sapientia praecipuum. Nempe sensum conscientiae. Qualis enim prudentia, qualis ratio, quale iudicium, ubi conscientia obstupuit? Atqui unde hoc totum, quod a Christianae religionis principiis sic abhorrent: nisi quod a Satana prorsus sunt inebriati, ut nullo iudicii Dei timore, nulla peccati cogitatione tangantur? Dici iam prius, non alia via posse ad Dei sapientiam perveniri, nisi stulti fiamus mundo. Sed huius humilitatis, sicuti religionis totius, fundamentum est conscientia et timor Domini: quo sublato, frustra aedificium moliaris." (*De scandalis* (OS 2:173:18-28; CO 8:17)).

[13]Ähnlich schon K. Reuter, *Das Grundverständnis der Theologie Calvins* (Neukirchen-Vluyn: Neukirchener Verlag, 1963), 98.

[14]Z.B. in *De scandalis* (OS 2:198-200; CO 8:42ff.).

dieser Verwendung enthält auch bei Calvin der "religio"-Begriff eine rational und phänomenal nicht ganz fassbare "subjektiv-existentielle" Dimension.[15]

C. "Religio" als öffentliche Gestalt der Gottesverehrung

Insofern sich der Begriff "religio" in Calvins Verwendung häufig auf die phänomenal fassbaren gottesdienstlichen Vollzüge im weitesten Sinn erstreckt, eignet ihm eine wesentliche soziale Dimension. Er bezeichnet die in einer menschlichen Gemeinschaft geltende und praktizierte Gestalt von Gottesverehrung—einschließlich sozialethischer Normen—die sich in bestimmten "religiösen" Handlungen ausdrückt (Verbindung mit "caeremonia" und "cultus").16 Ein gelingendes politisches Zusammenleben ist nur auf einer in diesem Sinn verstandenen Grundlage ("religio") letztlich möglich.[17] Diese Überzeugung teilte Calvin mit seinen für das öffentliche Leben Verantwortung

[15]Einige Beispiele: "Quasi vero non optima doctrinae suae ratio Domino constet, quae in promptu se offert religiosius quaerentibus" (*Inst.* 2:5:4 (OS 3:302:7-8)). "Nam ut aliis parcamus, qui multo absurdius ineptiunt: Plato inter omnes religiosissimus, et maxime sobrius, ipse quoque in rotundo suo globo evanescit" (*Inst.* 1:5:11 (OS 3:55:26-29)). Im Vorwort zum *Psalmenkommentar* erzählt Calvin von seiner Rückkehr nach Genf mit den Worten: "Vicit tandem officii religio ac fides, ut gregi a quo avulsus fueram me restituerem ..." (CO 32:27). Der französische Paralleltext kommt dagegen ohne "religion" aus: "Mais à la parfin le regard de mon devoir, que ie consideroye avec reverence et conscience, me gaigna, et feit condescendre à retourner vers le troupeau ..." (CO 32:28). "Pietas erga Deum religio est" (*Kommentar zu Tit.* 2:12 (CO 52:423)). "Tantum erat animus rudimenta quaedam tradere, quibus formarentur ad veram pietatem qui aliquo religionis studio tanguntur" (OS 3:9:6-7; CO 2:9). "Omnibus Christi evangelium religiose colentibus. Ministri Genevensis ecclesiae gratiam et pacem, veraeque pietatis incrementum a domino precantur" (Titel des Vorworts zum lateinischen *Katechismus 1538* (CO 5:317/8). "Veteres religiosius interdum simplicem quoque veritatis confessionem in hac parte reformidant, quod verentur ne impietati fenestram de operibus Dei irreverenter obloquendi aperiant" (*Inst.* 2:4:3 (OS 3:292:30ff.)). "Omnibus enim seculis haec irreligiosa religionis affectatio (quia humano ingenio naturaliter insita est) se prodidit, ac etiamnum prodit: quod homines comparandae iustitiae rationem praeter Dei verbum semper comminisci gestiunt" (*Inst.* 2:8:5 (OS 3:347:2-5)). "Ubi decenter fidei audaciam, quae Dei misericordiae innititur, cum religioso timore coniungit, quo nos affici necesse est quoties in conspectum divinae maiestatis prodeuntes, ex eius splendore, quanta sit nostra obscoenitas, intelligimus" (*Inst.* 3:2:23 (OS 4:33:19ff.)). Vgl. OS 4:70:24; 4:33:20; 2:200:29.

[16]So taucht der Begriff "religio" in der *Institutio* von 1536 nicht zufällig bei der Behandlung des 2. Gebotes (OS 1:43) und bei der Frage der (falschen) Sakramente (etwa OS 1:217) auf, in Begriffsfeldern von "imagines," "idololatria," "superstitio," "circumcisio," "cultus." So auch im *Katechismus 1537/38* (CO 5:328, 352). Vgl. *De scandalis* (OS 2:198ff.).

[17]Schon im lateinischen *Katechismus* von 1538 heißt es im Abschnitt über "de magistratu": "Tota autem eorum prope sollicitudo in hoc incumbere debet, ut publicam religionis formam impollutam conservent, ut populi vitam optimis legibus forment, ut suae ditionis bonum ac tranquilitatem publice privatimque procurent." (CO 5:354).

tragenden Zeitgenossen, und fand sie sowohl in der antiken Literatur[18] wie im Alten Testament[19] deutlich ausgesprochen. Ein "humanes" Zusammenleben ohne Basis einer öffentlichen "religio"—und diese war seit dem "Cunctos populos"-Edikt von 380[20] auch im Westen das trinitarische Christentum—war auch für Calvin undenkbar. Die Anrede an den französischen König als "rex christianissimus"[21] war keine Leerformel, sondern Benennung einer mit diesem Amt gegebenen Aufgabe: Die politische Gewalt trägt in ihrem Herrschaftsgebiet vor Gott Verantwortung für die öffentliche "religio"—nicht aber für den "persönlichen" Glauben der einzelnen Menschen.[22] Calvins Polemik gegen die "Epikuräer," "Lucianer," "Atheisten," und "Libertiner"[23] richtete sich nicht nur gegen deren Gottesvorstellungen, beispielsweise die "epikuräische" Vorstellung von einem "müßigen" Gott,[24] sondern wuchs auch und gerade aus der Sorge um die (sozial-)ethisch zerstörerischen Konsequenzen, die sich in seinen Augen daraus ergeben.[25] Dem entspricht auf der anderen Seite sein Bemühen, die evangelische Bewegung von dem römischerseits erhobenen Vorwurf zu befreien, eben gerade solchen, letzlich die Gesellschaft zerstörenden "impii" in die Hände zu arbeiten.[26]

---

[18]"Ac primo quidem hoc dictare naturae sensum, ut in omni politia bene composita principium teneat religio, et legum praesidio integra servetur, testes sunt ipsi increduli. Legantur philosophi, quicunque hoc argumentum tractarunt. Certe incipiunt a divino cultu, et eo religionis genere quod optimum esse putabant: ut secundum eos barbarus sit et insipidus legislator, cui pietatis erga deos prima non est cura ... Nam quum rectae politiae finis sit, legitimi inter homines ordinis conservatio, neglectus autem pietatis ordinem hunc ita dissipet, ut extra ipsam bruta sit hominum vita, mutilam esse gubernationis formam constat, in qua negligitur religio: et magistratus nonnisi dimidios esse et umbratiles, qui forensibus tantum negotiis intenti de asserendo Dei cultu non cogitant." (CO 8:474).

[19] In duas enim partes, quibus tota continetur iustitia, Legem suam sic divisit Deus, ut priorem religionis officiis, quae peculiariter ad numinis sui cultum perinent, alteram officiis charitatis quae in homines respiciunt, assignaverit. Primum sane iustitiae fundamentum, est Dei cultus ... Frustra igitur sine religione venditatur iustitia ... Neque modo est praecipua ipsius pars, sed anima quoque, qua tota ipsa spirat et vegetatur; neque enim citra Dei timorem inter se homines aequitatem ac dilectionem servant." (OS 3:352:12ff).

[20]Vgl. *Corp. Iur. Civ.* Bd. 2: *Iust.* 1:1:1 S. 5a.; *Cod. Theod.* 16:1:2 pr., S. 833 Mommsen.

[21]Vgl. z.B. das Vorwort zur *Institutio* (OS 3:9:2).

[22]Vgl. etwa CO 8:470.

[23]Vgl. O. Fatio, Introduction, in: Jean Calvin, *Des scandales,* édition critique par O. Fatio (Genève: Droz, 1984), 7-41.

[24]*Inst.* 1:16:3 (OS 3:190:15-16).

[25]Calvin steht damit sowohl im theologischen wie im juristischen Konsens seiner Zeit und einer langen Tradition seit Justinian, vgl. Justinian, *Novell.* 77 (*Migne Patrologia Latina* 72:1002).

[26]Vgl. *De scandalis* (OS 2:198-204; CO 8:42-48). So taucht der Begriff "religio" in der Darstellung seines persönlichen Werdeganges im Vorwort zum *Psalmenkommentar* nicht auf, wohl aber dort, wo er von den "Anabaptistas ac turbulentes homines" spricht, "qui perversis deliriis non religionem modo sed totum ordinem politicum convellerent" (CO 31:23).

Die als selbstverständlich anerkannte, notwendige öffentliche "religio" muss aber in Calvins Verständnis von der "vera religio" her inhaltlich gefüllt werden. Die gesamte öffentliche Gestalt und Organisation der Kirche als das Herz der "religio" eines christlichen Gemeinwesens ist damit von entscheidender Bedeutung. Entsprechend verstand Calvin den Katechismus von 1537/38 (und damit den in Genf beginnenden Unterricht darin) als Schritt zur Wiederherstellung der wahren "religio" in der Stadt, wie aus dem Vorwort deutlich wird, denn mit der bloßen Predigt des Evangeliums ist es noch nicht getan.[27]

D. Die *Institutio religionis christianae*

Calvins *Institutio* will bekanntlich ein Unterricht in der christlichen "religio" sein. Zugleich erläutert Calvin in der Vorrede seine Absicht mit den Worten:

> Tantum erat animus rudimenta quaedam tradere, quibus formarentur ad veram pietatem, qui aliquo religionis studio tanguntur.[28]

Einerseits kann "aliquo religionis studio" offenbar einfach das ernsthafte Interesse an Fragen der Gotteserkenntnis und der Gottesverehrung—sicherlich letztlich durch Gott selbst bewirkt—bezeichnen. Der "religio"-Begriff meint somit an dieser Stelle eine Zuwendung zur Beschäftigung mit Gott in einem weiten Sinn als Vorstufe zur "vera pietas."[29] Andererseits weist der Titel der *Institutio* darauf hin, dass dabei nicht nur individuelle Glaubensinhalte behandelt werden, sondern christliche Gotteserkenntnis und Gottesdienst im umfassenden Sinn. Der Ausdruck "fides," den Ernst Feil anstelle von "religio" im Institutiotitel als seiner Ansicht nach angemessener vorschlägt,[30] würde für Calvins Unternehmen entschieden zu kurz greifen, auch wenn er theologisch zweifellos bedeutend mehr Gewicht besitzt. Es ging Calvin (und das im Verlauf der verschiedenen Überarbeitungen der *Institutio* zunehmend) um die Darstellung der "summa religionis"[31] oder der "Philosophie Chrestienne,"[32] in der eben auch die Sakramente, die Ordnung der Kirche und die christliche Obrigkeit einen wesentlichen Platz einnehmen.

---

[27]"Quanquam post abominationem papismi, verbi virtute hic prostratam, senatusconsulto edictum fuerat, ut sublatis superstitionibus, earumque instrumentis, ad evangelii puritatem urbis religio componeretur" (CO 5:319).

[28]OS 3:9:7-8.

[29]Interessant ist in diesem Zusammenhang Calvins *Kommentar zu Apg.* 17:17, wo berichtet wird, wie Paulus mit den Proselyten spricht ("Disputabat igitur in Synagoga cum Iudaeis et religiosis ..."): "Secundus inde gradus ad gentiles erat, qui gustata legis doctrina, quamvis nondum vera pietate rite imbuti essent, colebant tamen Deum Israel, et discendi cupidi non respuebant, quae ex Mose et Prophetis scirent desumpta esse. Quia autem talis docilitas ingressus erat ad fidem, imo quoddam fidei initium, honorifico titulo eos dignatur Spiritus qui primis tantum rudimentis leviter aspersi proprius ad verum Deum accesserant: Religiosi enim vocantur" (CO 48:404).

[30]Feil, *Religio I*, 260.

[31]OS 3:6:21.

Trotz des weiten Umfangs des "religio"-Begriffs ist mit seiner Verwendung im Titel der *Institutio* auch eine klare Abgrenzung vollzogen: Einer spekulativen (scholastischen) Theologie ist damit eine praktische, auf den Lebensvollzug (der christlichen Gemeinde wie des Einzelnen) bezogene christliche Lehre entgegengestellt, ohne dass damit dieser letztere zum Ausgangspunkt oder gar zur Norm christlicher Lehre erhoben würde. Er steht vielmehr unter der kritischen Frage nach der "vera religio."

II. Die Grunddistinktion von falsa und vera religio

Bereits in der *Institutio* von 1536, in der Behandlung des zweiten Gebots (Bilderverbot), und in der Behandlung der (falschen) Sakramente, erscheint der Begriff "religio"—präzisiert als "vera religio"—als Gegenbegriff zu "idololatria" und "superstitio."[33] Die Unterscheidung zwischen "religio" und "superstitio," zwischen "vera," "pura," "germana," "sincera" "religio" einerseits und "falsa" "religio" andererseits, die Calvin, wie erwähnt, sowohl aus dem Studium der antiken Schriftsteller wie aus der Alten Kirche geläufig war, rückte ab 1536 zunehmend stärker in den Vordergrund, und damit überhaupt erst der "religio"-Begriff selbst. Nicht nur die "Duae epistolae" zeugen davon—Calvin stellte ihnen ein Motto aus 1. Könige 18 voran[34]—besonders der Katechismus von 1537/38 ist durchgehend von dieser Unterscheidung, oder besser: von diesem Gegensatz bestimmt.

Dieser "Neuansatz in Calvins Denken,"[35] der keine theologische Umorientierung ist, wohl aber eine größere systematische Gewichtung des ersten (und des nach reformierter Zählung zweiten) Gebotes, geht, so lässt sich vermuten, wohl (zumindest auch) auf den Anstoß des sich an Zwingli orientierenden Farel zurück, unter dessen Einfluss Calvin seit August 1536 stand.[36] Die Aufgabe der Neuordnung der Genfer Kirche, mit der sich Calvin plötzlich betraut fand, mag zum steigenden Interesse an dieser Unterscheidung das Ihre beigetragen haben, ging es doch in der praktischen Frage nach dem rechten Gottesdienst,

---

[32]OS 3:7:31-32.

[33]OS 1:43, 217.

[34]"Usquequo claudicatis in duas cogitationes? Si Dominus est Deus, sequimini eum: si autem Baal, sequimini illum." So lautet der Titel des ersten Briefes: "De fugiendis impiorum illicitis sacris, et puritate Christianae religionis observanda" (OS 1:287).

[35]So E. Saxer, *Calvin Studienausgabe,* Bd. 1:1, hg. E. Busch et al., (Neukirchen-Vluyn: Neukirchener Verlag, 1994), 136.

[36]Die Parallelen im Aufbau des Katechismus zu Zwinglis *De vera et falsa religione commentarius* (Z 3:628-911) sind denn auch deutlich. Farels Hochschätzung von Zwinglis *Commentarius* ist bekannt (Vgl. G. Locher, "Farels Sommaire und Zwinglis Commentarius," in P. Barthel, R. Scheurer, R. Stauffer, éd., *Actes du Colloque Guillaume Farel,* 2 volumes (Geneva, Lausanne, Neuchâtel: Revue de théologie et de philosophie, 1983), 1:137-46. Ders., "Die Lausanner Disputationsthesen als Dokument Zwinglischer Theologie," in E. Junod, éd., *La dispute de Lausanne (1536)* (Lausanne: Bibliothèque Historique Vaudoise, 1988), 91-103.

den religiösen Gebräuchen, dem rechten Umgang mit den Sakramenten usw. ständig um die Unterscheidung zwischen *(vera)* "religio" und "superstitio." Aus der wahren Gotteserkenntnis soll der wahre Gottesdienst fließen (das Ernstnehmen der ersten Dekalogtafel führt zum "Wort" als Kriterium aller Gotteserkenntnis[37]). Calvin sah sich hier in die Kontinuität der Kirchenväter gestellt, die gegen die (heidnische) "falsa religio" die (christliche) "vera religio" ins Feld führten und ihm so die Sprache vorgaben.[38] Die Unterscheidung von "vera" und "falsa" "religio" wurde dann der Grundthese Calvins, dass der Mensch zur Gotteserkenntnis bestimmt ist, eingeordnet. So lautet die französische Überschrift über den 1. Abschnitt: "Que tous hommes sont nez pour cognoistre Dieu"[39]—in der lateinischen Fassung wiedergegeben mit: "Omnes homines ad religionem esse natos"[40]—bevor im nächsten Abschnitt der Unterschied zwischen "vraye et faulse religion" behandelt wird. Dass es nicht um den "religio"-Begriff als solchen geht, zeigt sich aber bereits daran, dass im zweiten Abschnitt der lateinischen Fassung, überschrieben mit: "Quid inter falsam ac veram religionem intersit," die Begriffe nicht durchgehalten sind. Wo man den Ausdruck "vera religio" erwarten würde, ist stattdessen von der "vera pietas" (in der französischen Fassung: "la vraie piété") und von der "veri Dei cognitio" die Rede. In der zweiten Institutiofassung (1539) erhielt das Thema "religio" schließlich seinen Platz im Rahmen der schon von 1536 her bekannten Dialektik von Gotteserkenntnis und Selbsterkenntnis. Kp. 1, die Lehre von der Gotteserkenntnis, ist dort überschrieben mit: "De cognitione Dei, quae primum est religionis fundamentum, et unde eius regula sit petenda."[41]

Der allgemein gebräuchliche lateinische Ausdruck "religio" wird nun von Calvin dazu in Anspruch genommen, um die universale, schöpfungstheologisch zu verstehende Bestimmung des Menschen zur Gotteserkenntnis (und dem darin eingeschlossenen wahren Gottesdienst) auszusagen.[42] Angesichts der unbestrittenen, und durch die Autoritäten der antiken Schriftsteller bestätigten gesellschaftlichen Bedeutung der "religio,"[43] geht es Calvin um das

[37]Die Farel zugeschriebene (vgl. Saxer, *Calvin Studienausgabe* 1:1:135), zugleich mit dem Katechismus erscheinende *Confession de la foy* beginnt mit dem Satz: "Premierement nous protestons que pour la reigle de nostre foy et religion nous voulons suyvre la seule Escripture" (OS 1:418; CO 12:85; *Calvin Studienausgabe* 1:1:208).

[38]Vgl. Augustins Schrift *De vera religione,* aber auch der bereits zitierte Text von Laktanz; besonders auch: Heinrich Bullinger, *De origine erroris in divinorum ac simulachrorum cultu* (Zürich, 1529).

[39]CO 22:33.

[40]CO 5:324/5.

[41]CO 1:279/280.

[42]Im Katechismus von 1542 kann Calvin aber dann auch wieder bei der Bestimmung des Menschen einsetzen, ohne den "religio"-Begriff zu gebrauchen.

[43]"Quoniam hoc communi sensu receptum est, si a vita nostra absit religio, miserrime nos vivere, adeoque brutis pecudibus nihilo excellere, nullus est qui a pietate cultuque Dei prorsus alienus videri velit" *Katechismus 1537/38* (CO 5:323).

kritische Messen aller behaupteten und praktizierten "religio" an der ersten Tafel des Dekalogs, und damit an Gottes "Wort." Auf dieses "Wort" als Leitfaden und Kriterium zielt jede Thematisierung von "religio" vom ersten Katechismus an bis in alle folgenden Auflagen der *Institutio* hinein.

Auch Calvins Erwähnung der Etymologie von "religio" steht nicht im Dienst einer allgemeinen, seiner Verwendung vorangehenden theoretischen Klärung des Begriffs, sondern im Kontext der Frage nach der "vera religio." Sie erfolgt in *Inst.* 1:12:1, das den Titel trägt: "Deum ab idolis discerni, ut solum in solidum colatur." Calvin stimmt dort zunächst Cicero zu, "religio" von "relegere" her zu verstehen,[44] womit aber nicht, wie Cicero meint, "wiederholt lesen" gemeint ist, sondern ein "Sich-aus-der-Zerstreutheit-Zusammennehmen," ein "Fuß-fassen," ein "Sich Sammeln," ein Sich-Halten an die von Gott gegebene Regel, Grundlage und Leitung. Wie Theseus im Labyrinth den Ausgang dadurch findet, dass er den Ariadnefaden wieder aufnimmt (relegit), und so zur Freiheit gelangt,[45] so ist die "religio" als das Sich-Sammeln aus dem haltlosen Umherirren und der Zerstreutheit, das Aufnehmen des Fadens, der aus dem Labyrinth in die Freiheit führt zu verstehen[46]—das Aufnehmen des Leitfadens des Wortes Gottes zur Orientierung in der Schöpfung.[47]

III. Das Problem des "semen religionis"

Am meisten Aufmerksamkeit hat Calvins Verwendung von "religio," zumindest im deutschsprachigen Raum, sicherlich dort erlangt, wo vom "religionis semen"[48] die Rede ist.

> Hinter dem Fremdwort "Religion" ... verbirgt sich mehr oder weniger verschämt oder unverschämt das Bekenntnis, dass man es als moderner Mensch nicht mehr wagt, prinzipiell und primär und mit erhobener Stimme von Gott zu reden. Diesen geistesgeschichtlichen Zusammenhang könnte ich heute auch mit der schönsten dialektischen Verständigung über den gar nicht so üblen Wortsinn von "religio" nicht loswerden. Vielleicht kommt einmal eine Zeit, wo man wieder harmlos und unbefangen, ohne

---

[44]Und nicht von "religare," dessen Substantiv ja "religatio" heißen müsste. Auf "religare," "verbinden" führt übrigens Bullinger den Ausdruck zurück (*Sermonum Decades quinque* (1552) 4:5, fol. 227).

[45]Vgl. Ovid, *Met.* 8:173.

[46]Vgl. OS 3:105:17-23.

[47]Vgl. dazu: "... fulgorem divini vultus [gemeint ist das Schöpfungszeugnis Gottes] ... esse nobis instar inexplicabilis labyrinthi, nisi verbi linea in ipsum dirigamur ... Itaque saepius David superstitiones e mundo tollendas docens, quo pura vigeat religio, Deum regnantem inducit ... regnandi nomine non potestatem significans qua praeditus est ... sed doctrinam qua sibi legitimum principatum asserit: quia nunquam evelli queunt ex hominum cordibus errores donec plantata fuerit vera Dei cognitio" (*Inst.* 1:6:3 (OS 3:63:31-64:10)).

[48]Inst. 1:3:1 (OS 3:38:5-6).

erröten zu müssen, von Religion wird reden dürfen, wie Zwingli und Calvin es getan haben. Heute ist eine andere Zeit.[49]

Diese Sätze aus Barths Göttinger Vorlesung vom Sommersemester 1924 lassen etwas von der Perspektive erkennen, unter der um die Bedeutung der "Anknüpfung" bei der "religio" durch Calvin und um das Verständnis des "semen religionis" als möglicher Beleg für seine "natürliche Theologie" gestritten wurde.[50] Es ist die Perspektive eines Religionsbegriffs und eines damit verbundenen Problemkontextes, der seine Ausprägung erst unter westlich-neuzeitlichen Bedingungen erhalten hat und erhalten konnte. Eine systematische Inanspruchnahme der Verwendung des "religio"-Begriffs in Calvins *Institutio* muss allerdings diesen zunächst in Calvins eigenem, anders gelagerten Problem—und Erfahrungshorizont aufsuchen, und kann erst von der dort gefundenen Gesamtintention her, also indirekt, Calvins Meinung zu einem ihm nicht vorliegenden Problem zu erschließen suchen. Mit Recht hat sich Ernst Feil in seiner umfassenden Studie zum Ziel gesetzt, den vorneuzeitlichen Religionsbegriff von späteren interpretatorischen Verzerrungen zu befreien.[51] Wenn seine Quelleninterpretationen auch vertieft werden könnten, scheint mir die Tendenz einer Absetzung des vorneuzeitlichen Gebrauchs von "religio" von demjenigen, wie er etwa in Schleiermachers *Reden* vorgetragener Frömmigkeitslehre begegnet,[52] doch richtig zu sein. Wenn Calvin vom "semen religionis" spricht, geht es ihm nicht darum, darzulegen, dass es so etwas wie eine "natürliche Religion" bzw. allgemein verbreitete "Religiosität" gibt. Dieses Phänomen ist—sogar bei den "Epikuräern"—unbestritten.[53] im Horizont seiner Behauptung, nur in Gottes eigenem "Wort" sei die Regel und die Grundlage dessen zu finden, was mit Recht "vera religio" genannt zu werden verdient, ist die Pointe seiner Argumentation die Inanspruchnahme des schon von "heidnischen" Gelehrten bezeugten und bedachten Phänomens menschlicher "religio" durch seine, vor allem auf

---

[49]Karl Barth, *Unterricht in der christlichen Religion,* Erster Band: "Prolegomena, 1924," hg. Hannelotte Reiffen (Zürich: Theologischer Verlag, 1985), 225.

[50]Vgl. z.B. R. Seeberg, *Lehrbuch der Dogmengeschichte* Bd. 4 (4. Aufl.) (Basel: Benno Schwabe, 1954), 561; P. Brunner, "Allgemeine und besondere Offenbarung in Calvins Institutio," *EvTh* 1 (1934), 189-216; G. Gloede, *Theologia naturalis bei Calvin* (Stuttgart: W. Kohlhammer, 1935); P. Barth, *Das Problem der natürlichen Theologie bei Calvin,* ThEx 18 (München: Chr. Kaiser, 1935). Weiter: B. A. Gerrish, "Theology within the Limits of Piety Alone: Schleiermacher and Calvin's Notion of God," in Ders., *The Old Protestantism and the New. Essays on the Reformation Heritage* (Chicago: University of Chicago Press, 1982), 196-207; I. Werner, *Calvin und Schleiermacher im Gespräch mit der Weltweisheit* (Neukirchen-Vluyn: Neukirchener Verlag, 1999, 247-55.

[51] Feil, *Religio I.*

[52]Vgl. z.B. Schleiermacher, *Über die Religion. Reden an die Gebildeten unter ihren Verächtern (1799),* Kritische Gesamtausgabe Bd. 2, Schriften aus der Berliner Zeit 1796-1799, hg. G. Meckenstock (Berlin: W. de Gruyter, 1984), 197:2-19.

[53]"extra controversiam" (Inst. 1:3:1 (OS 3:37:17)).

Römerbrief 1 fußende theologische These der faktisch nicht realisierten, und dennoch bestehenden universalen Bestimmung des Menschen zur Gotteserkenntnis. Diese Bestimmung ist dem Menschen, was schon unverdächtige Zeugen bestätigen, ins Herz gelegt, und damit kann sich dieser dem Anspruch Gottes des "innerhalb" wie "außerhalb" des Menschen aktiv-präsenten Schöpfers in keinem Fall entziehen. Calvin will nicht um der Plausibilität des "Christlichen" willen an Allgemeinem "anknüpfen," sondern umgekehrt das Wesen des Allgemeinen, für ihn selbstverständlich verstanden als Bezug des Menschen zu Gott dem Schöpfer, vom streng biblisch-christologisch verstandenen Besonderen her erschließen, und er erschließt es damit als dynamische, von der Dialektik von Schöpfungswirklichkeit und Sünde geprägte Wirklichkeit. In diese Wirklichkeit ist die menschliche "religio" einbezogen, die Calvin in Anlehnung an Worte Senecas[54] und Ciceros[55] konstatiert, aber nicht durch eine anthropologische Theorie fundiert.

Die neue Anordnung des Stoffes von 1559 lässt den Einbezug des Ausdrucke des "semen religionis" in das Argumentationsgefälle, welches auf die Bestimmung des Menschen zur wahren Gotteserkenntnis, zur "vera religio" zuläuft, nicht auf den ersten Blick ersichtlich werden. Bei genauerem Hinsehen ist sie aber deutlich: Zu Anfang der *Institutio* von 1559 geht es um die wahre Gotteserkenntnis im Horizont des 1. Artikels, welche Calvin in breiter Auseinandersetzung mit der—humanistisch an Cicero und Seneca—gebildeten und von dieser Lektüre auch geprägten Leserschaft expliziert. Das Argumentationsziel von Inst. 1:1-5 ist aber erst in Kp 6 erreicht: Gott der

---

[54]In Senecas *Epistulae morales* heißt es vom Verhältnis der Menschen zu den Göttern: "Non sunt dii fastidiosi, non invidi: admittunt et ascendentibus manum porrigunt. Miraris hominem ad deos ire? Deus ad homines venit, immo quod est propius, in homines venit: nulla sine deo mens bona est. Semina in corporibus humanis divina dispersa sunt, quae si bonus cultor excipit, similia origini prodeunt et paria iis ex quibus orta sunt surgunt: si malus, non aliter quam humus sterilis ac palustris necat ac deinde creat purgamenta pro frugibus" Seneca, *Ep.* 73; Zitiert nach: *L. Annaei Senecae ad Lucilium epistolae morales,* Tom I, hg. L.D. Reynolds (Oxford: Oxford University Press, 1965), 224.

[55]"Solus enim vidit primum esse deos, quod in omnium animis eorum notionem inpressisset ipsa natura. Quae est enim gens aut quod genus hominum, quod non habeat sine doctrina anticipationem quandam deorum? Quam appellat πρόληψιν Epicurus, id est anteceptam animo rei quandam informationem, sine qua nec intellegi quicquam nec quaeri nec disputari possit. Cuius rationis vim atque utilitatem ex illo caelesti Epicuri de regula et iudicio volumine accepimus. Quod igitur fundamentum huius quaestionis est, id praeclare iactum videtis. Cum enim non instituto aliquo more aut lege sit opinio constituta maneatque ad unum omnium firma consensio, intellegi necesse est esse deos, quoniam insitas eorum vel potius innatas cognitiones habemus; de quo autem omnium natura consentit, id verum esse necesse est; esse igitur deos confitendum est. Quod quoniam fere constat inter omnis non philosophos solum sed etiam indoctos, fateamur constare illud etiam, hanc nos habere sive anticipationem ut ante dixi sive praenotionem deorum (sunt enim rebus novis nova ponenda nomina, ut Epicurus ipse πρόληψιν appellavit, quam antea nemo eo verbo nominarat) hanc igitur habemus, ut deos beatos et inmortales putemus. Quae enim nobis natura informationem ipsorum deorum dedit, eadem insculpsit in mentibus ut eos aeternos et beatos haberemus" (Cicero, *De nat.* 1:16:43-17:45).

Schöpfer will in seinem Wort erkannt werden, was nicht bedeutet, dass sich das Geschöpf Mensch mit der Unkenntnis dieses Wortes "entschuldigen" kann. Hatte Calvin 1536 noch—wohl unter stärkerem Einfluss Luthers bzw. Melanchthons—gleich zu Anfang seiner *Institutio* formuliert: " ... legem in omnibus cordibus Dominus inscripsit et quasi impressit ... ,"[56] so wird diese Feststellung in der Ausgabe von 1539 weit nach hinten verlegt.[57] Stattdessen heißt es an vergleichbarer Stelle nun: "... inscriptum omnium cordibus divinitatis sensum ..."[58] Das Phänomen "religio" wird zu einem theologisch gedeuteten Hinweis auf die Universalität des Gotteswillens, der sich konzentriert im 1. und 2. Gebot ausdrückt. Es gibt so zugleich Antwort auf die humanistische Frage nach der "Bestimmung" des Menschen. Der erste Schritt dazu ist der Katechismus von 1537/38: "Quum nemo hominum reperiatur ... qui non aliquo afficiatur religionis sensu ..."[59] Der "semen religionis" ist für Calvin ein "existenzieller," qua Geschöpflichkeit gegebener Gottesbezug, der nicht erst durch rationale Argumentation oder durch Reflexion herzustellen oder auch nur zu entdecken ist, sondern sich in aller Erfahrung aufdrängt.[60] Calvins Interesse an der "religio" steht nicht im Horizont der Auseinandersetzung mit deren "Verächtern" überhaupt, wie sie seit der Zeit der Spätaufklärung auch im deutschen Sprachraum als notwendig erachtet wurde.[61] Ihm geht es vielmehr von Anfang an um Unterscheidung und Abgrenzung: um die Unterscheidung zwischen Gottesdienst und Götzendienst, zwischen Glaube und Aberglaube, die überall wieder neu zu vollziehen er als theologische Grundaufgabe ansieht, und der das, was man seine "bestreitende Anknüpfung" nennen könnte, dienen soll.[62] Berücksichtigt man die Bedeutung der rhetorischen Bildung

---

[56]OS 1:39.

[57]Vgl. *Inst.* 2:2:22 (OS 3:264:24-265:7).

[58]*Inst.* 1:3:1 (OS 3:38:10-11).

[59]CO 5:323.

[60]Womit selbstverständlich nicht ein an der neuzeitlichen Metaphysik orientierter Erfahrungsbegriff gemeint ist. Vgl. dazu die Interpretation bei: Chr. Link, *Schöpfung. Schöpfungstheologie in reformatorischer Tradition,* HST Bd. 7/1 (Gütersloh: Bertelsmann, 1991), 149-50.

[61]Vgl. z. B. J. J. Spalding, *Religion, eine Angelegenheit des Menschen* (1797/1799), hg. W. E. Müller, (Darmstadt: Wissenschaftliche Buchgesselschaft, 1997); Chr. Meier-Dörken, *Die Theologie der frühen Predigten Schleiermachers* (Berlin / New York: W. de Gruyter, 1988).

[62]Einige Texte dazu: "Sed in ordine prophetae hoc quoque notatu dignum est, non aliter evanescere pravas superstitiones, nisi dum obtinet vera religio. Nam quia pro sensus sui tarditate ad verum Deum non perveniunt, necesse est eos in suis mendaciis errare: quae sola Dei cognitio discutit ac purgat, non secus ac sol fulgore suo tenebras dispergit. Ingenita est hominibus religio aliqua: sed quia talis est non solum imbecillitas mentis nostrae, sed etiam caecitas ac stupor, ut conceptum deitatis sensum statim depravet: hinc fit ut religio initium sit omnium superstitionum: non id quidem sua natura, sed quia obtenebratae sunt hominum mentes, ut verum Deum ab idolis non discernant" (CO 32:44, *Kommentar zu Psalm* 97:7).

Calvins und das rhetorische Gepräge auch der *Institutio,* so ist weniger die Aufnahme des religio-Begriffs erstaunlich als der Verzicht auf alle "captatio benevolentiae" in den Ausführungen über die "Religion." Calvin versucht, auf der Basis von Römerbrief 1 das paulinische Argumentationsgefälle im Kontext des Humanismus seiner Zeit zur Geltung zu bringen. Auf dieser Linie müsste man wohl Calvins sachliches Anliegen aufnehmen, ohne einzelne seiner Aussagen anachronistisch im neuzeitlichen theologischen Diskurs für die Notwendigkeit oder umgekehrt Unsachlichkeit einer religiösen Interpretation der Wirklichkeit in Anspruch zu nehmen.

Zu Apg. 17:17: "Disputabat igitur in Synagoga cum Iudaeis et religiosis": "Ordinarium Paulo erat ubicunque Synagogas habebant Iudaei, illinc facere exordium et Christum suae genti offerre. Secundus inde gradus ad gentiles erat, qui gustata legis doctrina, quamvis nondum vera pietate rite imbuti essent, colebant tamen Deum Israel, et discendi cupidi non respuebant, quae ex Mose et Prophetis scirent desumpta esse. Quia autem talis docilitas ingressus erat ad fidem, imo quoddam fidei initium, honorificio titulo eos dignatur Spiritus qui primis tantum rudimentis leviter aspersi proprius ad verum Deum accesserant: Religiosi enim vocantur. Sed meminerimus hac nota discerni ab aliis, ut in nihilum redigatur tota mundi religio. Vocantur spiritualiter Dei cultores, qui nomen dederunt Deo Israel: illis solis tribuitur religio: ergo nihil aliis fit reliquum praeter ignominiam atheismi, utcunque in superstitionibus anxie se torqueant. Et merito: quicquid enim splendoris ostentent idololatrae, si excutiatur interior eorum affectus, nihil illic reperietur praeter horribilem Dei contemptum, merumque esse fucum patebit, quod se idolis blandiri simulant" (CO 48:404).

Zu Apg. 17:26: "Iam Paulus quorsum conditum fuerit humanum genus Athenienses admonet, ut hoc modo invitet atque hortetur ad considerandum vitae suae finem. Haec sane turpis est hominum ingratitudo, quum vita communi fruantur omnes, non reputare quorsum Deus illis vivere dederit. Atqui belluinus hic stupor maiorem partem occupat, ut minime reputent, cur in mundo locati sint, nec illis in mentem veniat coeli terraeque opifex, cuius bona ingurgitant. Ergo Paulus postquam disseruit de natura Dei, hanc admonitionem opportune inserit, debere homines sedulo ad Dei notitiam attendere, quia ideo conditi sunt et ad hunc finem nati. Breviter enim hanc illis vivendi causam assignat, ut Deum quaerant. Porro quia non una in mundo religio vigebat, sed distractae erant gentes in varias sectas, varietatem istam ex corruptela natam esse admonet. Huc enim spectat meo iudicio quod dicit, ex uno sanguine fuisse omnes creatos. Debuerat enim consanguinitas et eadem generis origo vinculum esse mutui inter eos consensus: atqui religio est, quae maxime conciliat homines vel dissociat. Unde sequitur, a natura descivisse qui ita in religione et Dei cultu sunt discordes, quia, ex quocunque oriundi sunt loco, vel quamcunque mundi plagam incolant, unus tamen omnium est fictor et pater, qui uno consensu ab omnibus quarendus est. Et certe neque locorum distantia, neque fines regionum neque morum diversitas, neque ulla divortii inter homines causa Deum sui dissimilem facit. In summa docere voluit, naturae ordinem fuisse violatum, quum religio inter eos divulsa fuit, ac dissipationem, quae inter ipsos apparet, testimonium esse eversae pietatis, quia a Deo communi patre defecerint, ex quo omnis cognatio dependet" (CO 48:414).

Providence in Calvin: Calvin's View of God's Use of Means *(media)* in His Acts of Providence

Pieter C. Potgieter

Calvin's most comprehensive discussion of providence is to be found in his *Institutes* (1559) Book I, chapters 16-18. There are, however, many references to God's acts of providence in his commentaries, his correspondence and other works of his.

His view is very well summarised in the *Catechism of Geneva:* The Father Almighty governs the world "by his Providence, determining all things by his will, ruling all creatures as seems to him good ... [A]s the world was once made by God, so it is now preserved by him ... [T]he earth and all other things endure just in as far as they are sustained by his energy, and as it were his hand ... [I]t is he alone who by wisdom, goodness, and power guides the whole course and order of nature ..."[1]

Thus providence is God's very active *gubernatio* of everything on earth. He is not only Creator, but also Provider and Guide. Calvin based this dogma on the very will of God. "It amounts to this: When it is said that God's will is the very cause of all things, his providence is upheld as guide of all man's considerations and works; thus it not only exerts power in the elect, who are guided by the Holy Spirit, but it also compels to submissiveness those rejected."[2]

For Calvin providence was not so much an issue to be explained, but rather a *confession* related to the very heart of faith. He shows a deep conviction and faith in the comprehensive sovereignty of God over all creation. Everything that happens, whatever it may be, finds some place in the eternal counsel of God. The power of evil which we so often observe and experience should always be seen in the perspective of God's grace in Christ. His work of recon-

[1]CO 6:16, 18.

[2]"Summa haec sit: quum Dei voluntas dicitur rerum omnium esse causa, providentiam eius statui moderatricem in cunctis hominum consiliis et operibus, ut non tantum vim suam exserat in electis, qui spiritu sancto reguntur, sed etiam reprobos in obsequium cogat" (*Inst.* 1:18:2 (CO 2:170)). Quite remarkable is what he says in the *Catechism* regarding wicked men and devils: "he does not govern them by his Spirit, he however curbs them by his power as a bridle" (CO 6:18).

ciliation will without any doubt overcome the powers of evil. The suffering of Christ is the fundamental reality for faithful and obedient existence of man.

Although much has been written on providence in the works of Calvin, the issue of God's use of *media* in his acts of providence has not been investigated in depth. On this topic Calvin himself states clearly that in overruling all things the providence of God works at one time with means, at another without means, and at another against means: "ut nunc mediis interpositis operetur, nunc sine mediis, nunc contra omnia media."[3]

1. *Media* of providence at "different levels"?

The above statement of Calvin immediately raises the question whether he in fact thought of the Word and the Spirit as *media* of providence. The *sine mediis* obviously implies a direct and immediate act of God, whether it be by the Father, the Son (Word) or the Holy Spirit.

Calvin's commentary on and other references to Genesis 1:2 are relevant in this regard. In the moving (hovering, Hebr. *m^erachefet*) of the Spirit upon the waters, he sees God, particularly the third Person of the Trinity (the Holy Spirit) at work to preserve his creation. But can one then say: the Spirit, and in other biblical passages the Word of God, are the *media* of providence? To my mind, no. The Spirit, just as the Word, is God, the working *agens,* and thus not a *medium* employed by God. There is, incidentally, indeed one reference in the *Institutes* where the *word* is indicated as *medium* or instrument of the Spirit ("verbum esse *organum* quo Spiritus ...dispensat" (1:9:3)). From the context it is, however, quite clear that he in this case refers to the spoken word as proclamation of the Gospel, and not to the eternal Word as Person within the Trinity.

But now, whereas the Hebrew text of Genesis 1:2 only refers to the presence of the Spirit hovering over the water, Calvin added attributes: power, secret efficacy, inspiration. Is Calvin then seeing these attributes as the true *media* of providence? This, however, again relates to the question of whether he sees these attributes as *essentiae* of God's being, or as *dona.* I will in another paragraph revisit this question.

At another level, Calvin's view on the use of *media* in God's acts of providence is clear. God works through the instrumentality of men (per hominum ministerium) or aided by inanimate creatures (ab inanimatis creaturis adiutus) to guide and govern the world.[4] Thus Calvin sees the ministers of God as his *organa* (instruments) joining the efficacy of the Spirit to their word, but then also makes use of natural phenomena as *media* in achieving his objectives, e.g. the power of the east wind (Exodus 10:13). An interesting illustration of God's use of *media* is found in one of his letters: on October 1, 1538, in view of

---

[3]Inst. 1:17:1.

[4]*Inst.* 1:17:7.

particular circumstances he wrote to the church in Geneva: "Furthermore you should consider that these things did not happen to you apart from the providence of God; He even makes use of the impious to do his work according to his good will."[5]

2. Word and Spirit

Reading through various passages on God's providence in Calvin, one is struck by the way in which he uses now Word and then again Spirit in the very same context. What he in one place ascribes to the Spirit, he in another attributes to the Word.

Calvin distinguishes between various workings of the Spirit. One of them is his universal working of sustaining and preserving everything.[6] Also, in *De aeterna Dei praedestinatione,* he refers to the threefold work of the Spirit: first of these is the general rule of the world.[7] In his commentary on John 1:5 he states the same of the Word (the Son) of God.[8]

On the other hand Calvin makes a clear distinction between the Son and the Spirit: how can the eternal Word *(Sermo aeternus),* who in order precedes the Spirit, be called his image?[9]

Calvin is very hesitant, though, almost wavering, when he deals with the nature of the distinction between the Father, the Son and the Holy Spirit. And yet he finds it unbecoming to say nothing of a distinction which Scriptures do point out. "The distinction is, that to the Father is attributed the beginning of action *[principium agendi],* the fountain and source of all things; to the Son, wisdom, counsel, and arrangement in action *[sapientia, consilium, ipsaque in rebus agendis dispensatio],* while the energy and efficacy of action *[virtus et efficacia actionis]* is assigned to the Spirit."[10]

3. Hidden motives of God

Calvin's frequent use of the Latin adjective *arcanus* (lit. kept from public knowledge, secret, hidden, mystical) may be significant. There are at least ninety-eight occurences of *arcanus* in the *Institutes,* mostly in conjunction with attributes or acts of God or his Spirit, for instance with *virtus, inspiratio, efficacia, vis, vigor, potentia, communicatio, ratio, operatio, significatio, stipulatio, iudicia, motus,*

---

[5]CO 10/2:252.

[6]*Comm. Rom.* 8:14 (CO 49:147).

[7]"[P]rimo loco statuenda est ... generalis mundi gubernatio" (CO 8:349).

[8]CO 47:7.

[9]*Inst.* 1:15:3.

[10]*Inst.* 1:13:18.

beneplacitum, praedestinatio, electio, segregatio, voluntas, gratia, revelatio, irrigatio, testimonium, consilium, influxus, benedictio, providentia, nutus, sapientia and recessus. Referring to his conversion to Protestantism, Calvin even applies this notion in a personal context: "God, by the secret guidance of his providence, at length gave a different direction to my course."[11]

He strongly rejects every endeavor of man presumptuously to examine or even judge the hidden motives of God. He knows what he does and he may use whatever means he prefers for his particular purpose. In Calvin's exposition of Job undoubtedly there is a marked tension between a revealed justice of God and a hidden justice. And yet, occasionally it does happen that the light of revelation even breaks through the confines of God's hidden counsel.

4. *Essentia* or *dona*?

Somehow, says Calvin, in order to keep everything up, God has to impart strength from heaven *(e coelo vigorem installaverit)*.[12] He says that the world is sustained by the same power by which it was once created *(eadem Dei virtute qua semel creata est)*.[13] The point in case here is whether Calvin sees the strength by which God does this as *essentia* to his being, or as *dona*. He is quite clear that God did not employ any external means in creating the world: God's Word and the spirit of his mouth *(verbum Dei et spiritum oris)* over against *(opposuit)* all external means *(externis omnibus mediis)*. In the same passage, however, he also states that the creation of the world leads us by direct consequence *(continua serie)* to God's providence, of which he then says that the world is controlled *(gubernari)* by his wisdom and power *(consilio et manu)*.[14] Can he in some way escape from seeing these attributes as means within God, in spite of his unambiguous rejection of Servetus's idea of creatures partaking of the Holy Spirit?[15]

In his commentary on Exodus 3:14 ("I am that I am") Calvin says: "God attributes to himself alone divine glory, because he is self-existent and therefore eternal; and thus gives being and existence to every creature... Wherefore, in order rightly to apprehend the one God, we must first know, that all things in heaven and earth derive at his will their essence, or subsistence from One, who only truly is. From this Being all power is derived; because if God sustains all things by his excellency, he governs them also at his will."[16] Still, it is not clear

[11]"Deus tamen arcano providentiae suae fraeno cursum meum alio tandem reflexit." (CO 31:21) (*Comm. Psalms,* Introd.).

[12]*Comm. Isaiah* 32:15 (CO 36:551).

[13]*Comm. Jer.* 27:5 (CO 38:542).

[14]*Comm. Psalms* 33:6 (CO 31:326).

[15]*Comm. Psalms* 104:30 (CO 32:95).

[16]CO 24:43-44.

how the transfer from God to creation takes place. Even Calvin's commentary on 1 John 4:7-8 and 16 ("God is love") does not shed light on the relation between his *essentia* and his *dona*. He merely states: "Here then he does not speak of the essence of God, but only shows what he is found to be by us ... This is as it were the minor proposition in an argument; for from faith to love he reasons in this way: By faith God dwells in us, and God is love; then, wherever God abides, love ought to be there. Hence it follows that love is necessarily connected with faith."[17]

Calvin says: In sending forth his Spirit to maintain life, God makes what was his own to be ours *(quod suum erat, nostrum facit)*; this however does not mean that a portion of God's Spirit *(aliqua eius portio)* should dwell in every living creature. Although Calvin is not very clear here, it seems that his intention is that what we see is a reflection of the lifegiving power of God *(in hoc speculo* [mirror] *lucere nobis vivificam Dei virtutem)*.[18] Is this perhaps the reason why Calvin time and again refers to the ***arcana*** *Dei virtute*? How this happens, will remain a mystery for us.

Dealing with the Trinity, Calvin states that it behoves us to look on the Holy Spirit "as his energy diffused indeed over all things, but still perpetually resident in himself."[19] A key to solve this may be Calvin's use of the term *inspiratio* in connection with God's providence.[20] Another clue may be what Calvin says about John 1:3: that the ***effect*** of his power *(eius vis* ***effectu****)* is known in the external operation *(externum actum)* of the Word.[21] Maybe his intention is this: God may immediately create something outside of himself to use as *medium* for revelation or for providence. Then it is no attribute but his creation—a finite image of his essential attribute.

---

[17]CO 55:352, 356.

[18]*Comm. Psalms* 104:30 (CO 32:96).

[19]*Catechism of the Church of Geneva* (CO 6:14).

[20]Cf. Commentaries on Gen. 1:2; Exod. 6:3; Ps. 104:30; John 1:4; Acts 17:28; *Inst.* 1:16:1 and 1:18:2.

[21]*Comm. John* 1:3 (CO 47:4).

THE *MEDIA* OF PROVIDENCE IN CALVIN

Genesis 1:2

> And the earth was without form and void; and darkness was upon the face of the deep. And the Spirit of God moved upon the face of the waters.

Comm.

And the Spirit of God. Interpreters have wrested this passage in various ways. The opinion of some that it means the wind, is too frigid to require refutation. They who understand by it the Eternal Spirit of God, do rightly; yet all do not attain the meaning of Moses in the connection of his discourse; hence arise the various interpretations of the participle *(merachepath)*. I will, in the first place, state what (in my judgment) Moses intended. We have already heard that before God had perfected the world it was an indigested mass; he now teaches that the power of the Spirit was necessary in order to sustain it. For this doubt might occur to the mind, how such a disorderly heap could stand; seeing that we now behold the world preserved by government, or order. He therefore asserts that this mass, however confused it might be, was rendered stable, for the time, by the secret efficacy of the Spirit. Now there are two significations of the Hebrew word which suit the present place; either that the Spirit moved and agitated itself over the waters, for the sake of putting forth vigour; or that he brooded overt them to cherish them. Inasmuch as it makes little difference in the result, whichever of these explanations is preferred, let the reader's judgment be left free. But if that chaos required the secret inspiration of God to prevent its speedy dissolution; how could this order, so fair and distinct, subsist by itself, unless it derived strength elsewhere? Therefore, that Scripture must be fulfilled, "Send forth thy Spirit, and they shall be created, and thou shalt renew the face of the earth," (Ps. civ. 30;) so, on the other hand, as soon as the Lord takes away his Spirit, all things return to their dust and vanish away, (ver. 29.).

LATIN TEXT

Genesis 1:2

> *Terra autem erat informis et inanis; tenebraeque erant in superficie voraginis, et Spiritus Dei agitabat se in superficie aquarum.*

CO 23:16

Et spiritus Dei. Locum hunc varie torserunt interpretes. Quod nonnulli ventum intelligunt, adeo frigidum est ut refutatione nulla indigeat. Qui aeternum Dei spiritum, recte id quidem: sed in complexu orationis Mosis, sensum non omnes assequuntur: inde varietas in participio *(merachephet)*. Dicam priore loco quidnam, meo iudicio, voluerit Moses. Audivimus, antequam Deus mundum expoliret, fuisse indigestam congeriem: nunc docet spiritus virtutem in ea sustinenda fuisse necessariam. Poterat enim haec dubitatio venire in mentem, quomodo inordinata moles staret, quum nunc videamus mundum temperamento servari. Ideo dicit, massam illam quamvis indisposita foret, arcana spiritus efficacia stabilem ad tempus fuisse. Iam duae sunt verbi hebraici significationes quae conveniunt praesenti loco: vel quod moveret se atque agitaret spiritus Dei super aquas, vigoris scilicet exserendi causa, vel quod incubaret ad fovendum. Quia utrumvis eligas ad rei summam parum refert, liberum sit iudicium lectori. Caeterum si illa rerum confusio arcana Dei inspiratione opus habuit, ne mox concideret: quomodo hic tam pulcher ac distinctus ordo per se consisteret, nisi aliunde vigorem mutuaretur? Ergo illud impleri oportet: Emitte spiritum tuum, et creabuntur, et renovabis faciem terrae: sicut ex adverso, simul ac spiritum suum aufert Dominus, omnia in pulverem suum abeunt, et evanescunt (Psal. 104:29).

Genesis 7:11

> In the six hundredth year of Noah's life, in the second month, the seventeenth day of the month, the same day were all the fountains of the great deep broken up, and the windows of heaven were opened.

Genesis 7:11

> *In anno sexcentesimo annorum vitae Noah, in mense secundo, in septimadecima die mensis, die ipsa, rupti sunt omnes fontes voraginis magnae, et fenestrae coeli apertae sunt.*

Comm.

Lastly, God raised for men a theatre in the habitable region of the earth; and caused, by his secret power, that the subterraneous waters should not break forth to overwhelm us, and the celestial waters should not conspire with them for that purpose.

CO 23:131

Denique in regione terrae habitabili Deus theatrum hominibus erexit; et fit arcana eius virtute ne aquae subterraneae ad nos mergendos ebulliant, et simul conspirent aquae coelestes.

Exodus 6:3

> And I appeared unto Abraham, unto Isaac, and unto Jacob, by the name of God Almighty; but by my name JEHOVAH was I not known to them.

Exodus 6:3

> *Apparui quidem Abrahae, Isaac, et Jacob in Deo omnipotente: in nomine tamen meo Jehova non sum cognitus illis.*

Comm.

Since, then, nothing is more peculiar to God than eternity, He is called Jehovah, because He has existence from Himself, and sustains all things by His secret inspiration.

CO 24:78

Quum ergo nihil Deo magis sit proprium quam aeternitas, vocatur Iehova quod a se ipso habeat esse, et arcana inspiratione omnia sustineat.

Exodus 10:13

> And Moses stretched forth his rod over the land of Egypt, and the Lord brought an east wind upon the land all that day, and all that night; and when it was morning, the east wind brought the locusts.

Exodus 10:13

> *Extendit itaque Moses virgam suam super terram Aegypti, et Jehova adduxit ventum orientalem in terram toto illo die, et tota nocte: et ubi advenit mane, ventus orientalis excitavit locustam.*

Comm.

And the Lord said unto Moses. Since Pharaoh was not induced to obey by the announcement of the punishment, its execution is here related. And first, Moses is commended to stretch out his hand to bring in the locusts, in right of the authority with which God had invested him; for the stretching forth of the hand is a token of power. He therefore adds, just beyond, that he stretched forth his rod, which we have before seen to have been given him as a royal sceptre. It is, then, just as if God had appointed him to be His vicegerent, and had subjected to him the sea, and earth, and air. But that he may sink down into the character of a minister, he does not say that the locusts came up at his command, but assigns the glory of the operation to the Lord alone. And this mode of expression is worthy of remark, since we learn from it that the ministers of God, although they bring nothing of their own, still do not lose their labour, because the efficacy of the Spirit is conjoined to their word; and still that nothing is detracted from the power of God and transferred to them, since they are but instruments,

CO 24:123-24

Tunc dixit Iehova Mosi. Quoniam indicta sibi poena non fuit adductus Pharao ad parendum exsequutio hic narratur. Ac primo quidem iussus est Moses manum extendere ut locustas accerseret, pro iure imperii quo Deus eum ornaverat. Manus enim extentio signum est potestatis. Ideo paulo post subiicit se baculum extendisse, quem ante vidimus loco regii sceptri fuisse ei datum. Perinde igitur est ac si Deus praefectum constituens subiiceret ei mare, terram, et aërem. Ut tamen subsidat in gradu ministri non dicit locustas erupisse ad suum mandatum, sed laudem operis vindicat uni Deo. Atque haec ratio loquendi notatu digna est, ex qua discimus ministros Dei, quamvis nihil ex se afferant, non tamen ludere operam, quia spiritus efficacia cum eorum voce coniuncta est, neque tamen ideo quidquam delibari ex Deo virtute quod ad ipsos transeat: quando nonnisi organa sunt quae Dei manu in usum suum applicantur. Sic Moses non frustra neque inaniter extento baculo praecepit locustis ut ascenderent quia statim apparuit effectus mandati. Neque tamen ipse creavit locustas, neque

which by God's hand are applied in His service. Thus did not Moses in vain command, as he stretched forth his rod, the locusts to come up; because the effect of his command immediately appeared. Still he did not himself create the locusts, nor attract them by the stirring of his rod, but they were divinely brought by the power of the east wind.

baculi agitatione eas attraxit, sed impulsu venti orientalis divinitus sunt adductae.

Exodus 14:21

> And Moses stretched out his hand over the sea; and the Lord caused the sea to go back by a strong east wind all that night, and made the sea dry land, and the waters were divided.

Exodus 14:21

> *Porro extendit Moses manum suam super mare: et Jehova fecit mare abire per ventum orientalem vehementem tota nocte; posuitque mare in siccitatem, quia divisae erant aquae.*

Comm.

Meanwhile it is to be remembered, that the sea could not be dried by any wind, however strong, unless it had been effected by the secret power of the Spirit, beyond the ordinary operation of nature.

CO 24:154

Interea tenendum est, nullo quantumvis impetuoso flatu potuisse siccari mare, nisi supra naturae modum arcana vi spiritus sui operatus esset.

Psalm 33:6

> By the word of Jehovah were the heavens established; and all the host of them by the spirit of this mouth.

Psalm 33:6

> Verbo Iehovae coeli firmati sunt et spiritu oris eius omnis exercitus eorum.

Comm.

By the word of Jehovah. That he may stir us up to think more closely of God's works, he brings before us the creation of the world itself; for until God be acknowledged as the Creator and Framer of the world, who will believe that he attends to the affairs of men, and that the state of the world is controlled by his wisdom and power? But the creation of the world leads us by direct consequence to the providence of God. Not that all men reason so justly, or are endued with so sound a judgement, as to conclude that the world is at this day maintained by the same divine power which was one put forth in creating it: on the contrary, the great majority imagine that he is an idle spectator in heaven of whatever is transacted on earth. But no man truly believes that the world was created by God unless he is also firmly persuaded that it is maintained and preserved by him. Wisely and properly, therefore, does the prophet carry us back to the very origin of the world, in order to fix in our minds the certainty of God's providence in the continual order of nature. By the figure synecdoche, he uses the

CO 31:326-27

Verbo Iehovae coeli firmati sunt. Quo nos ad reputanda Dei opera melius expergefaciat, ipsam mundi creationem nobis proponit. Donec enim agnitus fuerit Deus mundi creator et opifex, quis credat ab eo curari res humanas, mundique statum eius consilio et manu gubernari? Mundi autem creatio ad Dei providentiam continua serie nos deducit; non quod tam dextre ratiocinentur omnes, vel tam recto iudicio praediti sint, ut mundum statuant eadem Dei virtute, quae se in illo creando semel exseruit, hodie sustineri: quin potius major pars eum e coelo otiosum spectare fingit quidquid in terris agitur. Sed aliter rite nemo tenet mundum a Deo conditum, nisi persuasus quoque sit, ab eodem foveri et conservari in suo statu. Scite igitur et apte propheta, ut nobis certitudinem infigat providentiae Dei in continuo naturae ordine, nos ad ipsam mundi originem revocat. Porro, nomen coelorum synecdochice pro universa mundi machina posuit: quia (ut alibi dictum est) eorum maxime conspectu in admirationem rapimur. Ideo mox addit eorum exercitum: qua voce sidera et stellas intelligit,

term heavens for the whole fabric of the world, because, as I have elsewhere remarked, the sight of the heavens more than all the other parts of creation transports us with admiration. He therefore immediately adds, And all the host of them, by which phraseology, according to the usual method of Scripture, he means the stars and planets; for if the heavens were destitute of this ornament, they would in a manner be empty. In saying that the heavens were created by the word of God, he greatly magnifies his power, because by his nod alone, without any other aid or means, and without much time or labour, he created so noble and magnificent a work. But although the Psalmist sets the word of God and the breath of his mouth in opposition both to all external means, and to every idea of painful labour on God's part, yet we may truly and certainly infer from this passage, that the world was framed by God's Eternal Word, his only begotten Son.

usitato scripturae more: nam si hoc ornatu carerent coeli, quodammodo vacui essent. Coelos autem dicens verbo Dei conditos, potentiam eius magis amplificat, quod solo nutu contentus, neque accersiverit aliunde subsidia, neque etiam multum operae vel laboris impenderit ad tam splendidum et nobile opificium. Quanquam autem verbum Dei et spiritum oris tam externis omnibus mediis, quam laboris difficultati quae in Deo fingi posset, opposuit propheta: vere tamen et certo hinc colligitur, mundum per aeternum Dei sermonem qui filius est unigenitus, fabricatum esse.

Psalm 104:30

> Thou shalt send forth thy spirit, and they shall be created: and thou shalt renew the face of the earth.

Psalm 104:30

> Emittes spiritum tuum, creabuntur: et renovabis faciem terrae.

Comm.

The prophet describes step by step the destruction of living creatures, upon God's withdrawing from them his secret energy, that from the contrast he may the better commend that continued inspiration, by which all things are maintained in life and vigour. He could have gone farther, and have asserted, that all things, unless upheld in being by God, would return to nothing; but he was content with affirming in general and popular language, that whatever is not cherished by Him falls into corruption. He again declares, that the world is daily renewed, because God sendeth forth his spirit. In the propagation of living creatures, we doubtless see continually a new creation of the world. In now calling that God's spirit, which he before represented as the spirit of living creatures, there is no contradiction. God sendeth forth that spirit which remains with him whither he pleases; and as soon as he has sent it forth, all things are created. In this way, what was his own he makes to be ours. But this gives no countenance to the old dream of the Manichaeans, which that filthy dog Servetus has made still worse in our own day. The Manichaeans said

CO 32:95-96

Gradatim vero describit animalium interitum, ubi arcanum suum vigorem retrahit Deus, quo melius ex opposito continuam inspirationem commendet, qua vegetantur. Quanquam autem ultra progredi poterat, omnia scilicet in nihilum reditura esse, contentus tamen fuit hoc crasso et populari docendi modo, in putredinem concidere quidquid divinitus non fovetur. Dicit autem rursum quotidie mundum *renovari*, quia *spiritum suum Deus emittit*. Et certe in nova animalium sobole assidue cernimus novam mundi creationem. Quod vero spiritum, quem prius animalium esse dixit, nunc tribuit Deo, nihil in eo repugnantiae est: Deus spiritum qui penes eum residet, emittit quo visum est: simulac emisit, omnia creantur. Hoc modo quod suum erat, nostrum facit. Caeterum hoc veteri Manichaeorum delirio nihil suffragatur, quod in deterius nostra aetate auxit impurus ille canis Servetus. Dicebant Manichaei animam hominis particulam esse divini spiritus, et ex eius traduce nasci .... Prophetae autem nihil minus propositum fuit, quam Dei spiritum partiri ut essentialiter aliqua eius portio in singulis animantibus habitet, sed

that the soul of man is a particle of the Divine Spirit, and is propagated from it as the shoot of a tree; ..... Nothing was farther from the prophet's intention, than to divide the spirit of God into parts, so that a portion of it should dwell essentially in every living creature. But he termed that the spirit of God which proceeds from him. By the way, he instructs us, that it is ours, because it is given us, that it may quicken us. The amount of what is stated is, that when we see the world daily decaying, and daily renewed, the life-giving power of God is reflected to us herein as in a mirror. ...... Since then the world daily dies, and is daily renewed in its various parts, the manifest conclusion is, that it subsists only by a secret virtue derived from God.

spiritum Dei vocavit, qui ab eo proficiscitur. Interea nostrum esse admonet, quia nobis in vitam datus est. Summa huc tendit, dum videmus quotidie mundum deficere et renasci, in hoc speculo lucere nobis vivificam Dei virtutem .... Quando itaque mundus quotidie interit et renascitur in suis partibus, hinc colligere promptum est, nonnisi arcana Dei virtute subsistere.

Isaiah 32:15

> Until the Spirit be poured upon us from on high, and the wilderness be a fruitful field, and the fruitful field be counted for a forest.

Isaiah 32:15

> *Donec super nos effundatur Spiritus ex alto, et ponatur desertum in agrum cultum, et ager cultus instar sylvae reputetur.*

Comm.

With good reason, therefore, does Isaiah say that "the Spirit" will come from on high to refresh and fertilize the earth; and he alludes, I have no doubt, to that saying of David, "Send forth thy Spirit, and they shall be created, and thou wilt renew the face of the earth." (Ps. civ. 30.) Holding out this as an evidence that God is reconciled, he at the same time declares that the restoration of the Church proceeds solely from the grace of God, who can remove its barrenness as soon as he has imparted strength from heaven; for he who created all things out of nothing, as if they had formerly existed, is able to renew it in a moment.

CO 36:551

Non abs re igitur Isaias spiritum e sublimi venturum dicit, qui terram vegetando eius foecunditatem renovet. Nec mihi dubium est quin ad illam Davidis sententiam alludat: Emitte spiritum tuum et creabuntur, et renovabis faciem terrae (Psal. 104, 29). Caeterum quia signum hoc reconciliati Dei proponit, simul admonet instaurationem ecclesiae manare a sola Dei gratia, posseque sterilitatem corrigi, simul ac e coelo vigorem installaverit. Nam vel momento eam exsuscitare potest, qui omnia creat ex nihilo, ac si prius exstitissent.

Isaiah 40:7

> The grass withereth, the flower fadeth; because the Spirit of the Lord bloweth upon it: surely the people is grass.

Isaiah 40:7

Exaruit herba, emarcuit flos, quia spiritus Iehovae sufflavit in eo. Sane herba est populus.

Comm.

On the other hand, if the Lord withdraw his Spirit, all is reduced to nothing. Here Isaiah asserts what is exceedingly different, and appears to contradict David. But there is no absurdity in saying that all things are renewed by the power of the Spirit, and again, that what formerly appeared to be something is reduced to nothing; for we are nothing but in God, and,

CO 37:11-12

Si vero Dominus spiritum substrahat, omnia in nihilum rediguntur. Hic longe diversa praedicat Isaias, ac pugnare videtur cum Davide (Ps 104:30). Sed absurdum non est virtute spiritus omnia reparari: atque rursus eadem in nihilum redigi quae prius aliquid esse videbantur. Nihil enim sumus nisi in Deo. In eo autem ut incipiamus aliquid esse, ante convinci oportet nostrae

in order that we may begin to be something in him, we must first be convinced, and made thoroughly to know, that we are vanity. Therefore does the Lord breathe upon us, that we may know that of ourselves we are nothing.

Jeremiah 27:5

> I have made the earth, the man and the beast that are upon the ground, by my great power, and by my out-stretched arm, and have given it unto whom it seemed meet unto me.

Comm.

He adds, *by my great power and extended arm.* Why was this said, except that men might be awakened on hearing that the earth continues not as it is, but as it is sustained by God's power by which it was once created? The same power preserves men and animals; for nothing can remain safe except God exercises from heaven his hidden power. This, then, was the reason why these words were introduced.

Ezekiel 7:24

> I shall let in the most ruthless of nations to take possession of the houses; I shall quell the pride of the strong, and their sanctuaries will be profaned.

Comm.

For they are carried forth by a perverse disposition. For God has a wonderful reasoning, and incomprehensible for us, by which he drives them hither and thither: so that he however does not at the same time involve himself in any association with their error.

Matthew 12:18

> I will put my Spirit upon him.

Comm.

It is no doubt true, that there never was any portion whatever of righteousness in the world that did not proceed from the Spirit of God; and that was not maintained by his heavenly power.

John 1:3

> All things were made by him, and without him was not any thing made that was made.

vanitatis, et eius probe conscii simus. Propterea Dominus efflat in nos, ut nos ex nobis ipsis nihil esse intelligamus.

Jeremiah 27:5

> *Ego feci terram, hominem et iumentum quod super faciem terrae est, in virtute mea magna, et brachio meo extento; et dedi eam illi qui placeret in oculis meis.*

CO 38:542

Adiungit, *In virtute mea magna et brachio extento.* Quorsum hoc nisi ut expergiscantur homines, dum audiunt terram non manere in suo statu, nisi quatenus fulcitur eadem Dei virtute qua semel creata est? Eandem simul virtutem tueri homines et animalia, quoniam nihil salvum manere queat, nisi quatenus arcanam virtutem inspirat Deus e coelo? Haec igitur ratio est praefationis.

Ezekiel 7:24

> *Et venire faciam improbos gentium (hoc est, qui mali sunt et perversi inter gentes), et possidebunt domos eorum: et cessare faciam superbiam fortium, et polluentur sanctuaria ipsorum.*

OC 40:172

Nam ipsi feruntur pravo affectu: Deus autem habet mirificam rationem, et nobis incomprehensibilem, qua ipsos huc et illuc impellit: ut tamen se interea non involvat ulla culpae societate.

Matthew 12:18

> *Ponam Spiritum meum super illum.*

CO 45:332

Verum est, nihil unquam fuisse rectitudinis in mundo, quod non profectus sit a Dei spiritu et coelesti eius virtute constiterit.

John 1:3

> *Omnia per ipsum facta sunt, et sine ipso factum est nihil, quod factum est.*

Comm.

Accordingly, the ordinary mode of expression is here employed, that the Father *made all things* by the Son, and that all things are by God through the Son. Now the design of the Evangelist is, as I have already said, to show that no sooner was the world created than *the Speech* of God came forth into external operation; for having formerly been incomprehensible in his essence, his power became publicly known by its effect.

CO 47:4

Quare hic mos loquendi usitatus est, patrem omnia fecisse per filium, et a Deo per eundem filium omnia esse. Huc autem spectat evangelistae consilium (sicut dixi), quod statim ab ipsa mundi creatione sermo Dei in externum actum produerit. Nam quum in sua essentia prius esset incomprehensibilis, tunc eius vis effectu palam fuit cognita.

John 1.4

In him was life, and the life was the light of men.

John 1.4

In ipso vita erat: et vita erat lux hominum.

Comm.

In him was life. Hitherto he has taught us, that by the Speech of God all things were created. He now attributes to him, in the same manner, the preservation of those things which had been created; as if he had said, that in the creation of the world there was not merely displayed a sudden exercise of his power, which soon passed away, but that it is manifested in the steady and regular order of nature, as he is said to uphold all things by the word or will of his power (Heb. I. 3.). This life may be extended either to inanimate creatures (which live after their own manner, though they are devoid of feeling) or may be explained in reference to living creatures alone. It is of little consequence which you choose; for the simple meaning is, that the Speech of God was not only the source of life to all the creatures, so that those which were not began to be, but that his life-giving power causes them to remain in their condition; for were it not that his continued inspiration gives vigour to the world, every thing that lives would immediately decay, or be reduced to nothing. In a word, what Paul ascribes to God, that in him we are, and move, and live (Acts xvii. 28) John declares to be accomplished by the gracious agency of the Speech; so that it is God who gives us life, but it is by the eternal Speech.

CO 47:5

In ipso vita erat. Hactenus docuit, per sermonem Dei creata fuisse omnia. Nunc eorum quae creata fuerant, conservationem similiter illi attribuit: ac si diceret, non subitam modo eius virtutem, quae mox transierit, apparuisse in mundi creatione: sed in eo esse conspicuam, quod stabilis et fixus naturae ordo durat: quemadmodum ad Hebr. cap. 1 v.3 dicitur sustinere omnia verbo aut nutu potentiae suae. Caeterum vita haec vel ad inanimata extendi potest (quae suo modo vivunt, etiamsi sensu careant), vel de solis animantibus exponi. Parum refert utrum eligas: simplex enim sensus est sermonem Dei non modo fontem vitae fuisse creaturis omnibus, ut esse inciperent quae nondum erant: sed vivifica eius virtute fieri ut in statu suo maneant. Nisi enim continua eius inspiratio mundum vegetet, necesse erit quaecunque vigent, protinus decidere, aut in nihilum redigi. Denique quod Paulus, Act. 17 v. 20, Deo adscribit, nos scilicet in ipso esse et moveri et vivere, Ioannes sermonis beneficio fieri testatur. Deus ergo est qui nos vivificat: sed per aeternum sermonem.

John 1:5

And the light shineth in darkness; and the darkness did not comprehend it.

John 1:5

Et lux in tenebris lucet, et tenebrae eam non comprehenderunt.

Comm.

For there are two distinct powers which belong to the Son of God: the first, which is manifested in the structure of the world and the order of

CO 47:7

Duae enim sunt distinctae filii Dei virtutes, prior quae in mundi architectura et naturae ordine apparet: altera vero qua naturam col-

nature; and the second, by which he renews and restores fallen nature. As he is the eternal Speech of God, by him the world was made; by his power all things continue to possess the life which they once received; ....

lapsam renovat et instaurat. Ut est aeternus Dei Sermo, per eum conditus fuit mundus: eius virtute acceptam semel vitam omnia retinent ...

John 5:17

> But Jesus answered them, My Father worketh hitherto, and I work.

John 5:17

> *Jesus autem respondit illis, Pater meus ad hoc usque tempus operatur, et ego operor.*

Comm.

Yet He did not cease to sustain by his power the world which he had made, to govern it by his wisdom, to support it by his goodness, and to regulate all things according to his pleasure, both in heaven and on earth. In six days, therefore, the creation of the world was completed, but the administration of it is still continued, and God incessantly worketh in maintaining and preserving the order of it; as Paul informs us, that in him we live, and move, and are (Acts xvii. 28;) and David informs us, that all things stand so long as the Spirit of God upholds them, and that they fail as soon as he withdraws his support, (Psal. civ. 39.) Nor is it only by a general Providence that the Lord maintains the world which He has created, but He arranges and regulates every part of it, and more especially, by his protection, he keeps and guards believers whom he has received under his care and guardianship.

And I work. Leaving the defence of the present cause, Christ now explains the end and use of the miracle, namely, that by means of it he may be acknowledged to be the Son of God; for the object which he had in view in all his words and actions was, to show that he was the Author of salvation. What he now claims for himself belongs to his Divinity, as the Apostle also says, that he upholdeth all things by his powerful will, (Heb. i. 3.)

OC 47:111

Interea non desiit mundum a se conditum sua virtute sustinere, regere suo consilio, bonitate fovere, et cuncta suo arbitrio in coelo et in terra statuere. Ergo sex diebus absoluta fuit mundi creatio, regimen vero eius perpetuum est et assidue in tuendo et conservando eius ordine Deus operatur, quemadmodum Paulus docet in eo nos vivere, et moveri et esse, Act. 17,28. Et David stare omnia docet quatenus ea spiritus Deus vegetat, deficere autem simul ac eius vigore destituta fuerint (Ps 104, 29). Neque generali tantum providentia creatam a se naturam tuetur Dominus, sed singulas eius partes ordinat ac temperat. Praesertim vero suo praesidio servat ac tegit fideles, quos in fidem tutelamque suam recepit.

Et ego operor. Iam Christus omisso praesentis causae patrocinio miraculi finem et usum exponit, nempe ut inde agnoscatur Dei filius. Nam hoc in omnibus factis et dictis habuit propositum, ut se ostenderet salutis autorem. Hoc divinitatis proprium est quod sibi vindicat, quemadmodum etiam apostolus Hebr. 1,3 dicit, eum sustinere potenti suo nutu omnia.

Acts 17:26

> And hath made of one blood all mankind to dwell upon all the face of the earth, and hath appointed the times before determined, and the bounds of their habitation.

Acts 17:26

> *Fecitque ex uno sanguine omne genus hominum, ut inhabitaret super universam faciem terrae definivitque praestituta tempora, et terminos habitationis eorum.*

Comm.

And when he addeth also that God had appointed from the beginning those things which He had ordained before, his meaning is, that He executeth by the power of His Spirit those things which He hath decreed in His

OC 48:415

Quum vero simul addit Deum ab initio definisse quae ante ordinaverat, sensus est, ipsum manus suae virtute exsequi quae consilio suo decrevit, secundum illud: Deus noster in coelo omnia quae voluit fecit.

counsel according to that: "Our God is in heaven; He hath done whatsoever He would" (Ps. cxv. 3).

Acts 17:28

For in Him we live, move, and have our being; as certain of your poets said, For we be also His generation.

Comm.

..... and that we have our being in Him, inasmuch as by His Spirit He keepeth us in life, and upholdeth us. For the power of the Spirit is spread abroad throughout all parts of the world, that it may preserve them in their state; that He may minister unto the heaven and earth that force and vigour which we see, and motion to all living creatures. Not as brain-sick men do trifle, that all things are full of gods, yea, that stones are gods; but because God doth, by the wonderful power and inspiration of His Spirit, preserve those things which He hath created of nothing.

Acts 17:28

In ipso enim vivimus, movemur, et sumus: sicut et quidam vestratum Poetarum dixerunt. Nam hujus progenies etiam sumus.

CO 48:416-17

..... nos vero in eo subsistere quatenus suo nos spiritu vegetat et sustinet. Nam per omnes mundi partes diffusa est vis spiritus, quae tueatur eas in suo statu: coelo et terrae vigorem quem cernimus, animantibus etiam motum suppeditet. *Non qualiter phrenetici homines deorum plena esse omnia nugantur, imo lapides esse deos: sed quia admirabili spiritus sui vigore et instinctu Deus quaecunque ex nihilo condidit, conservat.*

Romans 8:14

For as many as are led by the Spirit of God, they are the sons of God.

Comm.

But it is right to observe, that the working of the Spirit is various: for there is that which is universal, by which all creatures are sustained and preserved ; (there is that also ...)

Romans 8:14

Quicunque enim Spiritu Dei aguntur, ii filii Dei sunt.

CO 49:147

Caeterum observare convenit, esse multiplicem Spiritus actionem. Est enim universalis, qua omnes creaturae sustinentur ac moventur ....

Hebrews 1:3

Who, being the brightness of his glory, and the express image of his person, and upholding all things by the word of his power, when he had by himself purged our sins, sat down on the right hand of the Majesty on high.

Comm.

And upholding (or bearing) all things, &c. To uphold or to bear here means to preserve or to continue all that is created in its own state; for he intimates that all things would instantly come to nothing, were they not sustained by his power. Though the pronoun his may be referred to the Father as well as to the Son, as it may be rendered "his" or "his own," yet as the second exposition is more commonly received, and well suits the context, I am disposed to embrace it.

Hebrews 1:3

Qui quum sit spendor gloriae et character substantiae ejus, portetque omnia verbo suo potenti, peccatorum nostrorum purgatione per seipsum facta, consedit in dextera magnificentiae in excelsis.

CO 55:13

Portetque omnia. Portare hic pro tueri accipitur, facereque ut in suo statu maneant creaturae. Intelligit enim omnia mox casura, nisi eius virtute sustinerentur. Quanquum pronomen demonstrativum ἀυτος (tam de patre quam de filio exponi potest: verti enum potest, vel ipsius, vel suae. Quia tamen secunda expositio magis est recepta, et optime quadrat contextui: ego eam libenter amplector.

REFERENCES TO THE *MEDIA* OF PROVIDENCE IN CALVIN'S *INSTITUTES* ETC.

1:9:3

For the Lord has so knit together the certainty of his Word and his Spirit *(Mutuo enim quodam nexu Dominus Verbi Spiritusque sui certudinem inter se copulavit),* that our minds are duly imbued with reverence for the word when the Spirit shining upon it enables us there to behold the face of God ... He employed the same Spirit by whose agency he has administered the word *(eundum Spiritum, cuius virtute Verbum administraverat, submissit),* to complete his work by the efficacious confirmation of the word *(qui suum opus efficaci Verbi confirmatione absolveret)* ... the Word is the instrument by which the illumination of the Spirit is dispensed *(verbum esse organum quo Spiritus sui illuminationem fidelibus Dominus dispensat).*

1:13:7

... when they (the apostles) tell us that the worlds were created by the Son, and that he sustains all things by his mighty word (Heb. 1:2) *(per Filium secula esse condita et portare omnia potenti suo verbo)*

1:13:12

To govern the world by his power and providence, and regulate all things by an energy that is inherent in himself (this an apostle ascribes to him, Heb. 1:3), surely belongs to none but the Creator. Nor does he (Christ, the Word, cf. § 11) share merely the government of the world with the Father, but also each of the other offices which cannot be communicated to creatures.

Et sane providentia et virtute mundum administrare, nutuque propriae virtutis omnia moderari, (quod illi dat Apostolus Heb. 1:3) non est nisi Creatoris. (Christus/Verbum) neque solam gubernandi orbis provinciam cum Patre participat, sed alia quoque singula officia, quae creaturis communicari nequeant.

1:13:14

With reference to the Hebrew *merahefet* in Gen 1:2 Calvin here says *Spiritum Dei expansum fuisse super abyssos, vel materiam informem,* (the Spirit of God was expanded over the abyss or shapeless matter), whereas in his translation and Commentary he uses *agitabat* and *agitaret,* (moved and agitated itself)

In the *Institutes* he further states: *Ille enim est qui ubique diffusus omnia sustinet, vegetat et vivificat in caelo et in terra. Iam hoc ipso creaturarum numero eximitur, quod nullis circunscribitur finibus; sed suum in omnia vigorem transfundendo, essentiam, vitam, et motionem illis inspirare, id vero plane divinum est.* (his being diffused over all space, sustaining, invigorating, and quickening all things, both in heaven and on earth. The mere fact of his not being circumscribed by any limit raises him above the rank of creatures, while transfusing his own vigour into all things, breathing them into being, life, and motion, is plainly divine.)

1:13.15

Calvin is critical of the ancient fathers' quote of Psalm 33:6 ("By the word of the Lord *(Verbo Domini)* were the heavens made, and all the host of them by the breath (Spirit) of his mouth") in order to prove that the world was not less the work of the Holy Spirit than of the Son. He sees spirit (breath) of the mouth as equivalent to word. *(Spiritus oris idem valeat atque sermo).*

1:13:17

... the Father made all things by the Word *(... Patrem per Verbum omnia creasse).*

1:13:22

Calvin strongly opposes Servetus' view: The most execrable heresy of all is his confounding both the Son and Spirit promiscuously with all the creatures *(quod tam Filium Dei quam Spiritum promiscue creaturis omnibus permiscet).*

1:13:24

The declaration of Christ that "God is a Spirit" (John 4:24,) cannot be confined to the Father only, as if the Word were not of a spiritual nature *(acsi Sermo ipse non esset spiritualis naturae)*

1:14:20

...we learn that God, by the power of his Word and his Spirit *(Dei verbi ac Spritus sui potentia),* created the heavens and the earth out of nothing .... at the same time, as all things were liable to corruption, providing for the perpetuation of each single species ...

1:16:1

... by faith we understand that the worlds were framed by the Word of God (Heb. 9:3) *(concinnatum esse saeculum Verbo Dei)*

1:16:1

By the Word of the Lord were the heavens framed, and all the host of them by the breath of his mouth (Ps. 33:6) *(Verbo Iehovae ... et spiritu oris eius)*

1:16:1

Thou sendest forth thy Spirit, they are created, and thou renewest the face of the earth (Ps. 104:30) *(Si rursus emittis spiritum, creantur ...)*

1:17:1

... secondly, that in overruling all things, the providence of God works at one time with means, at another without means, and at another against means *(ut nunc mediis interpositis operetur, nunc sine mediis, nunc contra omnia media)*

1:17:7

In this way he sends Satan to be a lie in the mouths of all the prophets in order to deceive Ahab (1 Kings 22:22) by the counsel of the young men he so infatuates Rehoboam, that his folly deprives him of his kingdom (1 Kings 12:10, 15.) Sometimes when he leaves them in possession of intellect, he so fills them with terror and dismay, that they can neither will nor plan the execution of what they had designed..... Every thing, therefore, which turns out prosperous and according to his wish, the Christian will ascribe entirely to God, whether he has experienced his beneficence through the instrumentality of men *(per hominum ministerium)*, or been aided by inanimate creatures *(ab inanimatis creaturis adiutus)*.

3:1:2

Christ is the eternal Word *(aeternus Sermo Dei est)* who is joined to the Father through the Spirit *(eodem Spiritu cum Patre coniunctus)*.

4:17:8

... Christ was from the beginning the living Word of the Father *(vivificum illud Patris verbum fuisse)*, the fountain and origin of life *(vitae fontem et originem)*, from which all things have always received life *(unde omnia ut viverent semper acceperunt)*. Hence at one time John calls Him the Word of life *(Quare Ioannes (1:1) nunc sermonem vitae nuncupat)* ...

John 1:1

Calvin translates: In principium erat *Sermo, et Sermo erat* apud Deum, et ille *Sermo* erat Deus.

He also uses *Sermo* in the *Institutes* (1:13:8) in this regard: *principio Sermonem apud Deum fuisse dicit. Constituimus ergo rursum, Sermonem extra temporis initium a Deo conceptum* ... (he said that in the beginning ... the Word was with God. We therefore again conclude, that the Word was conceived by God outside/beyond the beginning of time ...)

Refutatio Errorum Michaelis Serveti (CO 8:606)
In his refutation of Servetus, Calvin states: "There is nothing in heaven or on earth which the Spirit of God does not quicken by his presence and secret influx."

Nihil in coelo est vel in terra, quod non sua praesentia arcanoque influxu vegetet Dei spiritus.

Confessio de Trinitate propter Calumnias P. Caroli (CO 9:705)
For it is he (the Holy Spirit), who, wherever spread out, sustains, quickens and gives life to everything, who living in the faithful guides them in all truth, regenerates, sanctifies and finally will give them life to fullness.

Ille (spiritus sanctus) enim est, qui ubique diffusus omnia sustinet, vegetat et vivificat, qui in fidelibus habitans ducit eos in omnem veritatem, regenerat, sanctificat, et olim ad plenum vivificabit.

De Aeterna Dei Praedestinatione (OC 88:349)

Regarding the threefold work of the Spirit, Calvin says:

First of all should be stated for all eyes to see the general rule of the world, by which all things are cared for and given growth, so that the integrity of their nature may stand firm.

Primo loco statuenda est ante oculos generalis mundi gubernatio, qua foventur et vegetantur omnia, ut stet incolumis naturae eorum status.

Sermo Iob 1:12

God uses Satan as instrument of his wrath.

Calvin and Beza:
The Role of the Decree-Execution Distinction in Their Theologies

Donald W. Sinnema

Theodore Beza (1519-1605), as Calvin's successor in Geneva, exercised a profound influence in the church and academy during a tenure of leadership that continued for forty years after Calvin's death. In the recent surge of Post-Reformation studies, the issue of continuity and discontinuity between the two figures has been a matter of keen debate. Older scholarship tended to see Beza as breaking with Calvin's theology and moving in a more rigid and scholastic direction.[1] Recent scholarship has recognized more of a continuity between Calvin and Beza, while acknowledging some differences in emphasis.[2]

This paper examines just one aspect of the relationship between their theologies—the role that each gave to the distinction between God's eternal decree and its execution in the course of time. This distinction is, of course, a truism. It is one form of the idea that God's will is done. But it reflects the more specific royal imagery of a king who issues decrees and sees that they are carried out. As applied to God as King, this imagery is implicit in Scripture (e.g., Psalm 115:3, Ephesians 1:11) and can be found here and there throughout the history of theology.

[1]The emphasis on discontinuity is found, for example, in the studies of Ernst Bizer, *Frühorthodoxie und Rationalismus* (Zurich: EVZ Verlag, 1963), 6-15; Walter Kickel, *Vernunft und Offenbarung bei Theodor Beza* (Neukirchen: Neukirchener Verlag, 1967); Johannes Dantine, "Les Tabelles sur la Doctrine de la Prédestination par Théodore de Bèze," *Revue de Théologie et de Philosophie* 16 (1966), 365-77, and more recently, Philip Holtrop, *The Bolsec Controversy on Predestination from 1551 to 1555* (Lewiston: Edward Mellen, 1993), 338-40, 822-67.

[2]The recent emphasis on continuity can be found in Ian McPhee, "Conserver or Transformer of Calvin's Theology? A Study of the Origins and Development of Theodore Beza's Thought, 1550-1570" (University of Cambridge, Ph.D. thesis, 1979); T. Maruyama, *The Ecclesiology of Theodore Beza* (Geneva: Droz, 1978); Robert Letham, "Theodore Beza: A Reassessment," *Scottish Journal of Theology* 40 (1987), 25-40, and Richard Muller, *Christ and the Decree* (Grand Rapids: Baker, 1988), 79-96; idem, "The Use and Abuse of a Document: Beza's *Tabula Praedestinationis,* the Bolsec Controversy, and the Origins of Reformed Orthodoxy," in Carl Trueman and R. S. Clark, eds., *Protestant Scholasticism: Essays in Reassessment* (Carlisle: Paternoster Press, 1999), 33-61.

Since Beza places significant emphasis on the decree-execution distinction, several scholars have sought to identify the source of this emphasis in his thought. Because for Beza this distinction forms a causal structure, Ernst Bizer saw this as the influence of Aristotelian philosophy on Beza's thinking.[3] Johannes Dantine pointed to a similar distinction in Aquinas and suggested his influence on Beza.[4] John Bray concluded that Beza modified Aquinas' distinction to meet certain problems raised by Augustine and Calvin, with the result that Beza's distinction between decree and execution became his most significant original contribution to the question of predestination.[5] Ian McPhee thought that Augustine was a more likely source than Aquinas, but also suggested that Calvin's distinction between remote and proximate causes far more likely inspired Beza's distinction. He also stressed that Beza took up the distinction to address certain problems raised in the Bolsec controversy.[6] Richard Muller has likewise emphasized the Bolsec context, but also pointed out that Calvin himself used the decree-execution distinction, and that this was probably Beza's immediate source.[7] Muller's suggestion is most convincing. And yet, a question that begs to be explored is whether Beza simply followed Calvin's usage or developed the distinction and its implications in new directions.

Calvin

With his emphasis on God's will, Calvin assumed the distinction between God's eternal decree of his will and his carrying out of it in the course of history. Thus, here and there in his theology one finds explicit references to the decree and its execution. Depending on context, the idea may also be implicit in many of Calvin's references to "doing" God's "will." However, "executing God's decree" is a more limited concept for Calvin, since he distinguishes God's will expressed in his decree from his will expressed in his law or precept.[8]

As may be expected, one can find references to decree and execution especially in the context of discussions of God's providence. In the *Institutes,* for example, Calvin presents his view of providence as follows:

---

[3]Bizer, *Frühorthodoxie,* 161-62.

[4]Dantine, "Les Tabelles," 372. In the *Summa Theologiae,* I, Q. 22, a. 1 & 3, Aquinas distinguished within providence between God's plan of the order of things *(ratio ordinis)* and the execution of this order *(executio ordinis).*

[5]John Bray, *Theodore Beza's Doctrine of Predestination* (Nieuwkoop: De Graaf, 1975), 91, 123.

[6]McPhee, "Conserver," 69, 71, 76, 79-80, 310. In his *De Praedestinatione Sanctorum* 18, Augustine distinguished between predestination as the preparation for grace and grace as its actual endowment. See below for Calvin's use of remote and proximate causality.

[7]Muller, *Christ and the Decree,* 21; idem, "Use and Abuse," 47-48. Muller also notes that the distinction was available in the theology of the late medieval scholastics.

[8]On the two senses of God's will, see Calvin's Institutes 1:17:2; 1:18:3-4; 3:20:43; Commentary on Deuteronomy 29:29, Ezekiel 18:23, Matthew 6:10, and Romans 11:34.

> [W]e make God the ruler and governor of all things, who in accordance with his wisdom has from the farthest limit of eternity decreed *(decrevit)* what he was going to do, and now by his might carries out *(exequitur)* what he has decreed *(decrevit)*.[9]

For Calvin, God even uses Satan to carry out his providential judgments and that happens not by mere permission:

> [I]t would be ridiculous for the Judge only to permit what he wills to be done, and not also to decree *(decernere)* it and to command its execution *(executionem)* by his ministers.[10]

Similarly, commenting on Acts 2:23, Calvin states that "the wicked are very far from obeying God, in whatever way they execute *(exsequantur)* what God in himself has decided *(statuit)*."[11]

The idea that God carries out his will through Satan and the wicked is especially clear in Calvin's sermon on Job 2:1-6: "God not only allows and gives permission, but also executes his will *(execute sa volonté)*, both through Satan and through the wicked." "God accomplishes his will *(accomplit sa volonté)* through them, in such a manner that they are as instruments that he works with and uses." "It is indeed God who executes *(execute)* his commands and his decrees *(ses commandemens et ses decrets)* in this manner, but note that the evil cannot by any means be attributed to him."[12]

In his commentary on the Lord's Prayer petition, "Thy will be done" (Matt. 6:10), Calvin again speaks of God"s providence in terms of decree and execution. Noting that Scripture reveals God's will as twofold, he points out that in the one sense "God's pleasure is said to be done, when He executes *(exsequitur)* the hidden decrees *(decreta)* of His providence."[13]

---

[9]*Institutes* 1:16:8 (OS 3:198-99). Translations from the *Institutes* are from the McNeill-Battles edition. This passage first appeared in the 1539 edition.

[10]*Institutes* 1.18.1 (OS 3:220). This first appeared in the 1559 edition.,

[11] Calvin, *The Acts of the Apostles*, eds. D. W. & T. F. Torrance (Grand Rapids: Eerdmans, 1977), 1:66 (CO 48:40). This translation and various others are slightly amended for the sake of consistency in the translation of key terms. Calvin makes the same point in his comment on Acts 4:28: "God so orders all things by His own secret counsel *(consilio)* that He executes *(exsequatur)* what He has decided *(statuit)* even through the agency of the wicked," 126 (CO 48:93). Likewise, he states that "while God accomplishes *(peragit)* through the wicked what he has decreed *(decrevit)* by his secret judgment, they are not excusable" (*Institutes* 1:18:4 (OS 3:225-26)). In this same passage Calvin mentions an objection that accused his theology of making God the author of evil: "therefore men are undeservedly damned if they carry out *(exequuntur)* what God has decreed *(decrevit)* because they obey his will."

[12]Calvin, *Sermons sur le Livre de Iob* (CO 33:106, 104, 107). These sermons are from the years 1554-55.

[13]Calvin, *A Harmony of the Gospels: Matthew, Mark and Luke*, eds. D. W. & T. F. Torrance (Grand Rapids: Eerdmans, 1972), 1:208 (CO 45:198). The first edition of this commentary appeared in 1555.

Elsewhere in his commentaries Calvin also uses the decree-execution distinction in reference to God's providence. For example, on Psalm 115:3 he affirms that "nothing can prevent Him from fulfilling *(impleat)* whatever He has decreed *(decrevit)*."[14] And on 1 Peter 1:20 he makes the point that "by the coming of Christ God has carried out *(exsequutus)* what He had decided *(statuerat)*."[15]

In sections on providence in his book *Concerning the Eternal Predestination of God,* Calvin makes similar statements: "whatever He decreed *(decrevit)* He effects *(effectum reddit)*;" "what was divinely ordained *(ordinatum)* was fulfilled *(impletum)*;" "God accomplished *(perficeret)* by the hand of man what He decreed *(decrevit)*;" and unwilling people sometimes "fulfill *(impleant)* what His hand and His counsel decreed *(consilium decrevit)* ."[16]

Occasionally one can also find explicit references to God's decree, or plan, and its execution in Calvin's writings about predestination. In one passage in the *Institutes* he states:

> As God by the effectual working of his call to the elect accomplishes *(perficit)* the salvation to which by his eternal plan *(consilio)* he has destined them, so he has his judgments against the reprobate, by which he executes *(exequatur)* his plan *(consilium)* for them.[17]

Calvin's *Congregation on Eternal Election* (1551) contains one such reference: "the Father—who has elected us—wants to carry out *(avancer)* his plan *(conseil)* to a full effect *(effect)* and perfection."[18]

Regarding John's statement that the Father's will is that everyone who believes in the Son shall have eternal life (John 6:40), Calvin comments that "God's will is that those whom he has elected shall be saved by faith, and he confirms and executes *(exequitur)* His eternal decree *(decretum)* in this way."[19]

While Calvin frequently refers to God's decree or plan in such contexts, it is striking how seldom one finds explicit references to the decree-execution distinction in his predestinarian writings. For example, there is only one instance in his four chapters on predestination in the 1559 *Institutes.* There are none in

---

[14]CO 32:184.

[15]Calvin, *The Epistle of Paul the Apostle to the Hebrews and the First and Second Epistles of St Peter,* eds. D. W. & T. F. Torrance (Grand Rapids: Eerdmans, 1976), 248 (CO 55:226).

[16]Calvin, *Concerning the Eternal Predestination of God* (London: James Clark, 1961), 157, 173, 175, 176 (COR: *Scripta Ecclesiastica* 1:212, 244, 250).

[17]*Institutes*3:24:12 (OS 4:423). This passage first appeared in the 1539 edition.

[18]Calvin's *Congregation* (CO 8:100) is translated in Holtrop, *Bolsec Controversy,* 704.

[19]Calvin, *The Gospel According to St. John,* eds. D. W. & T. F. Torrance (Grand Rapids: Eerdmans, 1978), 162 (COR: *Opera Exegetica* 11/1:208). Commenting on John 10:16, Calvin similarly states: "For the secret plan *(consilium)* of God by which men are ordained to life is at length manifested *(patefacit)* in His own time by the calling" (267 (CO 47:244)). The commentary on John was first published in 1553.

the discussions on predestination in *Concerning the Eternal Predestination of God,* or in his commentary on Romans 8 and 9 and Ephesians 1.

On occasion, Calvin refers to God's decree and its execution when he deals with topics other than providence and predestination. For example, in discussing the differences between the persons of the Trinity Calvin points out that the Holy Spirit is "the power whereby he executes *(exequitur)* the decrees of his plan *(consilii sui decreta).*"[20] Angels are "celestial spirits whose ministry and service God uses to carry out *(ad exequenda)* all things he has decreed *(decrevit).*"[21] In his explanation of Ephesians 3:11, which refers to God's "eternal purpose *(propositum)* which he made *(statuit)* in Christ," Calvin comments:

> I take "to make" as "to decide," because he is talking not only of the execution *(exequutione)* of the decree *(decreti),* but of the ordination *(ordinatione)* itself, which, though it preceded all ages, was kept in the bosom of God till the manifestation of Christ.[22]

In a comment on Matthew 26:39, Calvin advises this rule in regard to appropriate petitions in prayer:

> We must hold to the rule, that where we have no certain and special promise, we must not ask anything except on condition that God may fulfill *(impleat)* what He has decreed *(decrevit),* which cannot be done unless we yield our wishes to His instruction.[23]

While the instances of the decree-execution distinction that I have cited are not a complete list of occurrences in Calvin's writings, these are the main places where the distinction is found. In addition, Calvin sometimes speaks of God executing his judgments *(iudicia).* However, these references are usually not about the execution of God's decree but relate to his judgments on evil-doers in the actual course of history.[24]

---

[20] *Institutes* 1:13:18 (OS 3:132). This passage first appeared in the 1539 edition.

[21] *Institutes* 1:14:5 (OS 3:157). This first appeared in the 1543 edition.

[22] Calvin, *The Epistles of Paul the Apostle to the Galatians, Ephesians, Philippians and Colossians,* eds. D. W. & T. F. Torrance (Grand Rapids: Eerdmans, 1965), 164 (COR: Opera Exegetica 16:209). This commentary was first published in 1548.

[23] *Harmony of the Gospels,* 3:152 (CO 45:724).

[24] Thus God executes his plan by means of his temporal judgments against the reprobate, Institutes 3:24:12. Examples of carrying out *iudicia* in this sense may be found in the *Institutes* 1:17:5; 1:18:1-2; 2:4:3; 3:20:15; 4:20:10; *Calumniae Nebulonis Cuiusdam de Occulta Dei Providentia* (CO 9:308, 310, 311); *Sermons sur le Livre de Iob* (CO 33:57). On the other hand, sometimes God's secret judgment refers to his decree, *Institutes* 1:18:4. In the *Calumniae* (CO 9:308) both senses are together in one passage: "God, who produces light out of darkness, inwardly rules them by his secret and incomprehensible judgment *(iudicio)* in such a way that he executes his own just judgments *(iudicia exsequatur)* through their wickedness."

In Beza's theology the decree-execution distinction is integrally linked to the categories of primary and secondary causality. It is thus worth exploring whether Calvin also makes such a linkage. On occasion Calvin does distinguish between remote (or first/principal/highest/hidden) and proximate (or second/middle/lower/evident) causes. The remote cause of something is in God's will; the proximate cause is found in creatures.

Calvin uses these causal categories most often in his discussions of God's providence. For example, he explains the causes of sin in relation to this all encompassing providence:

> Hence, since the criminal misdeeds perpetrated by men proceed from God with a cause that is just *(justa causa)*, though perhaps unknown to us, though the first cause *(prima causa)* of all things is His will, I nevertheless deny that He is the author of sin. What I have maintained about the diversity of causes *(causarum diversitas)* must not be forgotten: the proximate cause *(propinqua)* is one thing, the remote cause *(remota causa)* another. Then we shall know how great is the distinction between the equitable providence of God and the stormy assaults of men.[25]

What is striking about this passage is that Calvin is willing to call God's providential ordaining of sin a remote cause of sin, though God is by no means its author.

Calvin makes use of the same distinction in regard to the causes of Job's suffering. In a letter concerning the Bolsec controversy, he affirms that God exercises his power through Satan and the wicked as instruments of his wrath, and then counters an objection of Bolsec:

> This profane trifler cries out that God is involved in guilt when we allege that he governs all things by his providence. Removing, in short, all distinction between causes as remote and hidden *(causam remotam et absconditam)*, on the one hand, and as proximate *(propinquas)* on the other, he does not allow us to regard the sufferings to which holy Job was subjected as the work of God, lest he be held as equally guilty with the Devil and the Chaldean and Sabean robbers.[26]

Calvin also uses the remote-proximate distinction to explain how both God and Pharaoh could be the causes of the hardening of Pharaoh's heart:

---

[25]Calvin, *Concerning Eternal Predestination*, 181 (COR: *Scripta Ecclesiastica* 1:260). Elsewhere in the same work Calvin also discusses the cause of sin in terms of remote and proximate causation and stresses that the guilt of sin cannot be placed in remote causes (122-23, 156 (COR: *Scripta Ecclesiastica* 1:146, 148, 210)).

[26]Letter of Calvin and other Genevan pastors to the ministers of Switzerland (November 14, 1551), in Jules Bonnet, ed., *Letters of John Calvin* (Philadelphia: Presbyterian Board of Publication, 1858), 2:325 (CO 8:207). Calvin virtually reproduced this passage in his introduction to *Concerning Eternal Predestination*, 51 (COR: *Scripta Ecclesiastica* 1:6).

> ... if the will of God is the highest or remote cause *(summa vel remota causa)* of the hardening, man himself, who hardens his own heart, is the more proximate cause *(propior causa)*. I everywhere distinguish the first or remote cause *(primam causam vel remotam)* from middle and proximate causes *(mediis et propinquis)*.[27]

The distinction between remote and proximate causes may be found also in Calvin's treatment of predestination. Commenting on Romans 11:7, he makes use of the distinction to explain the causes of reprobation:

> Indeed, the cause *(causa)* of eternal reprobation is so hidden from us, that we can do nothing else but wonder at the incomprehensible counsel of God... It is foolishness to try to conceal beneath the garb of proximate causes *(propinquis causis)*, as soon as we hear them mentioned, this first cause *(primam)* which is hidden from our notice, as though God had not freely decided before the fall of Adam to do what He thought best with the whole human race.[28]

Calvin utilizes the same remote-proximate distinction when he discusses the causes of condemnation. For Calvin, reprobation should be distinguished from condemnation, since the former is God's eternal decree to condemn some people, while the latter involves temporal punishments or the final damnation. Thus, in the *Institutes,* Calvin advises that "we should contemplate the evident cause *(evidentem causam)* of condemnation in the corrupt nature of humanity—which is closer *(propinquior)* to us—rather than seek the hidden *(absconditam)* and utterly incomprehensible cause in God's predestination."[29] In response to Pighius who accused Calvin of teaching that the reprobate are condemned not because they were ruined in Adam, but because before Adam's fall they were devoted to destruction, Calvin replies:

> It is no wonder that Pighius should indiscriminately ... confuse everything in the judgments of God, when he does not distinguish between causes proxi-

---

[27]Calvin, *Calumniae Nebulonis Cuiusdam de Occulta Dei Providentia* (CO 9:306). Calvin wrote this work on secret providence in 1558 to counter Castellio. In other discussions on providence Calvin also distinguishes between God's will as the remote cause and certain creatures as the proximate or lower *(inferiores)* causes that he uses as instruments of his providence. See *Institutes* 1:17:6, 1:17:9 (OS 3:209, 213); *Concerning Eternal Predestination,* 168, 170, and 178 (COR: *Scripta Ecclesiastica* 1:234, 240, 254); *Treatises Against the Anabaptists and Against the Libertines* (Grand Rapids: Baker, 1982), 244 (CO 7:188).

[28]Calvin, *The Epistles of Paul the Apostle to the Romans and to the Thessalonians,* eds. D. W. & T. F. Torrance (Grand Rapids: Eerdmans, 1980), 244 (CO 49:216). Commenting on Romans 9:11, Calvin similarly states that the proximate cause of reprobation *(propinquam reprobationis causam)* is the curse inherited from Adam, whereas God has a just cause *(iustam causam)* for election and reprobation in his own will, 200-201 (CO 49:178). The idea of a proximate cause of reprobation appears only in the 1540 Romans commentary; thereafter Calvin did not develop the idea.

[29]*Institutes* 3:23:8 (OS 4:403). This passage first appeared in the 1539 edition.

> mate and remote *(causas propinquas et remotas)* ... We cannot avoid concluding that the first origin of ruin is in Adam and that we individually find the proximate cause *(proximam causam)* in ourselves. What can then prevent our faith from adoring from afar *(procul)* with due humility the hidden counsel of God by which the fall of man was foreordained, and yet acknowledging what appears closer *(propius),* that the whole human race in the person of Adam is bound to the penalty of eternal death and therefore subject to death? Therefore Pighius has not shattered, as he thought, the splendid and fitting symmetry *(symmetriam)* in which the causes proximate and remote *(causa propinqua et remota)* agree with one another.[30]

On occasion Calvin makes use of such causal categories also in contexts other than providence and predestination. For example, in discussing the causes of salvation on the basis of John 3:16, Calvin states that "we see how God's love holds first place, as the highest cause *(summa causa)* or origin; how faith in Christ follows this as the second and proximate cause *(causa secunda et propior).*"[31]

It is apparent from the preceding passages that Calvin was not accustomed to link the language of decree and execution with the categories of remote/first/highest and proximate/second/lower causality. Though he does speak of God's will, or decree, as the first cause in many passages, in these contexts he does not explicitly relate the execution of God's decree to proximate or secondary causality. Calvin typically uses these two sets of categories in different contexts. The only exception that I could find is a passage in the treatise *Against the Libertines*(1545), where Calvin examines the place of creatures in God's providence:

> He is sorely angry ... whenever we fail to look up to him, recognizing Him not only as the principal cause *(cause principale)* of everything, but also as the author, who by his counsel *(conseil)* disposes as He wills. Therefore, let us adopt this resolution: that prosperity and adversity alike, rain, wind, sleet, hail, good weather, abundance, famine, war, and peace are all works of God's hand; and that creatures who constitute lower causes *(causes inferieures)* are only means by which He fulfills *(accomplir)* His will *(volunté)*; ... not only does He avail Himself of insensible creatures in this way, in order to bring about *(operer)* and execute *(mettre en execution)* His will *(vouloir)* through

---

[30] *Concerning Eternal Predestination,* 100-101 (COR: *Scripta Ecclesiastica*1:102). Calvin again refers to the remote and proximate causes of condemnation on p. 116 (COR: *Scripta Ecclesiastica*1:132).

[31] *Institutes*2:17:2 (OS 3:510). In an interesting passage on the role of good works in salvation, Calvin even concedes that good works may be called "lower causes *(causas inferiores)*" of salvation. Since what goes before in the order of dispensation may be called the cause of what comes after, good works in this sense are a step leading to eternal life and are "as it were a cause *(causam quodammodo).*" The "true cause" *(vera causa)* or "first cause" *(prima causa),* however, is God's mercy or election (*Institutes* 3:14:21 (OS 4:238-39)).

them, but He also avails Himself of men and even of devils. So much is this so that Satan and evildoers are executors *(executeurs)* of His will *(vouloir)*.[32]

The foregoing examination reveals that Calvin willingly used the language of decree and execution virtually throughout his career. One can find these terms as a pair in his writings from 1539 to the end of his life, but their explicit use is only occasional. Calvin does not highlight the distinction; it is not prevalent is his writings, especially as compared with Beza. It most often occurs in Calvin's discussions of providence, where the distinction is most appropriate. But it is surprisingly infrequent in his treatments of predestination. Rather than serving as a significant set of technical terms for Calvin, decree and execution seem to be but one set of categories among many in his theology. One may conclude that decree and execution as a wedded pair of categories are not one of the pillars of Calvin's theology, and they certainly do not function as a key structural principle of his thought.

Beza

For Beza, the decree-execution distinction plays a larger role than for Calvin.[33] In Beza's theology the distinction forms the pillars of a comprehensive framework. It encompasses all of reality: whatever God by his will has decreed from eternity, he executes or carries out within the course of time, and everything that happens in time is the outcome of what he has eternally decreed.

It is important to note Beza's terminology in describing this framework. From eternity *(ab aeterno)*, that is, before the creation of the world, God by his will *(voluntas)* decreed *(decrevit)* or ordained *(ordinavit)* whatever would happen *(evenire)* in time *(in tempore)*. This eternal decree *(decretum)* or purpose *(propositum)* or plan *(consilium)* is to be distinguished from the execution *(executio)* of this decree which God himself executes *(exequitur)* or accomplishes *(perficit)* or effects *(efficit)* in the course of time. To execute his decrees God uses temporal means *(media)* to achieve the end *(finis)* to which he has destined all things. The intermediate *(intermedii fines)* or medial ends *(medii fines)* are salvation or damnation, but the ultimate end *(ultimus finis)* is God's glory. The individual elements of this scheme can be found here and there throughout Calvin's writings, but for Beza they form a cohesive framework.

A distinctive feature of Beza's position is that he closely links causal categories to the decree-execution distinction. Thus God's decree is the primary cause *(causa primaria)* or highest cause *(causa summa)* of what happens in time,

---

[32]Calvin, *Treatises Against Anabaptists and Libertines,* 244-45 (CO 7:188).

[33]In a forthcoming article on "God's Eternal Decree and its Temporal Execution: The Role of this Distinction in Theodore Beza's Theology," in Mack Holt, ed., *Adaptations of Calvinism in Reformation Europe: Essays in Honor of Brian G. Armstrong* (Aldershot: Ashgate Publishing, 2006), I elaborate on this theme in Beza.

and God executes his eternal decree by using *(utitur)* or working through *(per)* temporal secondary causes *(causae secundae)* or lower causes *(causae inferiores)* or middle causes *(causae mediae)* or intermediate causes *(causae intermediae)* or proximate causes *(causae proximae)* or instruments *(instrumenta)*. Such secondary causes produce effects *(effecta)* which may in turn be the cause of further effects. Thus Beza speaks of the order of causes *(ordo causarum)* or series of causes *(series causarum)* by which God executes his decrees in steps or stages *(in gradibus)* until the proposed end is achieved.

This whole cohesive complex of categories that combines decree-execution, eternity-time, means-end, and primary-secondary causality is what I am calling the "Trinitarian decree-execution framework." This is the basic framework that structures Beza's thinking about predestination, and it is readily apparent in his predestinarian writings, such as his *Summa Totius Christianismi, De Praedestinationis Doctrina,* and *Ad Acta Colloquii Montisbelgardensis.*

The decree-execution framework is clearly the fundamental structural principle of Beza's early *Summa Totius Christianismi* (1555).[34] Its central doctrinal section (chapters 2-6) is explicitly structured by the distinction. The chapter titles reveal that chapter two deals with the decree or plan *(consilium)* of predestination, chapters three to six with its execution. Chapter two begins with the significant statement that nothing comes to pass without God's decree *(decreto),* including evil (2:1). Here Beza distinguishes between the purpose *(propositum)* of election and election itself, and between the purpose of reprobation and reprobation itself, that is, between the decrees of election and reprobation and their execution (2:6, 7). The third chapter deals with the execution *(exequutione)* of God's eternal plan in what is common to the elect and the reprobate. Chapter four then focuses specifically on the order of causes by which the Lord executes *(exequendae)* election, while chapter five focuses on the order by which God executes *(exequi)* the plan of reprobation. Then chapter six covers the final execution *(executione)* of God's plan in both the elect and reprobate.

Since Beza wrote the *Summa* within the historical context of the Bolsec controversy, McPhee makes the point that Beza used the decree-execution distinction to counter Bolsec's confusion of election and faith, to separate God from sin, and to demolish the view that predestination is based on God's foreknowledge.[35] Richard Muller suggests that in the context of this controversy the distinction also countered the argument of members of his own classis at

---

[34]The full title in translation is: *The Sum of All Christianity, or the Description and Distribution of the Causes of the Salvation of the Elect and the Destruction of the Reprobate, Collected from the Sacred Writings.* The original 1555 edition of the *Summa* is not extant. The revised second edition of 1560 is reprinted in Beza's *Tractationes Theologicae* (Geneva, 1582), 1:170-205. Hereafter referred to as *TT.*

[35]McPhee, "Conserver," 66-84, 310.

[36]Muller, "Use and Abuse," 49.

Lausanne who refused to distinguish between reprobation and damnation.[36] While these points are convincing, it is clear that the decree-execution distinction has an even larger role in the *Summa*—it forms the structural framework around which Beza organizes his thinking about predestination.

The decree-execution framework continues to play a pervasive role in Beza's mature thinking on predestination, as is evident in his *De Praedestinationis Doctrina* (1582). This is the product of lectures Beza presented on Romans 9, a passage often viewed as the *locus classicus* of predestination. He begins by pointing out that in this chapter Paul deals with the primary cause *(primaria causa)* of salvation—God's eternal purpose *(propositum)*.[37] A lengthy preliminary discussion includes a section on "the middle causes *(medias causas)* God has laid out for executing the eternal plan of election" and a section on "the means by which God executes the plan of reprobation."[38] Throughout this introductory section and the detailed commentary that follows, Beza interprets Romans 9 in terms of God's decree and its execution through middle causes. Among the dozens of explicit references to the distinction, Beza sometimes highlights it as an important distinction that must not be confused. For example, in countering the view that predestination is based on God's foreknowledge of a person's faith or unbelief, Beza wrote:

> Those who disagree with us in this matter continually confuse God's decree *(decretum)* and its execution *(exequutione)*. Although this execution and its middle causes *(causae mediae)* follow God's decree (by the intervention of which causes God executes his eternal plans *[consilia]* in his own time, in the order of causes and effects), these people, on the contrary, suppose that middle causes are prior in God's mind and that God then forms his plan from a foreseeing of them.[39]

Not only does the decree-execution distinction form the structural framework of Beza's predestination thinking; to a certain extent this framework also functions in Beza's whole theology, as is evident in the most comprehensive and systematic of his works, the *Confession de la Foy Chrestienne* (1558).[40] Its confirmation section, which lays out the basic teachings of the Reformed faith (chapters 1-6), has a *literary* structure that follows the Apostles' Creed. Nevertheless, Beza's *theological* framework of Trinitarian decree-execution thinking surfaces at crucial points within this creedal literary structure. The Trinitarian creedal structure is not just literary, but also has theological significance. In

---

[37] *TT* 3:402.

[38] *TT* 3:404, 406

[39] *TT* 3:419. See also 421, 426.

[40] Beza wrote the original 1558 French edition of the *Confession* to convince his Catholic father of the orthodoxy of his Reformed faith. I am using the Geneva 1559 reprint. A modern English translation by James Clark is titled, *The Christian Faith* (Lewes, East Sussex: Focus Christian Ministries Trust, 1992).

this context decree-execution thinking can well correlate with a Trinitarian emphasis. It is the triune God who decrees and carries out the decrees.

A few examples will suffice. The first chapter on the Trinity includes an article on eternal providence, understood in terms of the decree-execution distinction:

> Nothing happens by chance and without the just decree *(ordonnance)* of God, although God is not at all the author of or is guilty of any evil... He even ordains and does *(ordonne & fait)* well and justly what the devil and humans do wickedly and unjustly (1:3).

Near the beginning of chapter three (Christ the Son of God), Beza includes two articles on the immutability of God's plan and its execution by secondary causes:

> IV. God is Immutable
>
> God is immutable in his plans *(conseils)*,[41] of which it follows that everything that happens to humans was ordained *(ordonné)* eternally by him, following what we said about his providence (3:4).
>
> V. The Plan *(Conseil)* of God does not Exclude Secondary Causes *(Causes Secondes)*
>
> That does not hinder but establishes secondary causes through which all things happen. For God, in ordaining that which must take place *(advenir)*, also ordains the means *(moyens)* through which he is pleased that such a thing takes place, even to the point that when some vice is found in the secondary cause, there is no vice in the eternal plan of God (3:5).

The second article of this chapter focuses on "the Son eternally ordained *(ordonné)* as the sole Mediator between God and the elect" (3:2). Correlated with this article—as its execution—are articles 17 and 21, which deal with Christ the Mediator as promised under the Old Testament Law (3:17) and as fulfilled when "the eternal Son of God, at the time ordained by the Father, took the form of a servant" (3:21). A similar structural correlation of decree and execution occurs in regard to the creation of humanity. Article 3:6, which states that God "eternally ordained *(ordonné)* to create man to manifest his glory," correlates with its execution in article 3:9: "The Lord, at the time that seemed good to him to execute his eternal plan *(executer son conseil eternel)*, created man, male and female."

Chapter five presents a rather lengthy treatment of the Church and its offices, but reveals hardly a hint of decree-execution thinking. Here it is apparent that Beza does not work out the implications of the decree-execution thinking in all parts of the *Confession*, especially in the doctrine of the church.

---

[41]Here the Geneva 1561 edition adds: "and cannot be mistaken in them or be prevented at all from executing *(executer)* them."

Chapter six briefly discusses Christ's return and the last judgment, but it does not describe these events as the final outworking of God's decree.

Beza's *Quaestionum et Responsionum Christianarum Libellus* (1570) also presents a rather comprehensive range of doctrines.[42] It begins with the end or purpose for which God placed us in the world, then treats the Word of God, the Trinity, the Son of God, and finally the way to eternal life. The latter soteriological section ends with a lengthy examination of the sources *(fontes)* of faith—providence and predestination (QQ. 170-213).

The sections on the Word, the Trinity, and on the person of the Son show little evidence of decree-execution thinking. But in the sections on providence and predestination, which make up fully one third of the work, the decree-execution framework is pervasive. I mention only a couple of examples. Beza summarizes his discussion of providence in this way:

> Nothing at all happens without God's will or knowledge (that is, by chance or accident), but totally as God himself decreed *(decrevit)* it from eternity, disposing all the intermediate causes *(causas intermedias)* powerfully and efficaciously, so that they are necessarily brought to their destined end *(destinatum finem)*, in respect to his decree. Nevertheless, he is not the author or approver of any evil, since he always acts most righteously, with whatever instruments he executes *(exequatur)* his work.[43]

In the final section, Beza goes on to describe predestination as "the eternal and immutable decree, preceding in order all the causes of salvation and damnation, whereby God has determined to be glorified by saving some in Christ by mere grace, but by damning others by his just judgment."[44] Beza emphasizes the necessity of distinguishing the decree and its execution as well as their different causes.

> For the decree to save the elect is different than the very glorification of the elect; and the decree to damn the reprobate is different than the damning of the reprobate, since the decree itself must necessarily be distinguished from its execution *(decretum ipsum necessario sit distinguendum ab eius executione)*. Therefore, the execution of the decree *(executio decreti)* of election (the salvation of the elect) depends upon faith apprehending Christ; and the execution of the decree of reprobation (the damnation of the reprobate) depends upon sin and its fruits... But, of the decree *(decreti)* of electing certain people to be saved by grace, and of reprobating certain people to be condemned by their own sins, we know no other cause than this one *(causam*

---

[42]Printed in TT 1:654-88. There is a modern English translation by Kirk Summers, *A Little Book of Christian Questions and Responses* (Allison Park, PA: Pickwick Publications, 1986). I follow the numbering of the questions in this edition.

[43]Q. 187 (*TT* 1:681).

[44]Q. 195 (*TT* 1:683).

> *hanc unam)*, that the most merciful and most just Lord wills to be glorified in this way.[45]

Since Beza is governed by the content of the biblical text in his exegesis, one cannot expect the decree-execution distinction to be as evident in Beza's exegetical writings as in his more systematic works. Yet the distinction does appear in these writings, especially—as one might expect—in comments on texts that relate to providence, predestination, or God's will, but also occasionally on texts where analysis in terms of decree and execution would not seem very pertinent.

Thus in Beza's New Testament *Annotationes* of 1556, one can readily find the decree-execution framework in his annotations on predestinarian texts such as Romans 8 and 9 and Ephesians 1.[46] Commenting on 1 Peter 2:8, which speaks of those destined to disobedience, Beza seeks to safeguard God from the blame of sin by use of the distinction:

> Indeed, most just is he who condemns no one except those in whom he has found the very cause of condemnation adhering in them. For (as I have often said) between God's decree *(decretum)* and the execution *(executionem)* of the decree the cause of damnation intervenes *(intercedit)*, namely the depravity of those who are damned by the just judgment of God, so that they can blame no one but themselves.

It is noteworthy that already in this early work of his career, Beza observes that he has "often *(saepe)*" used the decree-execution distinction to explain how God cannot be blamed for the damnation of the reprobate.

On occasion in his *Annotationes* Beza also uses the distinction to explain non-predestinarian texts, for example, Romans 3:24, 11:24, 1 Timothy 2:5, and 2 Timothy 2:21. A similar situation can be found in Beza's other exegetical writings. Especially in his commentary on Job the decree-execution framework figures prominently. One good example is his comments on Job 1:6. This text, which speaks of the day when the sons of God (angels) and Satan presented themselves before the Lord, does not seem to lend itself to analysis in terms of decree and execution. Yet regarding that day Beza comments:

> But this point is established, that God decides *(statuere)* nothing in time, but he has from eternity determined *(constituta)* all things in general and in particular and every single thing by his immutable and inscrutable plan *(consilio)*. Truly, as God has decreed all things from eternity *(ab aeterno omnia decrevit)*, so he has also prearranged *(praefixit)* for the execution of his

---

[45] Q. 202 (*TT* 1:686).

[46] *Novum D. N. Iesu Christi Testamentum. Latine iam olim a Veteri interprete, nunc denuo a Theodoro Beza versum, cum eiusdem Annotationibus* ([Geneva], 1556). I have found the distinction also in comments on similar texts such as Luke 2:34, Acts 4:28, 13:48, 1 Timothy 2:4, 2 Timothy 1:9, Titus 1:2, 1 Peter 1:2, 1:20, 2:8, 2 Peter 1:10, and Jude 4. This list is by no means complete.

decrees *(decretorum suorum executioni)* their moments of time, which he alone holds in his power (Acts 1:7) and which cannot in any way be hastened or slowed down. Therefore, in this passage God is not introduced as revealing a plan containing something new about Job (for he had determined *(definierat)* all that from eternity), but on the coming of that day which he had destined for executing his plan *(consilio exequendo destinarat)* for him, on that day finally he revealed that plan to Satan, otherwise ignorant of the whole thing, whose works he had determined would execute *(exequi)* it.[47]

Though Beza closely linked the decree-execution distinction to causal categories, he rarely used Calvin's precise distinction between remote and proximate causes.[48] In cases where Calvin was prone to use this distinction, Beza typically substituted an analysis in terms of decree and execution. This provided him with a more moderate solution to a sensitive problem: Who is to blame for the damnation of the wicked? While for Calvin God's decree is a remote cause of their condemnation, Beza denies that God or his decree is at all a cause of condemnation. Rather, he contends that the cause of the decree (which is God's will) must be distinguished from the cause of the execution of the decree.[49]

We say that the condemnation of those who are left in their corruption according to that eternal decree of God should not be attributed rightly to that decree. For even if what God decreed cannot but happen, and accordingly those who perish do not perish apart from that decree of God, the cause of the execution of that decree (that is, of the damnation of those who perish) is not that divine decree but their native corruption in which they were born, and the fruits of that corruption.[50]

---

[47]Beza, *Jobus, partim Commentariis partim Paraphrasi Illustratus* (London, 1589), 42. See also his comments on Job 1:21 and 2:1.

[48]Beza occasionally refers to "proximate" causes, but seldom of "remote" causes. In one instance Beza speaks of the "remote" and "proximate" causes of Adam's free will (*Ad Acta Colloquii Montisbelgardensis* (Geneva, 1588), 2:206).

[49]In one passage Beza points out that "I have taught already a thousand times" that the cause of damnation is different than the cause of eternal destination to damnation (*Ad Acta,* 2:188). This disjunction between the decree and its execution prompted Jacobus Andreas, Beza's Lutheran opponent at the Colloquy of Montbéliard, to probe what is indeed a soft spot in Beza's position: How is God's decree not the cause of its own execution? (*Ad Acta,* 2:161). For Beza's response, see 2:178-79.

[50]Beza, *Ad Acta,* 2:161. The translation (somewhat amended) is from Philip Holtrop's *The Potter and the Clay: The Main Predestination Writings of Theodore Beza* (Grand Rapids: Calvin College, 1982), 479. Similar statements about the different causes of the decree and of damnation are found in the *Summa,* 2.5, 6 (*TT* 1:176), *Annotationes* on 1 Timothy 2:5; *Quaestionum,* Q. 205 (*TT* 1:686); *Responsio ad Sebastiani Castellionis Calumnias* (*TT* 1:340); *De Praedestinationis Doctrina* (*TT* 3:406, 417); *Ad Acta,* 2:9, 147, 158, 163, 172, 213-14. Bray, in *Theodore Beza's Doctrine of Predestination,* 91, 116, and Muller, in *Christ and the Decree,* 81, incorrectly state, because of a poor translation, that for Beza the first cause of damnation is the decree.

Decree and execution have different causes, because for Beza sin intervenes *(intervenit)* between the decree and its execution in time.

> When I said that damnation is just, did I not sufficiently indicate that just causes of the damnation of those who are damned intervene between that inscrutable divine and eternal decree anteceding in order all the middle causes of its execution (which are subordinated to that decree of God) and their actual damnation?[51]

By placing the responsibility for their damnation solely on the wicked themselves and not on God, Beza's decree-execution distinction softens a hard edge in Calvin's thinking.

For both Calvin and Beza, God's decree is so all-encompassing that nothing happens apart from the decree, including evil. Both affirm that God ordained the fall of Adam and sin.[52] This creates a recurring problem for both of them—how to explain that God is not the author of sin. Calvin was willing to speak of God's will as the remote cause of sin, without implicating him in its guilt. Beza, on the other hand, avoids reference to God as a cause of sin in any positive sense.[53] Instead, he uses the decree-execution framework to provide a somewhat more moderate solution: God executes his decrees by use of secondary causes, and the human will intercedes between the decree and its execution.[54] Though moved by God, human agents as secondary causes or instruments also voluntarily move themselves, sometimes in a contrary evil direction. By moving evil instruments God is a concurrent cause of their actions, but not of the evil.[55] Hence the cause of sin is not the decree, but lies solely in humans themselves. Hence God cannot be blamed in any way.

In conclusion, compared to Calvin's occasional use of the decree-execution distinction, Beza clearly gave it a more prominent role. Calvin uses the distinction mostly in reference to providence and seldom in his discussions of predestination, as is common with Beza. By and large Calvin does not explicitly

---

[51]Beza, *Ad Acta,* 2:158. The idea that sin intervenes or intrudes between the decree and its execution is also found in *Quaestionum,* Q. 207 (TT 1:687); *De Praedestinationis Doctrina* (TT 3:417, 421); *Annotationes* on Luke 2:34 and 1 Peter 2:8.

[52]For example, see Calvin, *Institutes*1:16:3, 8; 1:17:3, 5; 1:18:3 (OS 3:190, 199, 206, 208, 225); *Concerning Eternal Predestination,* 123 (COR: *Scripta Ecclesiastica*1:146); *Treatises Against Anabaptists and Libertines,* 242, 244 (CO 7:186, 188); commentary on Psalm 115:3 (CO 32:184); and Beza, *Summa,* 2.1 (TT 1:171); Confession, 1.3; *Quaestionum,* QQ. 171-73, 183, 187, 202 (TT 1:677, 680, 681, 685); De*Praedestinationis Doctrina,* (TT 3:403); *Jobus,* 38, 77-78.

[53]On occasion Beza does speak of God as a "deficient cause" *(causa deficiens),* but not efficient cause, of sin (*Quaestionum,* QQ. 182, 202 (TT 1:680, 685)). As Q. 202 indicates, this means that "by God *forsaking* the will of men, sin comes to mankind, and remains and bears fruit in as many as it pleases God to *give them up* to their own lusts."

[54]Beza, *Summa,* 3:6 (*TT* 1:179).

[55]Beza, *Quaestionum,* QQ. 174-75 (*TT* 1:678). Cf. *Jobus,* 77-80.

link the decree-execution distinction to the various paired categories of primary and secondary causality, as is typical of Beza. In contexts where Calvin speaks of remote and proximate causes, Beza usually prefers to substitute an analysis in terms of the decree-execution distinction, to avoid the notion that God's decree is a remote cause of sin or of damnation.

With Beza decree-execution becomes an important technical distinction. This is clear not only from the countless instances where Beza explicitly uses these terms, but also from the fact that he often insists that decree and execution must be distinguished,[56] and that his opponents are wrong in confusing the two.[57] It appears that Beza has taken one form of biblical imagery that portrays how God as King relates to creation and elevated it to a dominant distinction of his theology.

For Beza the decree-execution distinction forms the heart of a causal framework that is clearly the governing structure of his thinking about providence and predestination. But it is evident that this framework often surfaces in his other writings as well, and it does so at crucial points in his most systematic work, the *Confession*. However, Beza does not develop the decree-execution framework and its implications thoroughly or consistently throughout every part of his theology. That is especially true of his treatments of the doctrine of the church.[58] Yet one need not expect this framework to be explicit in every part of his theology for it to be operative. With some qualification, one might conclude that the Trinitarian decree-execution framework is the dominant structural framework of Beza's theology. This marks a shift of emphasis, though not a significant doctrinal deviation, from Calvin, for whom the distinction functions as but one among many and does not play an overarching role.

If the decree-execution distinction forms such a framework in Beza's theology, that does not make it a predestinarian system. This framework encompasses more than predestination; it is also the framework for other doctrines, especially providence, which for Beza is broader than predestination.

Moreover, this framework for Beza is not a deterministic scheme with a strict chain of causality, but rather a framework with a distinctive twist. Between God's decree and its execution in time human agency and sin intervenes. By creating something of a disjunction between the decree and its execution, and ascribing separate causes to each, Beza can deny that God (or his decree) is a cause of sin or a cause of damnation. Though the decree-execution framework as a causal scheme is sometimes thought to lead Beza to a more stringent position than Calvin, on these two issues, at least, his distinctive rendering of the distinction helped him develop a more moderate stance than his mentor.

---

[56]For example, *Quaestionum,* Q. 202 (TT 1:686); *Annotationes* on 1 Timothy 2:5; *Responsio* (*TT* 1:339); *Ad Acta,* 2:9, 199.

[57]For example, *De Praedestinationis Doctrina* (*TT* 3:419, 421, 422-23, 426, 430).

[58]For Beza's treatment of the church, see Maruyama, *The Ecclesiology of Theodore Beza.*